Montserrat
in
England

MONTSERRAT IN ENGLAND

Dynamics of Culture

SHARMEN GREENAWAY

iUniverse, Inc.
Bloomington

Montserrat in England
Dynamics of Culture

iUniverse books may be ordered through booksellers or by contacting:

iUniverse
1663 Liberty Drive
Bloomington, IN 47403
www.iuniverse.com
1-800-Authors (1-800-288-4677)

ISBN: 978-1-4620-5878-5 (sc)
ISBN: 978-1-4620-5877-8 (hc)
ISBN: 978-1-4620-5876-1 (ebk)

Library of Congress Control Number: 2011918830

Printed in the United States of America

iUniverse rev. date: 11/03/2011

CONTENTS

Dedicated To:

All those who migrated from Montserrat, 'the homeland', from the late '90s onward.

Those who remained, and those who left but returned and were brave enough to rebuild the country or just to retire.

Those of us who dream of returning one day to our beloved Montserrat. I salute you and hope the dream becomes a reality.

The entire Montserrat Diaspora; we are in this together, and I hope this reflects the true experiences of our emergence into metropolitan England.

To my aunt Rose Macfoy for her tremendous support.

PREFACE

The people of Montserrat are very proud of their cultural heritage. Originally of African descent, a strong Afro-Irish mix is evident in their local dialect, cuisine, music, and folk dances. This book gives the reader an insight into the impact of out-migration on culture for those who left Montserrat after the volcanic eruptions started in 1995. It highlights some of the main challenges experienced by Montserratians in England and the impact on their socialisation, personal and career growth, and development. Written in short story narrative with the support of third-party feedback, the book captures aspects of the local folklore and customs which have shaped Montserrat over the years. A number of issues related to schooling, employment, and relationships have determined the status and personal esteem of Montserrat folk in England, driven by a range of intentional and circumstantial experiences. The extended family unit, and social and intimate interactions, are of great value to most people, and the disruption of these elements has been a huge loss to the migrant Montserrat community.

Destruction of the main tourist attractions on the island—including the Soufriere Hills Volcano, which provided great sightseeing in its dormant state, and the popular Hot Water Pond, with its bubbling sulphur springs thought to have numerous health benefits—have led to new sourced tourist attractions for the continued interest of nationals and visitors alike. While struggling to blend into metropolitan England and maintain appearances, Montserrat folk try as best as possible to hold onto their culture, speaking the island's dialect at every opportunity while sharing tips related to the cuisine and listening to music loved by those associated with the island.

An attempt is made to capture the virtues of Montserrat, with morale boosters and references to the way Montserrat functioned prior to the volcanic eruptions. Personal experiences are cited as a means of capturing the impact of life in England in candid narrative. Also known as the other Emerald Isle, as a result of its relationship and geographic imagery of parts of Ireland, Montserrat was often fondly referred to as a paradise where its people remained virtually unspoilt by subcultures and outside influences. It is interesting how the author of *Fire from the Mountain* summed up the general environment in Montserrat following the major eruption of 1997.

> *Symbolic of an old fashioned, God fearing society in which the values of an emancipated peasantry—individualism, independence, devotion to land and home triumphed over the circumstances.*

The island of Montserrat has been trying to recapture its previous state of development but continues to experience extreme financial challenges due to its small population. Its current population of approximately five thousand is said to currently include more migrants from neighbouring islands than natives. There are genuine concerns among some folk that the culture of the island will fade away as a result of the circumstances and the influences of subcultures. Has Montserrat become the melting pot of the Caribbean? Has the fact that Montserrat now has an open-door policy so impacted on the culture of the island and its reduced population, that Montserratians are now concerned?

Some schools of thought suggest that the term *loss of culture* is a non-existent state and argue that the constantly adapting and changing environments and circumstances are the most significant determinants of what the ever-evolving culture of a people is at any given time. Therefore it is arguable that the influx of migrants eager to replace the fleeing Montserrat folk has only sped up the inevitable cultural shift. The other real argument could be that the island folk are more tolerant to influences of Western cultures such as that of New York City, rather than those islands that have chosen to dig in while the island is at its lowest ebb. Because change is inevitable no matter how intense the arguments or how strong the resistance, one cannot discount the need to document the details of current traditions as a source of reference for future generations, since culture in its purest form cannot remain stagnant; many visitors and migrants, in their attempt to speak the Montserrat dialect, often distort its pronunciations in a way that is painful to listen to.

As a result a chapter in the form of a travellers' guide has been dedicated to our dialect, or Creole proudly referred to as Montserrat English, of which the words and phrases are not found in any dictionary. For those purposes, among others, I felt it pertinent to ensure that this book did not emerge as a solely academic resource, deeming it inaccessible to the majority. Rather it is a multi-purpose tool of short accounts of current times and a recount of the way things used to be. Just as the nights of jumbie storytelling brought tears to the eyes in its construct of tales of suspense of dead ancestors making their presence felt among the living, so too should this book keep alive the essence of the culture of the Montserrat people. Because Montserrat is not an independent state—it remains a British Overseas Territory—the term Montserratian used throughout this book is merely a symbol of the way we island folk describe our national existence. Many of the island's natives would happily describe themselves unreservedly as being 'proud Montserratian' as a means of establishing their position in the world and their perceived sense of self.

Acknowledgements

First and foremost, I give thanks to the almighty for granting us surviving mercies.

We are indebted to Her Majesty Queen Elizabeth II and her government, the United Kingdom authorities, who made the decision to extend a welcoming hand to us in our time of need. I dare not think what could have been our outcome had we not been supported the way we were.

To the other countries, including the United States of America and the Caribbean islands, and to the various organizations that gave aid and donations to the island in one way or another—we are grateful.

I am grateful to Sir Howard A Fergus, who took time out of his busy schedule to support me with the editing of this by reading the manuscript and giving constructive criticism. Sir Howard has contributed to my education in the past, and his experience as a well-published author has sensitised him, thus enabling him to provide general guidance and some critical analysis of this book. I feel privileged that he gave me permission to use the song 'Mother Land' in this book, because it reminds me of the way Montserrat was and still is to some extent.

To Sheryl A Samuel, who assisted with the editing of this book and tolerated the monotony of the entire process.

Thank you so much to Social Worker Udwal T Aymer for conducting the research and volunteering the use of the findings for presentation in this book. This resource is inevitably a valuable contribution to the history of Montserrat. Thank you for taking me into Sutton Forest, Birmingham, aspects of which reminded me of my treks into Broderick's Mountain and Chances Peak.

I am grateful to my Aunt Rose A Macfoy, Alison Wells-Inyang, Anita Wells-Sutton (Miss Annie from Webbs), Iris Lake-Ryan, Janice Panton of the Montserrat UK Government Office, and Joseph Cassell.

Thank you to Germaine Dublin, who provided essential and selfless support in our search for housing in Hackney in 1997. Many thanks to Michelle Lee for patiently listening to the stories and giving her usual commentaries, and also to Rose A Sullivan for her contribution of an old song from yester-year.

Special thanks to my colleague Hilary McDowell for assisting with correct wording for some sensitive issues.

Thank you to Rudi Page for his support and encouragement from early on, when we were still new to England. He has given valuable insight into the benefits of group projects and entrepreneurship.

I am most grateful to Agnes Hazel and Lucinda Sullivan for reading and providing valuable feedback on some aspects of the book.

I am indebted to Madge Donaghue, who worked closely with me to form and run the adolescent group in Montserrat (1996-1997) during the relocations to the north, and for other personal support she has given me.

To my past colleague, Nurse Roseline Farrell of Cork Hill, who on my trip to Birmingham reminded me that I was the first person who predicted that the volcano would erupt as a consequence of experiencing deep rumbles and ongoing tremors while living in the now extinct village of St Patrick's prior to the first eruption.

I also express my gratefulness to my ever considerate stepmother, Rachel Farrell, and sibling Joycelyn Farrell, who made it possible for me to have legal access to the United States.

Thank you very much to my facebook friends, who contributed in one way or another through cultural discussions and more.

Finally, a special thank-you to all those who gave authorisation to use their various stories and situations within this book.

Despite all the editing and the attempts made to rid the book of errors, I do apologise and beg for your tolerance of any additional errors you the reader will pick up on your journey through this book.

NB: A number of names have been withheld and changed in the book for anonymity and confidentiality.

ABOUT THE AUTHOR

Born in Montserrat in a village called Molyneaux, located on the east side of the island, Sharmen Greenaway is a health care professional who enjoys writing candidly. At age two she was taken to a village called Trials, where residents are proud to come from 'over the bridge' to the south of the island of Montserrat. She later moved further up to Brodericks-Fairfield, which has a fabulous view of Plymouth and surroundings. She grew up climbing mango trees and trekking to the highest mountain, Chances Peak, with her siblings during school vacations. Exploring the natural beauty of the hills and mountains under the volcano was a regular hobby which has etched timeless memories in her mind.

She later migrated to the United Kingdom following the volcanic eruptions, and she pursued higher education and career development in health care. This book is a compilation of shared experiences of fellow Montserratians who migrated to England and other parts of the world en masse around the same period, following the major volcanic eruption of June 1997.

Motherland

Montserrat, dear Motherland
Your children raise your standard high
In toil and tears to serve you well
A crowning jewel from God's hand.
Chorus:
O Montserrat, by nature blest
To you your children sing
Come well or woe, come friend or foe
To thee thy people cling

We pledge unstinted loyalty
To emerald hills and fruitful fields
To pass on to posterity
Our father's culture proud and free.

In one clear chord we sing of thee
May God be your eternal guard,
And make our land a house of hope
A haven in the Carib Sea.

Rise up and make our country great
With art and skill and sacrifice
With masque and drum we'll celebrate
Triumphant masters of our fate.

No pestilence shall mar our shore
No fount of sadness overwhelm
A people striving under God
Our spirits free forevermore.

(Reprinted with the kind permission of the author, Sir Howard A Fergus.)

INTRODUCTION

It is interesting how a member of the Diaspora who migrated to the United States viewed the displaced Montserrat circumstance. As we shared ideas and moaned over situations, it became clear that despite being in different locations of the world, we had similar issues and experiences. It was easy for me to agree with her that the principles of adaptation were a good concept to use as a framework for our thoughts on the ongoing Montserrat Diaspora situation.

The interest in theories related to adaptation came about as a result of the developments within the lives of Montserratians following migration to various countries during the erupting volcanic phase. Over time we have had many life-changing experiences, which at times led us to make varied decisions and adjustments to facilitate our survival. It is difficult for anyone to imagine being forced to leave a comfortable lifestyle, family, friends, social environment, and employment to take up residence in unknown lands with a diversity of cultures. Left with little choice but to adapt to new societies in which we had to develop a new existence, it was anyone's guess what the outcomes would be. 'Without exaggeration, this was much like a do or die situation and is an experience I am sure we will never forget,' commented one young lady on her experience of living away from Montserrat for the first time in her life.

Within the framework of this book, I make an effort to examine the experiences of the Montserrat folk from differing perspectives, their use of survival skills in adapting to various situations, and the levels of adaptation they achieved while trying to cope with their changing circumstances. I further try to capture the essence of the Montserrat culture and its meaning in the lives of a now displaced people. The cultural issues are of great importance because the majority of islanders left Montserrat only to be replaced by a number of non-nationals. It is not difficult to envision the loss of culture in a small island where the composition of residents is said to be almost two to one in favour of migrants. Although populating the island with whoever is willing to come is favourable from an economic perspective, the resulting impact of subcultures can ultimately create a watering-down effect on the natural cultures of the island. This issue is only lightly touched on here (hopefully it will be addressed in more depth in another forum), because the focus of this book is the effects of out migration and cultural preservation for those who left, rather than debating cause and effect of in-island issues.

Roy's adaptation model describes the person as an adaptive system whose output can be viewed as a response that may be either adaptive or ineffective. However, adaptation must be viewed as an ongoing, purposive response contributing to health and integration, while ineffective responses do not. Chin and Kramer describe survival as a priority goal followed by other goals that promote growth, ensure continuation of the species or society, and promote attainment of full potential. The MSN Encarta Online Dictionary further describes adaptation as the process or state of changing to fit a new environment, or different conditions or the resulting change. Adaptation is further defined by McEwen as the process and outcome whereby thinking and feeling persons, as individuals or in groups, use conscious awareness and choice to create human and environmental integration.

A number of theorists view adaptation as a tool often used as a coping mechanism, which can be either positive or negative. It can be described as stimuli in the environment that further serves to generate adaptive mechanisms informed by changes in situations, the impact of past experiences, and their resolutions; lessons learned; access to knowledge; and the development and maintenance of skills and general limitations. Needless to say, responses to particular stimuli will determine each person's adaptation level, which understandably does not remain stagnant but constantly changes as it adapts to the environment.

A young man claimed that despite his educational level and qualifications, he had to take odd jobs that were not consistent with his qualifications. He expressed his annoyance that he could not validate this degree from back home, meaning Montserrat. He stated that on investigating further, he found that many other migrants, despite being highly qualified in their countries, had to settle for jobs as taxi drivers, shop workers, or security officers; some remained on job seeker's allowance for a very long time. The resulting low morale from these and other such situations have had varied impact on the adaptive processes. Others' experiences have been more positive, and they've been able to carry over their respective qualifications from their countries. The young man in question was obviously unhappy with the situation in which he found himself. The fact that he was forced to migrate to this new environment due to circumstances beyond his control impacted his acceptance of the situation. Had he left the island of his own accord, aware that he had to use strategies to survive, would his response to the situation have been different? Needless to say his expectations for job opportunities were high when he left Montserrat, and he expressed his disappointment when he ultimately found himself in a vulnerable situation over which he had little or no control.

For many of the displaced, food was an area of great concern. The cuisine of Montserrat consists of highly seasoned foods influenced by the African, Irish, British, and Amerindian cultures, a legacy of the island's history. The less highly seasoned taste of some English dishes was one of the many changes in the migrants' lifestyles.

A young man cited his main problem was the dress code, especially of some young women. He claimed that during the summer and sometimes in winter, he was shocked to see how some women dressed and walked the streets. He referred to his issues as culture shock. It took a long time for him to accept this lifestyle given that he hadn't lived in a metropolitan country before; the people in Montserrat were still dressing conservatively then. In fact there were strict dress codes after some visitors had the inclination to sunbathe topless on the island's beaches and walk the streets of Plymouth in various states of undress. Once these guidelines had been put in place it was very rare to see anyone, whether visitor or national, inappropriately clothed, even on the beaches.

The first photo I saw of Montserratians at a function in England was one that prompted reviews that referred to their style of dress as that seen in the '50s, which appeared drab and out of style.

This review was felt to be unfavorable and out of place at the time. A popular newspaper also described the Montserrat fashion sense at that time as being that of the '50s in England. Things have greatly improved since, and Montserrat men and women are holding their own among the most fashionable the world over.

It's not just fashion that the cultures differ. A young lady remarked on the interaction of people with each other in the big cities. 'No one has time to say hello or offer assistance,' she observed. 'No one greets you, and if you greet them, first they look at you as if you are crazy. This is not my culture; we are like family and treat everyone with respect.' Despite her issues with all these changes, she has adapted well to British society. Like many others, she hasn't given up on her cultural beliefs and values, but has incorporated them into her current lifestyle. She is now married with two children who enjoy the best of both worlds. She eventually graduated with a degree.

Some adaptive processes have been viewed as less than ideal. It is difficult to tell if it would have made a difference whether or not a different geographical location would have brought about changed circumstances. At three years old, a young boy was abandoned by his young mother; his father was living separately from them. He was the eldest of three kids to a young mother who could not take care of the children. Making the decision to give one up for care, she left the three-year-old boy at an orphanage in the United States. The boy became a ward of the state and was shuffled from one foster home to the other. He never had the opportunity to settle long enough to become part of any family. As he grew older, he became increasingly angry and resentful at this state of affairs. Eventually he rebelled and on several occasions resorted to stealing and running away to hang with friends. He was returned by the police each time, but his behavior did not change.

Eventually the boy was befriended by a young girl whom he met at one of his gym classes. The girl introduced the young boy to her mother, and the family immediately liked his pleasant, easy-going manner. On hearing of his story, the girl's mother took the boy into her home temporarily, for foster care. The young boy believed this was a permanent arrangement and was very happy at the way he was treated—he was now getting the love he craved. After several months another foster home was found for him, and after begging to remain where he was, he reluctantly left his friend's home.

He soon disappeared from the new home, and some months later he was picked up by the police and charged with burglary. By age sixteen his contact with the law had become more frequent and serious, and he was now involved in a number of questionable activities. He was eventually placed in a safe facility and treated for unsociable behavioral issues. His anger increased over time, and he became more disillusioned and continued to act out his frustration in various negative ways. The boy never adjusted to his new environment, and it is hard to say if he will ever be in a position to lead a socially acceptable life. It is also difficult to tell whether he would have had a different experience had he been back in Montserrat.

There are a number of similar stories of poor adjustments and adaptive processes which sadden the heart.

CHAPTER 1

A Volcano Awakes

It was an early afternoon in July when the call came. There was a sense of urgency to the ring, but of course that could have been my imagination. I picked up the phone to the excited, shrill, high-pitched voice of my niece Shaunette.

'Aunty do you hear a grating, kind of rumbling sound, almost like thunder in the distance? Listen . . . ! Can you hear it?'

'Wait! Let me listen. What sound? I don't hear anything. Is it going to rain? What's the big deal? Are you all right?'

'Aunty, there's a strange sound coming from the volcano, like its groaning or something. I am in Plymouth, at Sturge Park, and they think the volcano is going to erupt. Put on the radio and listen to the news.'

This conversation was to replay in my mind over and over for years to come as the various scenarios and changes through the years formed a new way of life, both personally and culturally. By now one can imagine my concern and response to the information I had just received. I quickly tuned in to ZJB, the national radio station of Montserrat. All my worst volcanic fears were now becoming a reality. The volcano was rumbling ominously, and by the sounds of things there was going to be an eruption. The seismic centre in Trinidad monitored the earthquakes, and we were now officially on volcano eruption watch. My mind flashed back to all the pleasurable activities we'd been fortunate to enjoy on and around the volcano. Visitors, tourists, and locals alike took pleasure in the organised hikes, picnics, and other social interests it generated. There was never a dull moment growing up on this beautiful paradise of an island. The memories of some such moments vividly replayed in my mind; the volcano had been more than a dome filled with ominous gasses and fire, ready to explode. The volcano was to Montserrat what Madame Tussauds is to London, or the Statue of Liberty is to New York. It would therefore be amiss of me not to incorporate some of the now novel events that occurred around and on the volcano, before the eruption.

Hot Water Pond

The annual beach picnic was here, and we were ready to go. As we headed out, we made a quick check of the items in our rucksacks: sandwiches, drinks, snacks and other foods to picnic on, swimwear, cricket bat, and tennis ball. Everything was in order and we are ready to roll. It was Whit Monday, the day after Whit Sunday—a national public holiday and a day all children in Montserrat looked forward to. Well, more specifically the children of the Anglican Church who attended Sunday school. No one wanted to miss the annual day trip to Barton Bay, situated just below Sturge Park, with its black sand beach and pebbly shoreline.

Sturge Park, known locally as Bartfield, was the location for different types of entertainment and sports, including cricket matches (both local and international) and the annual Calypso and festival queen shows. Barton Bay wasn't the best beach on the island by any means because its shoreline changed from time to time, influenced by time and tide. Sometimes the beach was sandy all the way around, and other times it was very pebbly with the presence of seaweed and other deposits from the seabed. In fact, if anything it could have been one of the more risky beaches for children because one had to look out for suck holes and the occasional high waves that doubled one up.

The blue waters were very deep in some areas and could be dangerous if you couldn't swim. The thing about Barton Bay in those days was that when you got there, you simply enjoyed yourself all day; when evening came you didn't want to leave. We were totally in love with the beach; it had so much to offer, including the beautiful scenery enhanced by the landscapes of the well-manicured lawns of the Montserrat Springs Hotel. In fact my childhood love for the scenery was such that I subsequently held my wedding reception at the Montserrat Springs Hotel when I grew up.

The tennis courts on the beach provided recreation for many, and there were treasure holes all over for digging out the hiding soldier crabs, which children enjoyed as a pastime while building sandcastles all around them.

The beach was the home of many large, pretty, pink and white seashells, some tinged with hints of brown. Children and adults alike took shells of different shapes and sizes home to paint and decorate. People set the shells on the centre of tables at home as part of the decor, ageless and fixed. They were only removed for cleaning, then repainted and replaced in their prominent positions for all to admire but not to touch.

Looking back, I now realise that those were actually huge conch shells from our own beaches, and I can't recall the last time I saw one. These shells were not things I used for decoration in my own home, but were rather part of the era of my mother's generation and my childhood. I suppose they didn't make the transition into the more modernised tastes of my generation. I do wonder if they are still on the beaches of Montserrat, though, and whether they changed in character, size, and shape. I endeavour to make looking for conch shells a priority on my things to look for list the next time I visit Montserrat.

That will be the reassuring evidence that no equal migration occurred among these sea creatures as was the fate of the Montserrat people. On getting to the pickup point the bus was waiting and in no time everyone was on board singing 'I Love to Go a Wandering', a much-loved, catchy song often sung at Girl Guides and Boy Scouts camp fires. It would have been nice to get some sugar cake from Miss Moot, who lived not far from the pickup point, but there was no time for that. We didn't even get any menthol from Mr Mills in Kinsale as Salt fish-tail (pronounced 'Sarl fish-tiarl' in local dialect) had been standing down at the roadside giving us the usual cheeky look. He was something of a character and could appear scary to children at times by the way he looked at them. The exception was when he was singing the road march for the annual Calypso competition. People loved his 'road march' songs, which were catchy and jumpy, making them favourites for the bands during the popular Christmas festival. One by Lard Alfredo was my favourite: '*Wake up, girl, this marnin', stap your nasty snorin', peep out through the window, see then jumpin afro. Jump up, girl, jump up. Jump up, girl, jump up . . . Shake out you afro.*'

We were on our way to the beach destination and looking forward to having fun. As we passed the Montserrat Secondary School and rounded the corner at the large Anglican Church in Plymouth, we drove past the cemetery, which we locally called burying ground, with its many tomb stones and flowers dotted around a large patch of land. We continued on around the south side of the fences that enclosed Sturge Park, where everyone took in the beauty of the big houses up at Richmond Hill.

I often wondered why they called it Richmond Hill and thought maybe only rich residents lived on the sloping mounded hill. But we actually knew some children in the Anglican Church who lived up there; they didn't appear that rich. Maybe we would ask them if their Sunday school was at the beach today, I thought dreamily as my mind flipped idly from one thing to the next. As we arrived at our destination, the bus came to a sudden stop, and everyone jumped off shouting thank-yous before speeding hastily in excitement to the welcoming but very hot black sand beach. Almost all beaches on Montserrat have black sand, a result of the volcanic activities in the past. The exception was Rendezvous Beach in the far north of the island, which had calm, shallow waters and white sand. The colour of the black sand didn't bother Montserratians; we were very proud of our unique black sand beaches because it was part of our heritage.

Within minutes the group had taken up their usual positions under the big tamarind tree, which yielded sour tamarind fruit, not far from the tennis court. We listened keenly but impatiently while the Sunday school teachers gave instructions of the dos and don'ts of the day. Heads nodded impatiently, giving assurance of order and discipline. With relief everyone hurriedly scattered to engage in their activities of choice for the day.

Hot Water Pond beckoned a group of us. The water flowing from the hot, steaming springs actually originated from one of the island's many volcanoes. They had taught us at school to value these natural phenomena, which formed part of the earth's natural resources. Geography lessons were always very informative though scary at times. One thing was certain, and that was the value of this pond, which was tremendous. Despite assurances of dormancy the volcano had appeared to be active then because the water was always bubbling and steaming vigorously in various locations.

Other parts of the pooling water, situated in a valley above the sandy beach, were greenish in colour, very warm, and stagnant. We placed our bare feet in the water and played in the almost too hot pools. The water was not crystal clear but still gave the impression of being quite clean and fresh. Green moss could be seen covering the bottom of the pools in some areas and almost felt like velvet underfoot. The smell of rotten eggs emanated from it, but it wasn't overpowering or in any way offensive to us. Geography class taught us that the odour came from sulphuric gases released by the volcano through vents in the earth's surface. The gases travelled from depths way below the earth's surface, trying to relieve the building pressure under.

All this was of little importance to us then; it was all part of our heritage and taken for granted as such. It appeared very peaceful in this area, which was amazing since the hotel just above had many guests or tourists constantly walking about and enjoying the benefits of the pond. Montserrat folklore suggested that the pools and springs have a number of positive healing properties. It was said that if you suffered from certain ailments such as arthritis and other skin conditions, you dropped some pennies in the water and lay down in it. This should start the ultimate healing process, triggered by the minerals in the water. I must confess that I have never met anyone who have said they were healed there, but there must be some truth to this because not only nationals but overseas visitors kept coming from different countries to benefit from the healing properties of the sulphur springs.

We had a special love for this little valley because it had such a peaceful and serene atmosphere. There were also huge cacti, and if you caught one flowering, it was a viewer's delight. Some cacti flowered only once every ten years. If you wanted to meditate and relax, this was the place to come to. Furthermore one could use some types to make 'calita' or use the aloes for cleansing. A number of school children view their worse nightmare as when they are given a dosing of aloes close to the end of the school holidays after consuming numerous mangoes. Twice more during the day we returned to the hot springs to play and watch the bubbling water in awe. We came during breaks from playing bat (cricket) and dodge ball, and bathing in the sea. I got doubled up twice that day, swallowing loads of water as the big waves crashed over my head and hauled me out to sea, tossing me around in circles. That was a scary experience, but in the end the wave quickly rolled back out to sea, and I had to hurriedly climb over the big bank in the water and head towards the shore before the next wave caught me.

It was strange how this part of the seabed was just as hilly as the land itself. On entering the sea, there was a sudden drop over a bank, and then you found yourself in deep waters very close to the shore. One could even imagine there might be mountains way out in the deep of the sea, waiting to be pushed up into land the way Montserrat had been thousands of years before our time. I imagined it would take only one big earthquake to make this happen. Some of the boys attempted to get around Bransby Point by jumping from stone to stone. On reaching the corner, those attempts had to be aborted because the water touched the cliff, blocking entrance to Foxes Bay. Later that evening, tired but happy, we heard the whistle signalling it was time to go home.

I proudly look back at the fun opportunities we had then on the land of my birth. Montserrat was so unspoilt, almost a paradise, and now imagine we were just waiting unawares for it all to disappear in an eruption. My mind wandered again and again to more visual memories of the fun and adventure that the Emerald Isle of the Caribbean had offered throughout my youth and adult years. I couldn't bring myself to focus on the voice on the radio or the person on the other end of the phone line that had disrupted my equilibrium. What was going to become of us on this tiny island, which was little more than a dot on the map? Would the volcano destroy the entire island? Would it ever go back to being dormant, or would it continue its activity like some volcanoes do? There were many outstanding questions and no answers in sight then—nor are there answers to this day. There are only more questions accompanied by a sense of loss and concern of the unknown future of Montserrat.

What if we never hiked up to Soufriere again? This was too serious and unthinkable to even dwell on in my mind. Whether you were a nature lover or not, you would be drawn to the deep mysteries of the Montserrat volcano. There was never a time when it didn't offer something unique to interest the curious, the scientifically motivated, and the romantic. At that moment another novel experience flashed through my mind that I couldn't ignore. Nature was to make a change that determined that Soufriere hikes would never occur in the same way again in the history of Montserrat.

There had always been something to do and places to go in Montserrat. One could hardly get bored. Girl Guides during the early teen years afforded the opportunity of fostering discipline, meeting new friends, and being creative. Activities included building tents, camping out, and earning badges by completing various aspects of creativity. Learning to tie new knots and exploring the out of doors were some of my favourites. The following account highlights one aspect of guiding that I enjoyed in and around the volcano in Montserrat.

Hike to Soufriere

One Saturday we set off for the pre-planned hike to the Soufriere Hills Volcano (Soufriere) in St Patrick's. It was going to be a long walk, and we had our rucksacks on our backs, which made the journey appear even longer. The journey itself was full of surprises that enhanced the enjoyment of the hike—what with climbing the hilly terrain and happening upon the various creeping, crawling, and flying inhabitants of the trees and undergrowth. This was nature at its best and a mini safari for the imaginative. From a distance one could smell strong sulphuric gases, like rotten eggs, but it wasn't an offensive odour.

There was always an adrenaline rush for me, almost a phobia, as I thought of the majestic mountain that housed the huge crater of a volcano. It just stood there, lush and green in its splendour; beautiful on the outside but oh so treacherous with its balls of fire and gases ready to explode at its nucleus. Of course it was known to be dormant, or that's what we had been taught. Furthermore the older folk claimed never to have seen it erupt in their lifetime. Still, one couldn't stop one's heart from beating fast when approaching the huge crater.

The sides of the road leading up to Soufriere were covered with beautifully green foliage, expanding all the way up to the crater. No wonder they referred to Montserrat as the Emerald Isle of the Caribbean! I just loved the place. Vines were hanging down from way up in trees that appeared to ascend up to the sky for an eternity. Look up and one could see a chameleon; they were very green when they adopted the colours of the leaves around them. Amazingly a huge chameleon jumped from a broad chainy bush and onto a tree trunk, and all of a sudden it wasn't green anymore but had turned brown like the bark. I didn't really care to get too close to it, though it was not dangerous because it didn't bite. Still chameleons were no tiny house lizards and their size was a bit daunting to many. These iguana's or large lizards were so tame that they appeared oblivious to our presence—but then we were not really so close as to reach out and touch them.

There was a time when I actually thought that the Amerindian or Carib name 'Alliougana' meant 'land of the iguanas'. I suppose it was the 'gana' at the end that created that perception. I wasn't disappointed to learn that Alliougana actually meant 'land of the prickly bush'. The name was appropriate given the number of prickly bushes (locally called cusha) that used to dig into my bare feet as I ran wildly with the wind in Brodericks Mountain.

We certainly took no heed at the shouts from parents to put shoes on. I wondered if the Caribs, who were the first known human occupants to live on Montserrat, ate the iguanas for food. Some Montserrat folk also thought they were delicacies when fried like chicken. I had tasted the fried leg once before, but it was just not my idea of a delicacy. While eating it all I could think of was mountain chicken (frog's legs), which I had also eaten in the past. The mountain chicken is actually the national dish of one of our neighbouring islands, the Commonwealth of Dominica. It had tasted nice, but I never, ever tried to eat it again. In the same way I couldn't eat the iguana again. The Caribs, an Amerindian people whom the Spanish explorer, Christopher Columbus met when he arrived on Montserrat in 1493, couldn't have had the variety of meats we have now. There is no indication that the Spaniards brought the iguanas to Montserrat; therefore they must be native creatures.

My mind returned to the hike, and the enjoyment and wonders it evoked. There were numerous creatures to see today and so many birds; it was amazing. The oriole, the island's national bird, clearly enjoyed the nectar from the flowers as it flew around in quick bursts of flight, dipping its beak to drink, then fly, dip, lift, and fly. Such a beautiful bird it was that I just had to watch its graceful flitting movements and busy activities. Though shy, it didn't run from us but continued with its search for nectar as if oblivious to our presence. There were no rabbits or agouties in sight today; I guess they were hiding from us, shy creatures that they were. Had there been dogs in our company, they would have hunted them out from their hiding places so we could have a glimpse.

This place was so lovely; one could imagine the Garden of Eden looked just like it. It was all lush green and beautiful, every inch of it. It was so good just to look at the sugar apple and soursop trees, full of fruit just about to ripen. Mangoes were all around, the fruits getting ready to ripen and change to a yellowish orange. The birds had already started eating their fill, but there was more than enough for man and other creatures.

A number of us stopped to pick some manciport from the overhanging pregnant tree. The fruits were brown and a bit scruffy to look at on the outside, but once the skin was removed the orange fruit inside was extremely nutritious and delicious. There were a couple of cocoa trees nearby, so I jumped up and picked some pods. When opened, seeds and thick juicy nutrients oozed out, which was tasty. We would take the seeds home to dry and grind into a powder, then use them to make cocoa tea with milk fresh from the cows. Sometimes we added cinnamon and nutmeg for flavour, and it gave off an aroma that could be recognised from a distance. There was nothing more energising than drinking a fresh cup of Creole cocoa boiled in cow's milk for breakfast.

By the time we got to the mound-like crater of the volcano, everyone was fully sated with the fruits they had picked and eaten on the trek there. The guavas here were amazingly sweet, and every single fruit was free for the picking. Where else could this be possible? Only in Montserrat; land of the free and blessed. Mounting the crater had brought us closer to the steaming brooks running gently in the gully below. The smell of sulphuric gases got stronger, and we were cautioned to be careful. A number of us took out raw eggs, which were placed in puddles of boiling hot water coming from small vents in the earth. The eggs were cooked in no time as we watched in fascination. It was strange that we weren't worried that a bigger vent would open up and blast us off the face of the earth. But of course nothing happened, and at the end of the day some of us were tired, happy, in love with this natural phenomenon, and planning for the next time we could come back to climb the monster volcano and cook eggs in boiling hot water springs. Montserrat boasted of ecological beauty that many countries only dream of. As its people remained in form, so did the natural beauty of the island too. For all intents and purposes, it was almost unspoilt by any development and outside influences, but it was still invaluable as a resource.

Needless to say, this blessed natural beauty kept entertaining and luring tourists and natives alike up until that fateful day many, many years later.

The Volcano Erupts

It had been almost three years since I had married and moved away from home. We had moved into the attractively renovated police quarter, which was situated upstairs from the St Patrick's Police Station. It was convenient and spacious inside, well decorated with my favourite neutral and earth colours, and there were loads of space outside. I was able to plant a tiny vegetable garden despite the poor soil in that little patch. The soil in that area was not a reflection of the fertility of the entire locale, because the soil higher up in the hills of the south were extremely fertile and produced bountiful vegetables and root foods such as cabbages, dasheen, tania seed, and sweet potatoes. The thing I enjoyed most about this area was actually being able to return home after work in the hot afternoons to peace and tranquillity.

There was hardly any bother or disturbance despite the fact that the downstairs of the building was in fact a police station. My only next-door neighbour, who was the district nurse in post at that time, had been no bother at all. In fact it was good to have her living so close; we had been friends and batch mates back in our student days, when we would be told off by the matron for being too thin and not eating properly while living in the dormitories. Aside from that she had been my partner in crime many a night, when we sneaked out from under the watchful eyes of the Austrian matron who ensured that we kept the curfew. The matron had patrolled the corridors every night to make sure we were all safely indoors. Safety in this case meant no access to the boys, since most of us were very young women ranging from seventeen to twenty-one. We were entrusted into her care, a responsibility she took rather seriously.

Life went on as normal, and at some points it would be so blissful on Montserrat that it felt almost like paradise. But of course as the saying goes nothing lasted forever, and especially not happiness or contentment. It all started with an increase in the smell of sulphur in the air. All my life growing up in the Broderick's, Fairfield, and Trials area, the strong odour of sulphuric gases would drift across from the south from whatever direction the wind was blowing. We lived at the base of Chances Peak, part of the Soufriere Hills mountain range that housed the volcano, and we were accustomed to it. We were never very concerned because the volcano had been 'sleeping' forever, and no one expected that it would ever 'wake up'. Not even the stories of the people in nearby Martinique and their fate after Mount Pelee erupted had scared us into thinking we might find ourselves in a similar situation one day.

For some reason on the weekends, when I was at home in St Patrick's, I had been noticing an increase in sulphuric smells coming from the hills. I drew my husband's attention to the intensity of the scent, which actually left a burning sensation in my nostrils when I inhaled. Of course he was not concerned, and to give him his due, not many things alarmed him. In fact he had previous experience with a different type of volcanic eruption in St Vincent, and he was prepared for anything. I was the total opposite, and my senses became alert instantly to the changes around me. Perhaps a combination of my personality, my Girl Guides motto 'Be prepared', and aspects of my career discipline (for which a high element of being observant is necessary) made me ultra sensitive. My increased sense of alert was obvious because the sulphuric emissions appeared to have intensified over time.

The interesting thing about the emissions was the frequency, which were merely intermittent and may have accounted for the resultant changes being ignored or taken for granted by most people in the south. I did not communicate my observation with anyone in the south; I was too busy to socialise in that area because most of my activities were based in the capital, Plymouth. Then the sounds started in such a way that only the overly sensitive would have picked them up. Late at nights I would lay in bed listening to a low, grating sound coming from deep within the earth's surface. Likened unto the sounds of a muted blender on low speed, it appeared to come from a far distance and just went on and on in the still of the night. The earth appeared to be shaking a bit at times, but not usually enough to be overly recognised. The first time I experienced this I woke my partner with a nudge and asked, 'Did you feel that? Can you hear that sound?'

He had not heard or felt a thing. But then that was not surprising because he always slept very deeply after playing football during the daytime. This occurrence continued, though not every night, and it was not felt in the daytime due to the noises and movements of the town. I had become very concerned about the anticipated threats of the volcano by then. I thought it was groaning and would erupt at some point. I didn't express those fears to anyone else for a very long time—not until I was certain. When I did report my experiences to my colleagues at the clinic where we worked their scepticism was obvious. I dreaded going to bed at nights for fear of what the stillness would reveal. My only fitful sleep came about when I was cuddled and wrapped up really close to my partner. For some reason the closeness gave me a false sense of security.

Surprisingly I was relieved though fearful when the tremors started getting stronger, and everyone could feel them. It confirmed that some geological activity was actually taking place under the earth. I continued to feel and experience the increasing sounds and motions in the still of the nights when there was no other sound or movement about. There was no telling what the future would bring. A few years back an evangelist had visited Montserrat to share his news of a vision he had for Montserrat. He had described his vision of the island of Montserrat being consumed by a ball of fire. He was not believed by the locals and simply left after he shared his vision, his mission accomplished.

By now the seismic centre in Trinidad had made it public that they were investigating the increased tremors, but we got the impression that they were not worried that it had anything to do with the volcano. I totally disagreed, of course, and had made it known to my work colleagues by this time that I thought the volcano was going to erupt. This did not mean I held claim to supernatural abilities by any means, for I have none, but my senses had been heightened to the extent where I was convinced that an eruption was a certain possibility. What reinforced my thought processes was what I saw one day on my drive to the village of Molyneaux in the east of Montserrat.

I was on my way to visit my grandmother, who unfortunately passed some months after the eruption started. I noticed a difference in the terrain as I drove down the steep, winding road from Dyers. My maternal family originated from Molyneaux, and my grandmother, whom we called Mama, was still living there. I visited her frequently and liked to look at the foliage and rugged landscape along the way. In an intriguing way it was so different to anywhere else on island, and I often tried to analyse it. The soil on the ridges above the road had holes in them, something I had never noticed before. The foliage was made up of medium-height trees, and the soil was of clay, which got really muddy when it rained. The terrain comprised mainly of hills, gullies, ghauts, streams that resembled rivers when it rained, and cliffs and ridges. There was hardly any flatland at all. People living in this area owned vast amounts of land, and my grandmother was no exception. Additionally there were a large variety of fruit trees all around—mangoes, guavas, coconuts, oranges, and more, all free for the picking; hence no shop in the area found it necessary to sell fruits. At some point during the drive, I turned to my companion and asked, 'Have you noticed that the land looks parched and dry? Do you see those holes in the sides of the land? Looks like it's just too hot under the earth and the land is trying to breath.'

I expressed my thoughts that something was going to happen in Montserrat. I did think that the volcano was going to erupt. As usual my companion tried to reassure me that the volcano was dormant. The volcano had erupted in his native St Vincent some years before, and his experience of pending eruptions had been different than the current circumstances.

My concerns did not decrease despite his reassurances, and that weekend I convinced him that we should move away from the area. The police station we lived at was situated directly under the mountain that housed the volcano. If the volcano was to erupt and I was convinced it would sometime soon; we were living too close for comfort. We lived only about a twenty-five-minute walk away from Soufriere. Later we were to learn that the initial eruption did not occur on that end of the mountain range but on the other end, at Gages and close to the village of Molyneaux, where we had moved prior to going north. St Patrick's was totally destroyed in a later eruption.

On my insistence, we moved back into my childhood home in Fairfield. My parents and siblings who were still living at home welcomed us without question when I told them of my concerns. The extended family unit was embraced by Montserratians and always welcomed. In fact many grown men and women only moved out of the childhood home when they got married. Fairfield is situated like a sandwich between the villages of Broderick's and Trials, and it lies just under the island's highest mountain, Chances Peak, which is part of the Soufriere Hills mountain range. Until I moved away from Fairfield months later, I had not given much thought to the fact that it was part of the volcanic range of mountains about which I was concerned. The fact that I grew up in Fairfield and had climbed Chances Peak many, many times during may have accounted for my lack of insight.

A few months after moving back home, we subsequently moved up to Molyneaux. My sister had returned to French St Maarten to live, work, and manage her rentable apartments. Dad, like many island men, had fathered children with a number of women, which resulted in me having fourteen siblings in total. My sister's two children were left with me to finish their education in Montserrat; the island boasted an excellent education system for children. The part French, part Dutch island of St Martin was better known for its tourism and duty=free shopping prices, and it was not ideal for educating children. Additionally, although the children spoke French fluently, the language barrier was still going to be a hindrance to learning.

Things were running smoothly, and the two children were amazingly easy to manage. Eventually the summer holidays came and I sent the children off to St Martin to spend time with their mom. I must say that since I had moved away from St Patrick's the sounds coming from deep within the earth at night, accompanied by tremors, had become an experience of the past. I was more relaxed now that the earth's movements had calmed down, and I was starting to think that maybe my fears were unjustified, that the volcano was not going to erupt after all. My days were pretty much occupied with work during the weekdays and my role as Girl Guides leader some evenings. On the weekends I travelled back to my original village of Fairfield and Broderick's to play female cricket, taking pride in my role as fast bowler and occasional wicket keeper.

Life continued as usual, and my partner and I bought two prime pieces of land on the island. One was located in Windy Hill, where the soil was fertile and the foliage lush, green, and beautiful. The air was cool and pure, the atmosphere peaceful and serene; I just loved that area. The second piece of land was situated in lower Broderick's in a much sought-after location. The land was awfully expensive but was not very fertile, nor was the scenery great, so it was just an investment of capital. This was also a fairly newly developed area and had the promise of attracting an elite neighbourhood.

It was not hard to choose where we actually wanted to live based on the scenery and benefits of the soil around, and we subsequently secured a mortgage and had the land in Windy Hill excavated. The excavation turned out very expensive because there were extremely tall trees with huge trunks that had to be removed. We decided to keep a few to add to the aesthetics of the area. The soil was very fertile here, so I knew my gardening hobby would certainly thrive. The foliage was absolutely amazing, and we were totally surrounded by Eden on earth. This was also a new development, which meant we could set the trend for future buildings and neighbours.

This series of events surrounding the purchasing of lands, securing mortgages, and building was in full swing leading up to the volcanic events. A number of persons lost these properties to the volcano; some areas were burnt or buried, and others were inaccessible. Most have had to repay the mortgages despite starting new lives and existences in different areas and different countries. The insurance companies pulled out at the beginning of the eruptions, and the financial losses among Montserratians have been great, with no way of recovering any of it. Like many we were looking forward to building a beautiful house and enjoying our surroundings for the rest of our lives. These losses were hard to withstand.

The drama had started that early afternoon in July, when the unwelcome call from my niece came. 'Aunty, there's a strange sound coming from the volcano; it sounds like it is groaning or something. I am in Plymouth at Sturge Park, and they think the volcano is going to erupt. Put on the radio and listen to the news.'

By now you can imagine how alarmed I had become. I quickly tuned in to ZJB Radio (or Radio Montserrat as we call it), the national radio station of Montserrat. So it was that all my worst fears were becoming reality. The volcano was rumbling ominously in town, and people were scared. I couldn't hear it from where I was in Molyneaux, but my heart still raced in anticipation of the worse. The seismic centre in Trinidad was monitoring the volcanic activities, and we were now on volcano watch. Or should I say, eruption watch.

With my heart pounding, I packed an overnight bag as advised by the media, and I tried to call my husband. He was a police officer and wasn't easy to contact. When I did make contact with him, he confirmed my worst fears. The volcano was rumbling ominously, and no one knew what was going to happen next. My on-going concerns from so many months back; the very reason for my relocation to perceived safer grounds, were all confirmed in a matter of minutes. I called around to ensure my relatives and friends were aware of the new developments and preparing to move. My elderly grandmother was alive then and lived about a mile up the hill from where I was living. She couldn't walk because her leg had been amputated below the knee due to diabetes-related complications. We had to take her to safety by lifting her to the car; she was a big woman, but we managed. She too was scared of the volcano. I knew her to be a strong woman, and her show of weakness served to increase my own concerns.

We all moved up to my niece's place at Windy Hill, which appeared to be a suitable haven at the time. She and her partner had newly built their home there. Later we all had to move again when we learnt it was one of the most unsafe areas to be. Following that fateful day, we kept moving back and forth similar to our predecessors, the Amerindians known as the Caribs and Arawaks. They moved from place to place, island to island, hunting for food.

Early in 1995, a number of ceramics, stone tools, shells, and human skeletons were found during an archaeological dig in the village of Trants. They were felt to be remains of the Amerindians who first lived on Montserrat. These findings resulted in a number of whispers and talk among locals. The general thought was that the disturbance of the site and removal of the materials would bring bad luck. It was not long after this that the volcano erupted, which for some might be confirmation that the disturbance of the Amerindian site had brought retribution to the island's people. Some locals made comments and noises to express their displeasure that these archeological findings had been removed. They had better put them back and leave them alone', ('Dem betta put dem back and lef dem looan') was the thought expressed by some locals. Of course no one took heed, as not everyone on island was superstitious, especially not the archaeologists and those at the Montserrat National Trust where the artefacts were kept. Those findings still remain at the Montserrat National Trust. The village of Trants, from where the archaeological findings were taken, along with the island's WH Bramble Airport (previously known as Blackburn airport), were located in the area that was totally destroyed by the volcano.

As time went on, things went from bad to worse, and the ash kept falling and the volcano continued rumbling on and off. From time to time people panicked, not knowing whether the volcano would destroy the entire island or go back to its dormant state. Most people followed the government's advisor to move to safety in the north and return each time it was perceived to be safe. The volcano, when it decided to rumble and spew out ash, created great terror among Montserratians at home and abroad. The thunderous ash clouds were often accompanied by a mix of fire and gases, which raced swiftly down the mountain and into the villages and out to sea. When this occurred, the affected areas became black, and visibility was often impaired.

It was sometimes hard to determine the final destination of the pyroclastic flows. Ash clouds that affected everything in the pathway, including animals and people, sometimes went as far as Puerto Rico an overseas territory of the USA located in the Caribbean. The ash caused chaos in the skies as well, putting fears in the hearts of pilots and travellers alike; plane engines could be affected by the unassuming particles. Despite the danger, there was an element of wonder and beauty to the volcanic eruptions. At nights a number of islanders would observe the glow of lava and huge boulders rolling down the side of the volcano. My favourite spot for this viewing was Jack Boy Hill, although I must confess that I was often scared when looking at it, even from a distance. Despite this one cannot deny the magnificence of its midnight glows, which entertained people as they glued their eyes to the glowing lava dome and red hot rocks. During the daytime the mountain could be seen emitting smoke from its cavity, while its side was bare and scarred, devoid of the once forest-like foliage and trees. The resulting output of ashes created a delta in the sea, adding some land to the island of Montserrat, which is clearly visible from a distance. It will be a very long time before it can be determined if this new piece of land will be habitable in the future.

During the height of the eruption, my observation of its ultimate beauty passed me by without much thought of how attractive it really was when seen by eyes not marred by fear or dissatisfaction at its ongoing activity. I sometimes wonder how it were that there weren't more accounts of accidents over the cliffs following these eruptions. I am grateful that there weren't more severe consequences resulting from manoeuvring the rugged, hilly terrains in panic. Montserrat is extremely hilly, and there are no protective barriers between a number of roads and the edges of steep cliffs while heading towards the north. People were known to drive almost recklessly in panic while trying to make quick escapes in cars covered with thick ash deposits. No one wanted to be caught in the thick clouds for fear of the consequences. As a result of the mountainous terrain and edgy roads, the islanders are known to be very skilful drivers. More surprising is the fact that more related illnesses hadn't occurred among individuals as people panicked at the sight of the natural wonder of the erupting volcano. It is no wonder that Montserratians are considered to be a very resilient people, with some of the best survival instincts known to man. Throughout the eruptions they continued to show great instincts, using coping mechanisms developed through trial and error. There was some element of risk taking, which the government tried to check through strict guidelines and the posting of officers at checkpoints to deter people from remaining in or returning to areas deemed unsafe. Some individuals had to be removed by some element of force to preserve life and keep down the death toll and injury rate.

As the volcano continued sending mixed signals, and various scientists from different parts of the world tried to understand and predict its activities, normal routine for the island's people continued in a disrupted, uncertain state. Life as we knew it was never going to be the same, but no one knew this at the time, as hopes of the volcano going back to sleep was strengthened through the fervent prayer of the faithful and spiritual reassurances based on the experiences of persons in neighbouring islands. Persons living beyond the village of Salem leading to the north experienced fewer disruptions from ash, pyroclastic flows, and evacuations, but they were no less affected.

Numerous earthquakes and tremors occurred throughout the island, although the location of the epicentre would always determine which areas experienced the heaviest shakes. Damage to some buildings was evidenced through the cracks in the cemented walls, but none ever collapsed or had such structural damage to declare them unfit for dwelling. There was no report of buildings collapsing from these earthquakes because buildings were built strong enough, using modern techniques that enabled them to withstand strong earthquakes. During the years of the volcanic eruptions, earthquakes in Montserrat generated by volcanic activity created some of the most frightening moments of my life. Montserrat is a part of the island arc at a meeting point of two converging tectonic plates, where the earth's crust floats on semi-molten rock; earthquakes are regular occurrences. Despite this, we islanders were accustomed to feeling earthquakes and tremors, reacting to it, and forgetting about it because another one wouldn't normally be felt for months or years.

The many earthquakes and tremors which accompanied the volcanic eruptions differed in frequency and intensity, and as such they created an element of fear because of the constantly anticipated threat. In some twenty-four-hour periods, quakes were recorded in the hundreds and varied in intensity. We sometimes knew one was coming by the ominous rumbling sounds that preceded it. Continuing life as usual on a day-to-day basis became the trend; many tried to appear strong, and others reacted badly to the stress of it all. I continued like everyone else, until one day I finally decided enough was enough. I needed a break from all this packing of bags and moving back and forth. I had grown tired of encroaching on my uncle's space in Salem and running every time ZJB Radio gave the command. We had been lucky to have my uncle and aunt, who were living in the safe area of Salem. Uncle Ben ran a restaurant and bar downstairs, and the living quarters upstairs was big and roomy. He embraced my family and made us feel welcome and comfortable. When the going got rough, he too eventually returned to England where he had spent most of his adult life.

After leaving Salem my family rented a house in St Peter's and only went back to Plymouth to shop and work while it was still safe. St Peter's was felt to be very safe because it was surrounded by the mountain ranges of the Centre Hills. It was easily protected, and one couldn't see the volcano from St Peter's. Despite this, St Peter's still experienced its share of ashes generated by pyroclastic flows; the wind direction was often responsible for this. By this time the entire island, but mostly the south and east of Plymouth including Plymouth itself, appeared to be in chaos.

It was December 1995, the earthquakes had intensified, coming harder and faster, and there were premonitions of gloom and doom. It was possible that something terrible was going to happen, and I couldn't take any more of the ongoing uncertainty. With this in mind, I planned my belated honeymoon with the husband and flew to St Vincent for two solid weeks. By then my grandmother, who had moved several times from the village of Molyneaux to escape the volcano, had passed, and it was time for the burial. I was just too anxious about the increasing earthquakes, which were becoming more severe in intensity, to remain for her funeral. Additionally my best friend was getting married the following week, and I was too uncomfortable with the situation to attend her wedding. Sadly these things played on my mind in St Vincent, and I felt really selfish to have gone away at such important times, but I felt justified and reassured myself that I needed to do it for self-preservation. The period of respite in St Vincent worked well to relieve my stress, and I returned to Montserrat rejuvenated for a time, though still watchful at what the volcano might do next.

On my return to Montserrat, I learnt there had been some extremely heavy rainfall, huge ash fall, and many strong earthquakes. My visiting relatives from the United Kingdom were still on island and couldn't wait to get away from it all. Then one day after I returned to the island, the volcano let loose in such ferocity that army planes were sent in to evacuate people from the island. The place appeared to be in chaos as a number of Montserratians and visitors frantically packed their bags and headed for the airport. I hustled my aunts and uncles who were visiting from England into the army airplane and bid them good-bye with a sigh of relief. My thought at this time was for their safety; with them gone I had less people to worry about.

Life continued on Montserrat with its usual disruptions and commands to evacuate all areas south of Belham. It was 25 June 1997, and we were almost two years into the volcanic crisis when the biggest eruption occurred. That was the fateful day when nineteen persons lost their lives. I stood watching transfixed as a charred body was removed from the helicopter, hoping someone would wake me up if I was dreaming. I am unable to describe how I felt then; there could have been a feeling of emptiness and hopelessness. My job was to save lives, but the first individual I saw was charred in a fixed position—no life left to save, just a mummy to remember in my dreams. The feelings of sadness among other things would come much later. The capital Plymouth and other villages, including the airport, were destroyed, and the south and east of the island had become an exclusion zone. It was no longer inhabitable and wouldn't be for an indeterminate period.

I was part of the mass casualty team trained to be on standby to triage and treat anyone injured or burnt by the massive pyroclastic flows. Despite the simulations and ongoing preparation, I must admit that I never actually expected anyone to lose their lives in the eruptions. I had anticipated minor injuries and was ready for this like everyone else on the team. The north of the island was meant to be safe and became our haven of safety. My village was no longer accessible, and my properties no longer existed. The careful, ongoing monitoring and instructions to move to safer areas had been reassuring, and those who followed the instructions remained safe, although many were displaced.

Homeless

Up until the events following the volcanic awakening, I had never witnessed such a homeless dilemma in the history of Montserrat. Homelessness was practically unheard of, and the few people who were known 'street people' did so by choice. For those who had housing issues, the government had strategies for coming to their aid, providing appropriate accommodation to meet their needs. Homelessness was never an issue, especially not for working class people and certainly not for those who had the means to otherwise purchase their own properties. Montserrat is a very small island, and a very large majority of people were living in the east, west, and south of the island prior to the volcanic activities. The south of the island, including the capital Plymouth, was the most developed and was the home of the island's only hospital, Glendon Hospital and secondary school. Thousands of people were displaced as two-thirds of the island was declared unsafe and made into an exclusion zone monitored and patrolled by police officers. Some of us were fortunate enough to rent vacant properties in the north; others sought temporary accommodation with relatives.

Many Montserratians became homeless by national standards and were housed in shelters in schools and churches. Some of those shelters had limited facilities, creating discomfort and dissatisfaction over time. The purpose for which they had been built did not include hundreds of occupants at any given time. Because all businesses in the exclusion zone had either closed or relocated, there were a large number of jobless people. There was not much to keep people occupied, which created much stress and anxiety. School resumed in the north in makeshift accommodation in some cases, but young people were restless and unoccupied. The junior secondary school in Salem became the main secondary school. There was limited access to televisions and other means of entertainment. People were focused on survival and worried constantly about returning home and whether properties and possessions had been burnt or destroyed. Only limited belongings had been allowed and encouraged in the moves. Even if they could have brought them along, the space to store them was unavailable. No one knew what the future held for them and their families. Many had no relatives to rely on and hadn't a clue what would happen, and they could never return home.

A nurse and I were concerned for the well-being of the young, especially those aged eleven to twenty, and we started a group for adolescents in St Peter's. The group was a welcomed distraction and was well attended by a large number of displaced young people. The majority of members were from the east, mainly Streatham and Windy Hill. After some time a number of young people from the local area started attending regularly as the topics generated great interest and benefits. The aim of the group was to provide an outlet for young people to discuss issues affecting them, thus providing and maintaining a medium for stress relief through group support and one-on-one sessions where indicated. All topics were encouraged, and special attention was given to relationships and sex education. The group was a success, and I am happy to say that none of those young people involved in the group reported becoming pregnant while in Montserrat despite their reduced circumstances.

Additionally, in circumstances where young people could have become bored with little space and not enough recreational activities to challenge them, the group became a point of reference for extracurricular activities. Most of those kids ended up in England and from all accounts are doing pretty good for themselves, managing well in this multicultural state.

CHAPTER 2

Migrate to England

The rest of the story has been well told over and over again of how Britain eventually stepped in and gave the evacuation order to relocate Montserratians to the United Kingdom. It was announced that provisions for housing and support had been organised for those who didn't have relatives to assist them. British Royal Naval ships were often seen way out at sea in those days, patrolling the waters around Montserrat in readiness to evacuate the people off the island if necessary. Thankfully those ships were never used for this purpose, and most people left the island on a ferry to Antigua on their way to England, America, and other Caribbean Islands.

The W. H. Bramble airport with its single-plane airstrip had been destroyed by the pyroclastic flows. The only port of exit from Montserrat was by sea via a hired ferry, with the possible use of a helicopter in emergencies. Reports suggest that two-thirds of the island's population (which was approximately twelve thousand at that time) left Montserrat for safer pastures in the late '90s.

It is not surprising that some Montserrat folk were very reluctant to leave, because they had visions of foreigners moving into Montserrat and taking over their nice houses and hard-earned properties, some of which had been in families for generations. Fear of the unknown also played a part in people's decisions to remain on the island. Meanwhile, some of those who left returned when they realised it was business as usual in Montserrat despite the losses and the ongoing instability of the volcano. Some individuals left because they had no accommodations or jobs, leaving them with little choice but to relocate to greener pastures for economic reasons.

Despite the monitoring of the volcano, its activities were still unpredictable. There were mixed messages coming from different scientists. The English scientists had different predictions than the Americans, and some thought the volcano was a super volcano while others thought it would go back to dormancy after the big event. If it was a super volcano that meant it would have a massive eruption, sending tidal waves to other countries, causing huge losses of both lives and properties.

I needed to get away from the whole thing—the uncertainty of when the volcano would have a massive explosion or go back to sleep, the ash, the eruptions and earthquakes. Life was a mess, yet one was still expected to carry on as normal. There was no break anywhere, no respite for anyone. At some point the Chief Minister in post met with the nurses and suggestions were made for the professionals to be given a break to leave the island do some studies and return later; allowing another group to do the same. This appeared ideal given that there were talks of volunteers coming in to be of service to the hospital. Unfortuantely nothing came of these suggestions at the time and it was business as usual for all.

The proximity to the volcano was just too close for people to be able to relax their guard completely. I decided to leave the island for a few months, not just a few weeks; only I didn't know for sure how or where I would go. The year before, 1996, on a visit to the United States, my concerns were intensified by the anxiety of those who followed the happenings on the news, and I had to force myself to return to Montserrat. It was amazing how fellow Montserratians that were living away from the island actually thought the worst was going to happen; they were even more fearful then than the people who actually experienced the eruptions. Most people I came into contact with expressed fear of the pending volcanic eruptions and strongly encouraged me not to return to Montserrat. I almost gave in to the sympathetic invitations to stay whilst visiting Boston. Still, I decided I needed to get back to Montserrat to my family and work.

My loyalty to kin outweighed my need to feel safe and secure, and with a heavy heart I boarded the plane, obediently returning to Montserrat when my holiday came to an end. By then my daughter, who had been flown out to St Vincent to continue her secondary education away from all the drama and disruptions, had returned to live with us in the safe zone. Unfortunately she felt she wasn't getting the attention she needed from her parents. We were just too busy, and given the nature of our jobs as essential service workers, we were more or less on call most of the time. One afternoon I got home from work feeling tired, after listening to the fears and anxiety of others. My job automatically brought with it the role of supporting others to manage their stress and anxiety. The job was not an easy one because my colleague had already left for England, leaving me to manage the entire case load and demands of the job. As I walked into the house one evening, my daughter appeared very quiet and thoughtful, and she had a fierce look on her face. I greeted her lovingly as usual and wondered what we were fighting about today. She hardly fought about anything, so this was serious, I thought. 'Hi,' I said light-heartedly without looking at her. 'What's up, with you?'

She looked pointedly at the paper lying in front of her on the table, glanced up at me, and said, 'I am writing a letter.'

'Okay,' I replied. 'You're writing to a friend in St Vincent?'

'No,' she replied, 'I'm writing a letter to your boss.'

My heart skipped a beat and I said, 'What did you say'? She repeated the statement without batting an eyelid. I walked towards her and reached out a hand for the letter, saying, 'Let me take a look.' Letter in hand, I sat down and read it. The girl had outlined her issues, mainly being her mom had no time for her family and especially her daughter. The letter was well written, showing that a lot of thought had gone into it. She had given examples of occasions when the volcano had erupted, and she had been left on her own. Also, the hand radios and beepers we service workers carried were going off constantly. She also noted that for all intents and purposes, I was always working because I brought the noisy radio and beeper home. According to her, because the other parent in the house was also a part of the essential services and always on call, there was no one to care for her in an emergency.

She shared great insight into her discontent, and that was when I knew that I had to make a decision in the interest of the family. It was time to take another break from Montserrat. Choosing between the United Kingdom and the United States was not easy. We had ties in both countries, and the American relatives had said we would be welcomed anytime. The British relatives hadn't said much about anything, but I didn't expect them to turn us away. Even if they did, the British government had said to come, and we would be housed. After looking at the pros and cons, Britain won because it offered financial support, free access to health care, educational and job opportunities, and housing.

We set off to London on the ferry on a bright, hot, sunny day, and oh, what a journey that was. The island did not use a ferry service for transporting people in this way prior to the eruptions, so this was a new experience for us. First I stood on the pier at Little Bay, looking up at the hills in the distance and vowing I would be back soon on my beautiful island. I wasn't going to stay in England too long, but rather get the young lady settled in school, leave her with relatives if they would have her, and return home as soon as possible. For some reason I felt very sad, as if I was leaving behind the best part of me forever. Little did I know I was going to be away for a very long time.

The journey to Antigua was anything but uneventful; in fact it was a sailor's nightmare. The seas were rough, and my girl, like many others on board, was seasick and scared. As the ship leapt and bounded across the wide open seas, I held her in my arms and sang the way I used to when she was a baby. I can still picture myself singing in the midst of the storm one of my mom's favourite hymns: 'Peace, peace, sweet peace the gift of God's love.' That ritual of singing and praying during tough times was to continue during the early stages in England. Sometimes it would be happy songs and then sad songs. When the homesickness and loneliness was at its worst, I would put on some Soca music out of Montserrat from the Mighty Arrow's albums and sing, dance, and cry to the music. The journey to England on the British Airways 747 was long but smooth and uneventful. At Gatwick my dear, welcoming aunt and uncle met us, took us home, and made us feel welcomed. We stayed in the southwest of London, where there was a strong cultural mix of whites, blacks, and Asians. There was no culture shock for me, though, because I was a seasoned traveller who had made two prior journeys to England. My daughter was also an experienced traveller who had spent many holidays in America and various islands. Despite this being her first time in England, she adjusted very quickly as I knew she would.

A young lady left Montserrat for England with her family in late 1996. She had recently left school and was not yet experienced in the world of work, but she had great promise and wanted to be an artist. She intended to perfect her skills in drama and fashion when she got to England. Despite her positive outlook for the future, she tells the story in poetic form of how she felt and the emotions she displayed as she took the journey away from her beloved Montserrat.

The Journey

By Alison Wells-Inyang

Reluctantly I left my warm cocoon,
My birthright,
A place that nurtured and protected me.
Together we were one.
We rode life tides,
Enjoyed its carefree pleasures,
Rebuked the rebelliousness
That lurks within its path.
We laughed,
We loved,
We cried,
We shared.

Accommodation

A certain young woman and her daughter left Montserrat in 1997 with the intention of starting afresh in England. The husband remained in Montserrat waiting for the wife to settle; his plan was to remain financially viable so he could provide support until they settled in. They had mortgaged a property in the east of Montserrat and moved in only months before the volcano erupted. The property was no longer accessible, although not yet destroyed by the volcano. The villages around it had been badly affected, and the area was unsafe even for a visit. The lady and her daughter arrived in England as hopefuls who knew a good life back in Montserrat, and they were house proud. She was heavily pregnant with her second child and needed a semblance of comfort suitable for one in her condition. She was surprised when she was offered a flat in a tall tower building which was in poor condition. Feeling she had no choice, she moved in but spent most of her time at her friend's home, which was more comfortable.

This is just one of the many stories I have heard, and some people have faced more difficult situations. Those with relatives to offer support had better luck because they had guidance from individuals who understood the system. The general consensus at the beginning of the migration process was that there would have been representation in place for the Montserrat community; however for most of the system did not appear to be very clear. This impacted greatly on their ability to provide the level of support needed by the migrants.

The issue of finding appropriate accommodation or any, for that matter; turned out to be more difficult than it had sounded before we left Montserrat. My dearest Aunt Rose and Uncle Dave, whom we had stayed with initially, waited on us hand and foot for two weeks while we became acclimated. By week two my uncle took us to the housing office to seek what I soon learnt was housing benefit. Surprisingly we were told the office knew nothing of the Montserrat situation—they had never heard of a volcanic island whose people were now provided for by Britain. We went away disillusioned. We were disappointed of course but not daunted and further research revealed that Montserratians in Hackney in the east of London were assisted with housing and other benefits without many problems. Diane Abott, the Member of Parliament in post then, was actively lobbying for the cause of Montserrat nationals who migrated to England and chose to live in Hackney. It was good to know that the Montserrat case was being championed not only by herself but another MP based in Tottenham.

Taking 2 double-decker buses to complete our three-hour journey, we headed off to Hackney to seek accommodation. We never even thought of taking the train because we hadn't mastered the use of the underground yet. On arrival in upper Clapton, Hackney, we initially shared an overcrowded house with a Montserrat family who had relocated there some months before and were already set up in the system. They had left late in 1996 before the major eruptions. The head of the household had just given birth to a premature baby that was conceived in Montserrat. A newly qualified nurse, she had migrated to England shortly after learning that she was pregnant. The baby boy, who eventually became my godson, was not big enough to fill my palm and had to be kept in the special baby unit at the Homerton University Hospital for several months. Needless to say, that baby was nurtured and has grown to be a lovely, healthy, and strong young man.

It was this family that gave us invaluable support for a short while and enabled and directed us through the correct processes and agencies to contact for accommodation. They were also supporting another family at the same time. It was to be another two weeks before we were offered housing in a flat, which was so run down and dirty that my daughter still reminds me to this day that it was the first time in all her life she had seen me cry. Yes, I cried unashamedly in front of the housing officer when I saw the condition of the flat; the tears just flowed and wouldn't stop. It wasn't that I was a proud person, as I consider myself to be very humble, but as with most Montserratians I would say figuratively that my home is my castle and must reflect that inside and outside. At a glance I couldn't figure out how this flat in such great need of redecorating could ever become close to anything I would be proud to call home. Further, if you lived in a terrible state such as this, some Montserrat folk would certainly look down on you and talk about you negatively.

I tried not to be too disappointed by the condition of the place and accepted the flat. I set to work single-handedly to make it habitable and a home for us. I was all alone in Hackney, with no family or friends to call on for the type of help I needed. Neither could I afford to pay to decorate the flat at that time. I decided on the only logical alternative: I had to do absolutely everything on my own. The bathroom was in a worse condition than the rest of the flat because it was full of mould and mildew. I had never removed and replaced wallpaper before, but with determination I repapered the entire bathroom and bedroom by myself. I was told it looked good by visitors and felt grateful for the compliments. One of the things I had to come to grips with was the size of the rooms in the flat. They were really small in comparison to those we were accustomed to in Montserrat. In fact the entire flat was only the size of some Montserratian living room and kitchen combined. This was something of a shock for a number of us, which created some fuel for discussions when we met up. Despite this I was still very grateful to have a place to call home and did not complain.

Social Interaction

A young lady remarked on the interaction of people with each other, or lack thereof. 'No one has time to say hello or offer assistance. No one greets you, and if you greet them first, they look at you as if you are crazy. This is not my culture; we are like family and treat everyone with respect.'

Despite all these changes, she has adapted quite well to this society. Like many others, she has not given up her cultural beliefs and values, but has incorporated it into her current lifestyle. She has since married with two children and recently graduated with a degree.

Like the young lady above, I initially found it difficult to adjust to the reserved attitude of neighbours in London. At first it came as a bit of a shock that no one greeted me or acknowledged my greetings. People in Montserrat are very friendly and helpful to all, no matter who they were or where they came from. I thought the Londoners appeared quite reserved. I was quite open about my thoughts and feelings then. I have since learnt that this is not always appreciated in England. After living in London for a year or so, I learned about the basis of the reserves of Londoners. On a visit to an area outside London, I ignored those I met, having adopted the behaviour. I was rather surprised when people greeted and chatted to me easily and politely.

The reality is that virtually everyone in London migrated into the inner city from another geographical location, be it another city in England or Europe or elsewhere—hence the term melting pot. People appear to be in a hurry to get somewhere and are focused on their own business.

This gross generalisation is proven to be just a stereotypical issue; when you actually associate with people through work and other social events, they are quite pleasant and polite. Upon evaluation I soon recognised that life in London was about getting on with it and trying to achieve your goals. For those living outside London, the atmosphere is usually calmer and more casual, with people politely queuing for buses and saying thank you on disembarking. People are known to take time to have a chat and greet each other. In some instances those living in villages could be related in some way or have known each other for ages, giving way to a more trusting and accepting existence.

Moving On

Settling in London was not easy, but willpower outweighed the challenges, and in no time I had a calm household, got a job, and started university. Pursuing a degree was one of the goals I dared not hope would become a reality back in Montserrat, because I would have to find the funding for tuition or join the queue waiting for some agency to provide the funding and offer a scholarship. Then I would have had to travel to one of the campuses of the regional University of the West Indies (UWI) based in Barbados, Cavehill, Jamaica, St Augustine, or some other country to study.

There was no university for locals on Montserrat, although the island did house the American University of the Caribbean (AUC) for foreign students studying medicine. The AUC has since relocated to St Martin. Migration to Britain contributed to our education in a very big way by offering funded opportunities for career and personal development. I soon got over my dissatisfaction at having to start from the bottom again in the same way a newly qualified person would. The other tertiary education provider on the island was a secondary facility on Montserrat called the University Centre, an affiliate of UWI. This created the opportunity for tertiary education through studies up to certificate level credits, which can carry over to a degree at one of the campuses.

Here in England the British government had allocated funds for Montserratians in England to pursue tertiary education at universities, and I had successfully secured a place at the London Metropolitan University in London, then known as the University of North London. I completed the honours degree in health studies in two years as the first step in higher education, and I then studied further for a master's degree. Thirteen plus years later, I am still in England planning to return to Montserrat sometime in the future but still not sure when or how.

As life stories go, with its ebbs and flows, I cannot say I have been disappointed by the outcome of my migrant status in England, except that I still miss the Montserrat I used to know most terribly at times. England is not a substitute for Montserrat, but like many I have embraced it as the next best thing and have adapted to its varied cultures while trying keeping my own cultures and values intact. On some days it causes an ache deep in my heart that leaves what feels like a gaping hole to know that so much of the Montserrat I knew and its culture no longer exists. The effects of life in Britain have created cultural challenges for Montserratians in general. Most have adapted quite well, but a small number have returned to Montserrat because they find it difficult to adapt to a new country.

The reasons most people gave for migrating was to meet their immediate needs for housing and jobs, provide schooling for children, and generally uplift the tidal wave of low morale created by the volcanic eruptions. It was never anticipated that the migrant society would be totally disruptive and that people would lose their sense of being Montserratians. However as is the case with any change, there has been some anticipated experiences that have not been very positive, and as people deal with challenges differently, each individual has had a story to tell. People were just too desperate for a better life and wanted to get out of Montserrat quickly. Looking for a chance to reduce the stress created by the erupting volcano, they had no time to think of the resulting impact on the culture. Still, the benefits of being in England have been tremendous despite the initial discomfort due to lack of direction (and support in some instances).

Whereas previous migration out of Montserrat during the '50s was attributed to a need to increase the economic status of the self and support relatives back home, for the migrants of the '90s it was about survival. The intent of most was to be away from Montserrat for a limited time and return home when the volcano goes back to sleep. Many that I know felt five years was a good time frame to aim to return to the island. Five years have come and gone twice over, and yet the majority of us are still in England and haven't made any plans to go back. The vast resultant changes, and the consequences of the eruptions and subsequent migration, were never anticipated in the least.

Montserratians in England as a whole have had to make huge adjustments to their way of life, the cultural norms and laws of the country. As to be expected, this has constituted a difficult journey for some, but others have been able to adapt successfully. Below I give an account of the cultural impact of schooling, parenting and discipline, and health care, as well as their impact on relationships and the quality of life.

Modern England

According to my Aunt Rose, who migrated to England in the 1950s after travelling by sea on a French ship, things are much better for immigrants now than they have ever been. Few planes if any flew to the Caribbean then, and the only people from Montserrat who had travelled as far as England were a few nurses and teachers. As such not much was known of the cultures and lifestyles of England. Aunt Rose told her story of having left Montserrat in a lovely cotton dress during the late summer of 1954.

She was to learn the error of wearing such an inappropriate dress when she got to cold, damp England. She mentioned that a number of enthusiastic folk were picked up from different Caribbean islands on the way to England; the goal was to find a better life and earn money.

The ship took about nine days to get to the port in England. She has seen many changes since then and is happy at the way things have shaped up since her arrival. She made no judgements as she gave an account of her many experiences as a West Indian in England. Blacks back then were not allowed to rent certain homes and would be told the places were already taken when inquiries were made. She thought that this was not necessarily the truth but more a case of blacks not being thought 'good enough' to rent such accommodations then. One must remain in one's place in those days if unlucky enough to be born outside the acceptable ethnicity. Despite her light skin and soft hair, she felt she did not fit. She made it quite clear that things have changed over the years and those extreme situations no longer exists. Additionally she has had her share of opportunities in England. She started out working at a chocolate factory and eventually trained to be a nurse, retiring in the '90s.

She fondly recalls her first week in England. With stars in her eyes in her early twenties, she was very enthusiastic and hopeful of a bright British future. She had enlisted to travel to England with the support of her large family, but she knew no one in England and had no idea where she was going to stay when she got there. Still, she was determined to find a better life, and with the sense of adventure common to the young, England was beckoning. She planned to return home eventually, once she had her education and career sorted. Luckily she met a young lady of Montserrat origins on the ship, and she was well organised. The young lady had good connections and was meeting friends in England. She liked Aunt Rose's easy-going, pleasant personality and asked her to join them. Feeling extremely lucky, Aunt Rose took up the offer, and that is how her future began.

On arrival in England, they met the woman's friends and subsequently settled at a flat in North London. Aunt Rose recalled that she was unprepared for the cool temperatures and had no cardigan or jacket. Her less than adequate cotton dress was unable to protect her, and she had her first shocking experience of real cold. A few days later Aunt Rose was introduced to a gentleman who offered her a job in a chocolate factory. She was happy to find employment so soon but would have preferred the opportunity to pursue nursing, which was her first choice. Following her more experienced companion's guidance, she accepted the factory job as a temporary means of supporting herself.

Left to find her way on the first working day, she got lost because she had no idea what door number she lived at upon returning from the factory. She hadn't realised that all the doors were painted the same colour then and had individual identifying numbers. Back in Montserrat all doors were individual to their owners, and no two looked alike. She had expected England to be the same. Scared and vulnerable in her new, unfamiliar environment, she had walked up and down the street for hours followed by two men in a big black car. This made her even more uncomfortable. The men politely asked if she wanted help, and because she did not know who they were and thought the worst, she firmly rejected their assistance. After many hours of walking back and forth looking at each door hopefully; she realised she was still being followed by the two men. Imagine her relief when she saw her friend coming up the street towards her. She later learnt that the two men were police officers.

She had virtually flown into her friend's arms with tearful relief. After that initial mistake, she quickly learnt her way around and took nothing for granted. She had discovered the difference of living away from Montserrat, and her powers of observation intensified. For survival she had to learn to adapt very quickly; her experience was not dissimilar to many who came to England in the '90s. West Indians back in the 1950s came to Britain mainly for economic reasons. The expectation then was that they would work and send money back home. The pound has always had a good exchange value against the Caribbean dollar and goes a long way, and the support of relatives was taken very seriously as an obligation. Like most people who migrated from their beloved lands, they intended to return to help support and rebuild the economy once they had earned enough. Some have successfully returned upon retirement, but others never did.

The trend continues throughout the ages, and from experience we are aware that many people never returned to their homeland for one reason or the other. Aunt Rose and many other Montserratians of the 1950s further reported how West Indians were kept in their places and had limited opportunities to progress due to work and family commitments. Some were known to start work as labourers from a very young age and couldn't realise their educational dreams as a result. A very small number were able to think outside the box, slip through the net, and end up in professional employment. Since the arrival of those who came in the '90s onwards to England, from time to time I have heard the phrase 'Because I am black', which reflects the way West Indians felt about the way they were treated. Looking on from a distance, it was obvious that a large number of blacks saw themselves as vulnerable victims of their race and circumstances, because discrimination was felt to be a very common occurrence by some.

However, by the 1990s when the volcano-driven migrants arrived in England, it was not very clear at times that the perceptions of being discriminated against were always as obvious as it had been in the '50s. It could be that new policies and guidelines seeking to create a state of equal opportunities in England have made individuals more conscious of their overt actions. Despite all the efforts made to control discrimination against ethnic minorities, there is obviously still a lot of work to be done to reduce the ongoing inequality.

Currently there is an obvious economic downturn, and many are feeling the effects. Is there any truth in these allegations, and if so, what are we to do about it? If one faces economic difficulties in England, and there is job loss, who do we turn to? It is obvious the motherland cannot support us. There are no jobs, no accommodation, and not enough educational institutions on Montserrat. Does that leave us homeless, nameless, and unwanted folk who, due to circumstances caused by Mother Nature, were pushed into another man's land? This is ultimately an ongoing dilemma, and we dare not think of what would happen in such circumstances.

Organisations, including the inner London hospital I started out working at, have been proactive in investing in people, and that included everyone who took up the offer of funds for continuing professional development. 'Investing in people' certainly became a buzz phrase for a short period, but current financial constraints have made it virtually impossible for organisations to continue with this type of support. Still, while the good times rolled, the benefits for most were tremendous—but as the saying goes, 'all good things must come to an end'. There have certainly been noises around equality and diversity, and a number of groups have cropped up over time with the intent to represent and provide support for individuals from black and minority ethnic (BME). These groups, along with the support of several unions, have served to change the fate of not only West Indians but those from other minority backgrounds.

So for all intents and purposes, I hardly ever hear that self-reducing term anymore, and Montserrat folk of this era appear to have had better overall support and motivation resulting in less emphasis on 'Because I am black'. Rather than sitting back pitifully, individuals are striving to keep up with everyone else, setting goals and finding ways of achieving them. That should not create a negative reflection on those who came before us, because through their experiences, subsequent stories and obvious warnings, those who came later were already made aware of the obvious pitfalls. It would have been more than disappointing had the negative experiences continued indefinitely without a struggle. These in no way suggest that there are no vulnerable individuals existing in the society; nor does it suggest an absolute cleansing from inequalities. It could be that the support systems available to those who choose to access it are being more effectively utilised.

The other not so obvious explanation could be that people are scared of speaking out and have come to accept their circumstances for what they are rather than rocking the boat. Some individuals have expressed fear of causing further problems by complaining of issues which affect them, and they would prefer to confide concerns to those whom they trust.

School and Discipline

Opportunities and experiences for Montserratians in England certainly appear better now than they would have been in the '50s and '60s. There is no longer such a thing as missing school or joining the labour force at an early age. It doesn't matter who you are in this country; the law stipulates that if you miss a day of school, someone has to pay, and that someone is usually parents. This passage does not discuss education in its entirety because that subject has been adequately covered and researched. The idea here is to give an insight into the various cultural issues that affect the progress and socialisation of the Montserrat child in England. Formal education as we know it is compulsory in the United Kingdom for all children of primary and secondary age groups.

Those who wish to attend university have access to student loans, which are available to those who qualify. Student grants are now a thing of the past, and as the cost of living increases in England, so does the cost of attending universities. It is uncertain how many will be able to afford the increasing costs of education in the future, but this is a common problem amongst all British children. Schools are not problem free, and a number of those children who arrived in the UK during the '90s and beyond have had their own unique set of discriminatory struggles which have affected them in various ways over the years. As is often said, *children will be children* and as such they are less able to control their emotions and responses to anything that is new or unusual, or appears not to fit in.

Discrimination and initiation to new schools is not unknown to Montserratians, but when combined with other issues it can become overwhelming. Some examples of this type of issue would be the boys attending secondary school in Montserrat for the first time. During the first week, their experience would be wide and varied, ranging from being knocked with knuckles on shorn heads to having to clean the shoes of senior boys. This form of bullying would last only for a short period and has not been known to have any long-term psychological effect. On the other hand, some Montserrat children attending schools in some areas in the inner and outer London areas have reported ongoing discrimination, resulting in feelings of isolation as they tried to adapt and fit in. They reported being bullied by other children at certain schools, and it continued for years.

Attempts to get parents to control the children who cause the problems have met with negativism, which in some cases resulted in feelings of dissatisfaction. In some cases the way the school handles the issues has left parents and students disgruntled and misunderstood. Although bullying and harassment is not unique to Montserrat children and is in fact a common experience shared by others in different parts of the world, the type and nature can have long-term psychological effects. For the Montserrat children, it is the combination of trying to adapt to a new society and way of life, combined with the bullying, that has caused those affected to have major setbacks. Some children have been known to stay away from school because these ongoing experiences have impacted their confidence and ability to socialise with other children. While some used coping mechanisms that worked for them, reinforced by family support at home, there were others who may not have had a very good stronghold at home and suffered social isolation as a result. Some children tried to work things out in their own way by fighting back, creating more tension and unrest. Because fighting is not tolerated in schools, these children have been suspended from time to time, resulting in more frustration and delinquent behaviours such as truancy.

Missing lessons has created major gaps in their education, making it difficult to catch up with their peers. Continued disruptions in their education may have resulted in otherwise intelligent children struggling without an obvious career path. At times there have been difficulties finding colleges willing to accept these children—who, by the time they reach college age, would have had a label of being badly behaved and disruptive. Many of those who managed to complete formal education have had so many issues in school that by the age of seventeen or eighteen they've built up poor records which ultimately follow then to every interview and put them in a bad light. Younger children who reportedly have had experiences of inappropriate responses from fellow students and parents have had to overcome many difficulties to survive in the system. Some have successfully moved to schools where they are more comfortable, but others have had to endure the unfavourable remarks and inappropriateness for a long time.

Moving schools brings with it other major issues related to distance of travel, and it compromises the parents' ability to pick them up after school. Where there are other children in the household attending different schools, trying to manage the situation favourably could be a very daunting one. A combination of culture shock and perhaps lack of support from persons of similar cultures may have impacted on educational attainment for some teenagers who arrived in Britain during the late 1990s. I say this because a number of children who were thought to have positive future potential back in Montserrat were not able to realise their dreams, leaving them feeling despondent and unsure of the future. There is no way of knowing if outcomes would have been different had things remained unchanged by volcanic activities and there was no migration.

The upside is that it has not been all gloom and doom for the children who migrated in the '90's. There are those who have been fortunate enough to successfully enrol in schools that are very multicultural and have children from similar and mixed minority backgrounds. Many of those schools are located in London and the bigger inner cities, where there are large mixes of ethnic populations. In some cases children may have been born in Britain to parents who migrated here some time ago. Overall it appears that children of Montserrat origin have been able to hold their own in many areas of academia, boasting similar successes in the education arena, and they have progressed despite migration and the adaptive changes they experienced. These children have remained focussed throughout and have gone on to attain various qualifications at universities and colleges. A large number hold prestigious jobs in the community and have been able to maintain successful social relationships.

It has been recognised that individuals learn at a different pace, and the Montserratian child—or even adult, who is a slower learner—has loads of opportunities for developmental support in England. Those who receive benefits will be offered opportunities for prevocational studies, leading to appropriate qualifications and enabling them to find jobs to take them off benefits, or 'the dole'. There are loads of opportunities for most of those who are genuinely interested in learning, and some options are free of cost. It's really up to the individual to make the best of every opportunity for personal development.

That brings us to the issue of discipline, which is the big issue on everyone's agenda. Instilling discipline in children is a very important aspect of the Montserrat culture, and I can recall a number of times back in the homeland when I would hear the biblical term 'Spare the rod and spoil the child' quoted as a way of justifying discipline. Children in Montserrat are expected to be obedient to parents and those in authority, or else they will certainly be punished. Punishment can take various forms, but the most common form remembered by most is the use of corporal punishment both at home and school. In Montserrat the ultimate embarrassment as a child is to be asked to choose their object of punishment to increase their shame and remorse at the wrong they had done. Choices can range from twigs called whips to rulers, belts, wires, and shoes. The severity of the punishment would vary depending on the seriousness of the crime. This is an acceptable form of punishment on the island and was no way deemed as abuse by most of the children who grew up on Montserrat. As can be expected, Montserratians who migrated to England continued to use this culturally appropriate form of punishment to discipline their children. Some continued this practice despite knowledge of the contrary laws of Britain, which is totally against corporal punishment because it is thought to be abusive, and from some accounts there have been those who have used corporal punishment with such force to cause long-term harm. Others used the practice out of ignorance of the law of the land, but the backlash for those caught has had similar emotional impact despite their level of knowledge or severity of punishment.

The state's laws on discipline for children have had a far-reaching emotional impact on parents and children, affecting the very core of their interpersonal relationships with each other. Parents' fears of disciplining their children via their usual methods have left them feeling disempowered to deal with issues such as truancy and delinquency. The thought of a social worker turning up at someone's home after being informed by a neighbour or a teacher at school that there is suspected abuse of a child is enough to deter many Montserratian parents in Britain. The following story is an account of the experience of a single mother of three sons of primary school age. The mother opened her door cautiously to a knock one day after she had set her sons down to dinner. On opening her door, she noticed a lady and a policeman standing outside. She asked, 'How can I help you? Is something wrong?' The lady at the door pulled out a card identifying her as a social worker and explained that she was there to question her about her children. Feeling apprehensive lest her sons had committed some crime, the lady let them in.

At the end of the visit, the mother knew that she had been accused of beating up her eleven-year-old son. She explained he had bruised his back falling down the stairs the day before. Apparently whilst changing for physical education, the bruising was noticed by the PE teacher. The teacher questioned the child and was assured by him that he had fallen down the stairs at home while messing about with his brothers. Not believing this, or perhaps just to cover her own back in case there was some truth to it; the teacher reported the matter to social services. Not surprisingly there was an obvious obligation to investigate the matter. On hearing the mother's side of the story, which was identical to that of the child, the social worker was satisfied that there was no evidence of abuse and hence no cause for alarm. However as per policy she couldn't just walk away without taking formal action, so she asked for two character references from the mother, which were supplied, and the investigation closed. The mother was informed that the case would be kept on record for future reference in the event of any further incidents involving the boys.

The mother was terrified and feels that as a result of this experience, she had lost her ability to discipline her boys the way she would like to in the future. Her greatest fear was that the boys would take advantage of the situation and end up threatening to call social services, as many children do when they can't have their way. Being a single female parent with three young boys, she was already placed at a disadvantage for not having a male role model in the home. Her fears intensified, exacerbated by the current gang culture among young men, where the loss of lives from violence was on the rise. This was certainly not a problem she would have had to deal with in Montserrat, and as such had limited reserves of experience to fall back on.

One of the disadvantages of coming from a small, close-knit society is that people are very easily identified by their stories. For many Montserratian parents and especially single mothers, the impact of migration and resettlement in Britain often places them at a disadvantage in using culturally appropriate means of disciplining children in a meaningful way. The adaptation process hasn't been easy and continues to create problems culturally and emotionally as they try to learn new ways to support their children through education and relationship-building strategies. The real dilemma for the Montserrat parent in Britain, whether of single household or nuclear and extended family units, is how to support children in such a community where kids are vulnerable and easily influenced by the impact of the number of subcultures. There has been no easy solution to this question.

Naturally some people question the use of corporal punishment as a means of discipline for Montserrat children in Britain. Can the continued use of this method of punishment be attributed to ignorance? Is it not important to understand the laws of the country within which you dwell? We admit that laws are there to protect rather than create problems, so what is the problem with us Montserratians then? Things are obviously not as clear cut as just accepting laws of a country and moving on. There is certainly more to it than that, when one considers the cultural implications for a people accustomed to a certain freedom of existence. Furthermore, just as conforming to a new set of laws doesn't take place instantly, in the same way most children would not instantly respond to a new type of discipline.

There are obvious consequences from both viewpoints, and only a well-organised support system would serve to provide the mechanism needed by both children and parents to make the transition into the British culture a more satisfying one. That brings us to another worrying thought on the issue of understanding. It is quite likely that people used the form of discipline they considered correct as a result of not knowing another way existed. In some cases it was not brought to their attention that the method was no longer appropriate outside Montserrat, resulting in them acting out of ignorance. Nevertheless a different school of thought carries the conviction that a number of people use their cultural background as a smoke screen to carry out crimes. This cannot be denied or ignored, but it still doesn't resolve the problem of strategic support for migrants on entry to the country through relevant contextual information sharing.

The solution might very well be in the organisation of communities equipped to support the young, especially those approaching puberty and adolescence in specific areas of concern. This, however, raises the issue of funding, volunteerism, and location. Of course there are a number of people out there trying to harness and support the floundering young Montserrat community in England, but they are very few and far between. We need commitment and financial sustainability to be able to provide a service to save young Montserratians before they become lost in the ever evolving subcultures of Britain.

Employment

In analysing the welfare status of Montserratians, it was revealed that many were able to secure low-paid jobs and were experiencing difficulties meeting their needs.

A young man claimed that despite his educational background, he had to take odd jobs that were not consistent with his qualifications. He was annoyed that he could not validate his degree from back home. On investigating further, he found that many migrants, despite being highly qualified in their countries, had to settle for jobs as taxi drivers, shop workers, or security officers; some remained on job seekers' allowance for a very long time. The resulting low morale from such situations have had varied impacts on the adaptive process. For others their experiences have been more positive, and they've been able to carry over their respective qualifications from their countries.

Finding employment related to prior training and experience in the workforce has not been an easy task for the newly migrated Montserratian in England. Many years later, people are still struggling to regain the status they once held in the workforce. The migration and resettlement processes have been fraught with work-related challenges that have etched deep, unhealable scars in their lives. Certain professions are regulated in Britain, and there are laws setting the qualification one must have to practice. This has resulted in a number of Montserratians finding it necessary to return to study for relevant qualifications within their fields, despite having gained similar qualifications in the Caribbean. Those who were trained teachers in the Caribbean—and almost every other professional who did not receive their original qualification in Britain—were told they had to earn a relevant qualification if they were to find a job within their field.

The exception to the rule was the qualified nurses from Montserrat. Nursing qualifications gained in many other countries are usually not recognised in Britain, requiring the holder to complete a conversion course before being allowed to work. However, the Montserratians already qualified as registered nurses on arrival in Britain were requested only to register with the regulatory body, the Nursing and Midwifery Council (NMC), after which they could apply for work. On the other hand, midwives were advised that they had to undergo a top-up course, or complete the entire eighteen-month course if preferred, before they could apply for related work. Those midwives who were also qualified nurses were able to find work as regular nurses, and the majority chose to specialise in other fields of nursing. It was disappointing to learn that nurses who had worked in senior positions in Montserrat prior to relocating were advised that they had to apply for the most junior job held by a qualified nurse in Britain. They started at the bottom of the ladder in the same position as a new nurse would find herself.

The upside to this was that Montserratian nurses were trained as generalists, and therefore it didn't matter what areas of specialty they found themselves in; they were able to adapt quickly, perform well in the clinical areas, and further develop their skills. As opportunities afforded themselves in England, those nurses eventually worked their way back up into senior positions.

Nurses who held nursing assistant positions in Montserrat and who were not yet qualified appeared to have benefited most, because they were afforded the opportunity to study and obtain registered nursing status. Being very motivated and already functional by nature of their previous Montserrat experience; a number of them soon climbed up the ladder into senior positions, holding positions as high as those previously considered to be their seniors back in Montserrat. The basis of this could very well be found in the difficulties in getting beyond band seven posts in England, given the competitiveness to gaining these higher positions. It is therefore not surprising that a number of persons are stuck at the same level and can see no clear pathway to moving beyond band seven. There is really no clear-cut solution to this type of stagnancy, and the answer may be looking for opportunities outside of nursing if individuals are so inclined or moving into teaching positions by obtaining further qualifications.

For a large number of Montserratians, their pathway to gaining work has been fraught with disappointment and frustration. That they had varying respectable positions back in Montserrat and are now given the impression that they are only fit for 'menial' jobs, or they need to go back to study for a qualification they already owned—the experiences have been just short of demeaning. Some choose to live off state benefits, or the dole, while others rose to the challenge and went back to study for relevant qualifications. Skilled workers, including those in construction and environmental fields, were also expected to gain qualifications in their relevant areas if they wanted a proper job that paid well. Some individuals who had not attended any studies for many years, and those who had never attended secondary school or college, found this a very daunting prospect. Others used the opportunity to develop new skills and gain new qualifications, which brought them satisfaction and self-respect. As can be expected, some individuals collecting benefits became dissatisfied with just sitting at home and waiting for handouts. Eventually many decided to go back to college and university to gain new qualifications, leading to satisfying jobs.

Still, there are others who would have liked to return to work but have been limited by the need to care for young children at home. Others were obliged to drop young children off and pick them up from school, having no support or resource to do otherwise. Back in Montserrat finding someone trustworthy to assist with children would not have been a problem, because the close bond between extended family and neighbours would have provided the necessary support in such cases. In Britain individuals worry continuously about children being safety cared for when left with nannies and caregivers. We also cannot forget the social worker knocking on the door, as this would be the reality if children of a certain age weren't picked up from school or were not supervised by parents in the correct way. Despite the obvious difficulties, caring and supporting the youth is a priority, the importance of which cannot be ignored.

As so nicely put by one of the Montserrat youth links on a popular networking site, many aspire to develop self personally and professional with an intention of repatriation back to Montserrat in order to support those at home. There is no doubt that pushing national pride now will enable these dreams to be a reality in the future.

Health Care

'Norse mi wantu piddle, bring di battle yah foo mi'. (Nurse I want to pass urine, bring the urinal for me).

Access to health care resources in England certainly reaches beyond any resource that Montserrat has or would ever be able to provide in the foreseeable future. Despite its cultivation of excellent, home-grown nurses and doctors, the dilemma of Montserrat as an overseas dependant territory of Britain is the lack of financial autonomy. The knock on effect of limited funding for health care equipment severely impacts the island's health care system, resulting in overseas travel to neighbouring islands, and even as far as England for specialist care and diagnostics. In fact specimens for biopsies are often sent to England, resulting in delayed diagnosis and treatment interventions. Despite this Montserrat has been able to boast 100 per cent maintenance in some areas of health care, such as immunization and vaccination.

Diseases were usually at a minimum in the years preceding the eruptions, to the extent that nurses studying for the three-year professional programme were sent to Jamaica for clinical experience. This ensured that they observed and learned to care for patients with various disorders not prevalent in Montserrat.

In England, Montserrat folk with their status as British citizens are eligible for free health care. Registration with a doctor referred to as general practitioner is the main criteria. Most specialist care is free on the National Health Service (NHS), dependant only on funding from primary care trusts. The unintentional drawback is usually the waiting times, but compared to what is offered in Montserrat, it still comes out on top. For those remaining on Montserrat, having to travel for care to neighbouring islands, and the accompanied cost, creates major problems for many. Needless to say, on the basis of being British those who remain in Montserrat do have some form of access to health care in England and can further benefit from the advanced services offered in the United Kingdom, where there is access to a wealth of private practices and specialist services. There is an obvious cost and method to accessing these services.

Culture plays an important role in access to any service, and health care is no exception. For the most part Montserratians in England have blended in and are able to adequately express most of their basic health care needs. The cultural barrier is not totally absent and often becomes apparent where there are deficits in cognitive states, as seen in dementia-related disorders, strokes, and neurological disorders. Even in the absence of cognitive impairment, some terminologies used in Montserrat often have a different meaning in England. The other key language barrier is the communication style and dialect of Montserrat, which is understood by all Montserratians whether at home or abroad, but not necessarily by everyone with which they come into contact. There is a free way of speaking among the island folk, and when communicating it is important to listen carefully to what is being said while checking body language at the same time. If careful attention is not given, the context of the message can be distorted to have a different meaning than that intended by the speaker.

The communicating Montserratian may make a statement which means one thing to a Montserratian and something else to the non-Montserratian. As such many a blunder has been made, and remarks and comments can be taken out of context as a result of general ignorance about the folk speech and intent. This dilemma has been observed by many who agree that the context and perceptions in communication with non-Montserratians is very important to getting the right message across. There is still a lot to learn about communicating the British way, and folks have had to deal with the consequences of remarks made loosely that had different meanings to the listeners. This can have negative consequences in health care, as well as with benefit agencies and other organisations. It is expected that individuals living in metropolitan London would fare better over time because professionals are more exposed to a larger mix of cultures and traditions. As time passes, many Montserratians are learning to communicate in a different way, although there are difficulties for the older members. Access to advocates though limited is also a possibility and can be accessed in some organisations.

There is an element of vulnerability because the English-speaking Montserratians come across as not needing advocates. Some may disagree with this since the majority of older folk are more versed at speaking the island's dialect. It can be argued that despite using English as the main means of communicating, the Montserrat dialect spoken on the island may actually be considered their first language. In fact some older folk find it difficult to have a proper conversation in English and often interchange between English and dialect, causing some difficulty to the listener. If this dilemma was understood by those with whom it matters, then for all intents and purposes older Montserratians would need advocates in various systems to allow them to maximise the benefits of certain aspects of health care and other services in England.

An area of some concern could be the care of the Montserrat elderly in England.

The common term '*Take me out of Montserrat, but you can't take Montserrat out of me*' gives new meaning to the way some older folk respond to issues, thus disclosing their attitudes towards life in England. Elderly folk in Montserrat are often part of the extended family and as such receive ongoing care in a loving and caring environment. The picture in England is sometimes much different, and more often than not the elderly may require placement in residential or nursing homes, where relatives live distances apart. Older folk may have very limited concepts of how things really are in England, resulting in unrealistic demands placed on the younger person because of expectations to be cared for in the same manner as they would have in Montserrat. Oftentimes raising the subject of residential and nursing home placement is met with the stubbornness of a brick wall and many unfavourable confrontations. This often results in very complex and challenging situations as feelings of guilt override good sense, and the elderly is allowed to remain at home rather than be forced to settle into an appropriate environment. The individual's capacity to make decisions is a very serious issue in health and social care. The other issue is where work pressures and family commitments create difficulties to the provision of care of the elderly at home, resulting in a nursing home being used as the alternative of choice. Prior to migration, when things were virtually unspoilt and family friendly in Montserrat, it was generally thought by older folk that if they were placed in a nursing home, they were being sent there to die. This attitude has not changed by any means despite the exposure to a more enlightened way of life in England. Though good sense dictates that the nursing home is the best option for safety, this is usually met by negative responses and resistance from the older folk. Other members of the family also have a tendency to blame the one member of the family informally identified as main caregiver.

A certain young lady had an elderly mother and a teenage daughter living with her in a tiny, two-bedroom flat. The mother was disabled and needed more care than the young lady could provide. The lady had a full-time job and studied at the same time to improve her qualifications in order to meet the demands of her job's continual professional development guidelines. Her husband, who remained in Montserrat, was planning to join her in England as soon as he could leave his demanding job. On recognising the difficulty of finding space to study in the small flat and the possible contribution to ill health and stress, she made the decision to move her demanding mom into sheltered accommodation. Being one of nine children and yet the only one providing support to her mom, for a number of reasons she based her decision on the need for self-preservation. Needless to say, her decision, although made for the correct reasons, made her very unpopular with her mom and some relatives. The siblings appeared to understand her circumstances, but some of her mom's siblings, of which there were a number of them in England, had no regard for her feelings as a young woman trying to adapt to a new environment, and they piled on the guilt.

One of the mom's many sisters went as far as to write a letter reinforcing her mom's ideology of being placed in a nursing home to die. Despite being retired and living in England for most of her adult life, the sister made no attempt to offer support of any kind to the newcomers to England; rather she allowed ignorance to reinforce negative thoughts of supportive placements. Now eleven years later, the mom is still alive and continues to live in the sheltered accommodation. Her health continues to deteriorate as she gets older, and further care in a different environment is needed. She has refused to leave the environment with the same entrenched belief that a move to another type of accommodation is a move to her death. Under the Mental Capacity Act, she has the capacity to make her own decision about where she lives.

The daughter decided that rather than go down the Depravation of Liberty route, she will allow her mother to make the final decision of placement. Is the issue of capacity overplayed? Should older people at risk of self-neglect and abuse of many types be allowed to make decisions about where they receive care? Is the issue of capacity a benefit or hindrance? Many would certainly prefer the description of hindrance when it relates to elderly placement and some aspects of care. Despite the resistance common to a number of older people, not only those of Montserrat origin, it is imperative that the correct decision is made in the best interest of the elderly folk in England. Care of the elderly is felt to be better offered within the community at home, and provisions have been made for this.

The concern is not necessarily that the care is inadequate, but more that many of those given the responsibility for direct care appear not to have much interest in the well-being of the elderly. This often leads to a number of disappointing challenges, such as carers turning up late or not completing tasks satisfactorily. The provision of care is often questionable on this basis, and frequent reviews by health care providers still fail to find the right solution to each individual need. In fact it is surprising that the emphasis often appears to be on funding rather than quality of care. Even when review of care is undertaken, the risk factors are often missed because it takes no less than a hidden camera to pick up all the inadequacies of some caregivers.

Ethnicity is by no means seen as a motivating factor in the provision of care to meet cultural expectations. Health care in England, especially in the larger cities, appears to be provided by a large number of caregivers from minority ethnic backgrounds; therefore it could be that the subject of more support in the form of training for carers should be addressed. This idea could be the answer to the ultimate provision of a more effective practice for older people. As pointed out by an official Montserrat representative in England, the situation is not unique to the Montserrat elderly but is one of the common themes of elderly care in Britain. However an improvement in practice support at a higher level would improve the experience of the elderly in England. Not for the want of trying efforts are still being made by those responsible to find the right solution.

Outlooks of health care in England are by no means regarded as a perfect system, and there are certainly mixed viewpoints about the benefits and outcomes of their various contacts within the system. Furthermore, just as individual experiences vary, so do the skills and experiences of health care professionals; therefore everyone's story must be taken on its own merit and judgements made accordingly.

Cuisine

One Montserratian notes, 'Caribbean foods are available in Birmingham, but some foods we are used to eating a lot of are not here, and they taste very different to what we are used to in Montserrat. They are quite expensive as well, so you cannot always buy all the foods we used to eat back home.'

For many the taste of food was an initial area of great concern. Finding the right places to buy ingredients to suit the taste buds of a people accustomed to highly seasoned foods was considered a huge problem. Although some variety of desirable tasting foods was available in restaurants, especially in the multicultural capital of London, there were other things to consider, including the cost of eating out and access. Most Montserrat folk preferred to eat home-cooked meals they had prepared themselves, and finding the right seasonings was another issue. Looking back, it would be pertinent to determine whether it was the general discontent driven by our circumstances that narrowed our outlook on the foods, reducing the natural explorative nature of many. The other aspect could be the sheer novelty of living in a European country where the change of lifestyle and enormity of size overwhelmed some, creating an initial apathetic response.

The cuisine of Montserrat consists of mainly highly seasoned foods influenced by the African, Irish, British, and Amerindian cultures—a legacy of the island's history. Ultimately mouth watering, the food encourages the diner to eat large portions at each sitting. The initial encounter with the cuisine in England had the opposite effect on the migrant community: the discontent with the food led to smaller appetites overtime. Additionally smaller portions are served when eating out in England, leading to reduced satisfaction and smaller appetites over time.

In fact on attending a workshop at the Viewpoint Hotel in Montserrat in 2001, my colleagues remarked on the small portions I ate. The food was delicious as ever and served buffet style; I could take as much as I wanted. Despite this my stomach had grown accustomed to eating smaller portions and filled up very quickly.

Years later in England, I count myself lucky to be in a place where the variety of cuisines available enables me to make any choice I want. London has so many restaurants, and whatever takes your fancy from one day to the next are only a few minutes away in some cases. Additionally there are now many more shops offering foods from the West Indies, such as dasheen, yams, green bananas, mangoes, and guavas. The goods are highly priced but are available in certain shops and some markets in Brixton and Hackney. Additionally there are a large number of Caribbean restaurants that serve up really tasty foods. I must confess that I have acquired the taste for a number of British dishes and have even learned to cook a few. It goes to show that it is only a matter of time before one adjusts to the environment. This is merely a subjective viewpoint, as for each individual the adaptation process has a different meaning.

Fashion

'Aiuo! Aiu look pan wuk yah! Look how dah gyel deh a wark harf neakid pan di rouad?' (Aye, look at this! Look how that lady is walking almost naked on the street).

As mentioned earlier, the differences in dress code was another cause for Montserratians. The first coat I bought was awfully fluffy and very masculine. I had no clue of what was fashionable in coats and also noticed that others had made similar blunders. It was initially difficult to choose the correct type of clothes, and I often went around looking like a fat elephant in the winter, wearing the longest and thickest clothing I could find. My first fur coat was awful, and when I think back I can't imagine myself wearing an animal and feeling as if I was well dressed. The thing I missed most then was having my hair done by professional hairdressers every two weeks. My hair was always well done and grew healthily with the regular care it received. On arrival in England, I started to care for the hair myself, which was most difficult given the change in weather and working patterns. I had more responsibility and fewer funds to spend on myself by then. I must confess that I am still searching for a hair dresser who makes me feel on top of the world after a day in the salon.

Despite the differences, the things we miss, and wanting things to remain the same, many aspects have greatly improved since, and Montserrat men and women are holding their own among the most fashionable the world over. For those living in England, who otherwise dressed conservatively and frowned on others that didn't, the desire to do so is long gone because one couldn't differentiate the attire of the young Montserrat from non-Montserratians.

A Taste of winter

Many Montserrat folk prefer to stay indoors during the winter months, only coming out for essentials such as food and health care. It had been really cold as I left work and headed for the motorway that would take me home. As usual I was looking forward to a weekend of relaxation and the opportunity to relieve my mind of the week's stress. On my way home I pulled off the motorway and popped into a supermarket, where I shopped for £85.00 worth of groceries. I had heard that it was going to snow heavily, and the advice was to stock up on groceries, especially dry goods, because there was no way of knowing what problems the snow would bring or how long it would last.

I really hadn't anticipated any problems, and if anything untoward occurred, I was convinced that my insurance was adequate to cover the cost of repairs. Still, having experienced two major natural disasters in the past, I was certainly going to be prepared for whatever drama this snow brought along with it. It was just one week before Christmas, and some of my associates were actually looking forward to a white Christmas. I most certainly was not. I was not looking forward to any winter at all and its associated cold, which left me pale and numb.

My real wish was to be in Montserrat, or in any sunny country for that matter, where my body could lap up the warmth and my brain could rejuvenate itself after long hours of labour. I had plans to leave London early in the morning of the twenty-fourth for a cottage in Devon with three associates, and I was hoping this would still be a reality. The forecast was that this winter was going to be harsher than previous years, but the promise of a warm cottage well away from London and the inner cities was an expectation which kept me going. We had it all planned: sitting by the cosy fireplace, roasting chestnuts in pyjamas, singing and praying while the rest of Britain lay frozen on the outside. With thoughts of the upcoming weekend and the benefits it promised, I packed my shopping into the boot of the car and set off once again for the motorway and the long journey home.

The traffic was hardly moving, and we crawled at the usual snail's pace, which stretched the journey from forty-five minutes on a good day to almost two and a half hours. Many people were in a hurry to get out of London to the comfort and warmth of their homes. Some were heading to the country for the holidays, and others were heading to the shops to buy Christmas presents. The economic downturn didn't seem to affect people's spending at Christmas. There were folks like me who were happy that their religious aspirations prohibited buying gifts for special religious occasions.

I finally arrived home, carefully parking the car and taking the groceries indoors. The first set of fine snowflakes were already falling on the grass only to quickly disappear into nothingness, as if it was just a figment of the imagination. The flakes looked so soft and beautiful; they reminded me of the cotton my family used to pick back in Montserrat at Broderick's, when I was a young child.

It was freezing indoors because the central heating timer had not yet kicked in. I turned on the fireplace and central heating up to warm the house quickly. In the meantime I turned on the tiny electric heater for a quick boost of heat; this would guarantee a warm living room in about five minutes. All this time I kept my coat and gloves on, for my fingers were numb and colourless. I looked outside into the cold darkness of the evening and observed the heavy snow falling, a sure sign of things to come. I thought of my dear old disabled mom in London sitting on the commode in her flat, on her own and waiting for one of her relatives or friends to give her a call, or for a carer to come in and help her to bed. I just don't know how she does it, sitting there all day and looking down the corridor for a glimpse of her friend Una. At this point she must be missing the Montserrat sunshine terribly like many of us.

I called her and was reassured that she was okay and hadn't a clue about what was going on outside. Her flat was nice and warm, and they would cover her from head to toe with her duvet, or what the Americans refer to as a comforter. We didn't need to use any of those things in Montserrat, but we knew of blankets, which turned up in the hundreds after natural disasters. Still, I worried about her, knowing that if her central heating broke or if her pipes got frozen, I was too far away to help, and she had no one to call on. This was a frustrating thought that can vex the spirit, so I decided to be optimistic about the whole thing. That night before going to bed I took one last look outside noticing how a white snow blanket had covered everything. It was not dark outside as the sheer whiteness of the snow set everything aglow. By the next day I turned on the TV and looked at the screen in amazement, as the announcer stated loudly and clearly that frozen Britain was at a standstill. There were queues at Heathrow and some of the other airports, and many flights were grounded. They were calling it 'freak winter weather'.

Snow in London was a common occurrence, but this year was the worst many of us had seen. Never had it been this severe for more than twenty years, claimed some Londoners and the media. Everything on the outside was totally white by this time, including the cars and rooftops. I grabbed my camera and decided to take a few still shots of this beautiful phenomenon. One couldn't deny the beauty as the snow fell down in clumps, covering everything in sight in a pure white blanket.

A few minutes later, as I walked into the bathroom, I heard the unusual sound of gushing water. It sounded as if someone was filling up a bathtub in the house. I flushed the toilet as a means of checking out the source of the gushing sound, and I noticed that the noise became louder and louder. Something was definitely wrong. It sounded as if it was happening somewhere at my feet, but I couldn't see anything. Looking up into the loft, I hoped the tank was still intact so I wouldn't be wet. I felt assured that it was not coming from the roof and raced downstairs with unaccustomed speed.

I checked the water meter and ascertained that it was also intact. At a loss, I opened the conservatory door not really expecting to find anything—and lo and behold the entire floor was covered with water. Looking towards the dryer, I noticed that the plumbing intended for the dishwasher had burst, and water was flowing like a water fall. It certainly reminded me of the Great Alps Waterfall in Montserrat as it fell beautifully from a great height offering bathing opportunities and photographic moments. Somehow I managed to lock off the stiff pipe at the meter, stopping the flow of water. Survival instinct kicked into place; I never forgot the lessons learnt during hurricane Hugo and the eruption of Soufriere Hills Volcano. I quickly managed to switch the pipe back on, filling every container I could find with water, just in case. Little did I know that I would need this water soon.

Trying to make contact with the water department was a nightmare. The automated system kept me on hold for hours with an annoying repetition: 'You are in a queue.' It notified me that the waiting time was longer than usual due to the extreme weather conditions. The advice was to call again the next day after 8.00 a.m. Having no luck with this, I eventually went to sleep around midnight, hoping to find a solution next day. The next morning I started the calling process again. This time it took about forty minutes for the call to be answered by a very helpful administrator, who advised that there was nothing they could do at the moment because they were overwhelmed with calls for maintenance of frozen and burst water pipes. Knowing that she must be telling the truth—after all, even the airports and public transport weren't coping well with the weather—I decided not to shout my frustration at her but called my insurance instead. The insurance company was more responsive; this was all about money, service, and clientele. They advised that they would visit the property within twenty-four hours. They kept their word, and it turned out that the pipe had become frozen like many others in the country and had burst as a result. The pipe was fixed in no time, and I was told to keep an eye on it because it could happen again.

Now how could I keep an eye on it when I had no control over the weather and the exposed pipes? The young man who completed the work was extremely helpful and polite. He even took his shoes off when he entered the house, showing what Montserrat folk would refer to as good manners. The state of the country and people's response reminded me of what we as Montserrat folk had been through over and over again in natural disasters, and at some point I wondered if the snow would stop anytime soon. If it didn't, and we ended up with a number of broken pipes and the central heating collapsed, what would happen to us? I supposed I could go to some homeless shelter, but where was that? And what of those who did not have transport? I really couldn't help thinking of worst-case scenarios; I had seen far too many disasters in my life not to worry a bit.

The worst winter I had experienced since coming to England continued, and I did not go to Devon for my weekend in a cottage. I was disappointed, but it was my decision not to go. The other associates went and experienced loads of drama and even got stuck in the snow. I was all by myself because I didn't want to risk being stuck in snow in a strange countryside. One of my associates said she refused to have her holiday spoilt, and nothing was going to stop her from going. Her response was not surprising, because she had paid for the cottage and made all the plans. I managed to roast some chestnuts in the oven and pretended I was eating breadnuts as I would have back home. Unfortunately the chestnuts got hard and tough very quickly and were hardly edible. It was my first time trying to roast them, and I obviously didn't have the right technique.

I couldn't help but wonder if it wasn't better to be in Montserrat with the volcano than in frozen England, where everything stood still and one worried about the big freeze and its consequences. When all is said and done, there will always be disasters wherever you are in the world, and the important thing is the emergency measures you put in place to manage the situation. My experience is echoed by a number of Montserrat folk in England; some actually claim to hate winters, while others have come to embrace it in their own way. People are not always very tolerant of the cold weather conditions, and some simply stay indoors, preferring to hibernate for long periods during the winter months. A number of people plan to travel to Montserrat for short periods over the popular Christmas festivities, but those who remain in England have learnt to carry on despite the cold winters. I personally tolerate the winters knowing that my favourite season, spring, is just around the corner.

Culture

Every Montserratian who migrated has experienced cultural displacement. The limited access to cultural traditions has been mourned and missed by most. Many reflect on the total loss of traditional celebrations considered to be the core of the Montserrat culture.

Certain traditions and cultures are very important to Montserrat folk. We look forward to celebrating Festival for three weeks, during December and January, which incorporates the renowned Calypso Monarch Show, the local festival Queen Show, and teenage pageants. John Bull[1] and Miss Goosy[2] dance to the steel pan and brass band music expressed through

---

[1]   A costumed man dressed with horns and a long stick.

[2]   A costumed lady on stilts.

traditional soca and calypso. Then there is the popular masquerade dancing the quadrille in colourful costume, with tiny mirrors shining and shimmying as they move to the beat of the African drum. These are traditions that have been with Montserrat for a long time, handed down by our ancestors, and we never expected to lose them. However, we certainly have not reached the stage where we have been able to recreate any of these in England. One can't help but wonder why some of these cultural practices cannot be recreated in this country. Surely Notting Hill Carnival would be an ideal place to initiate these events. Is leadership the problem, or is it motivation? Maybe it is time we stopped missing and started creating. Or have we actually moved on from our cultural traditions and now feel comfortable in mourning their loss with no real intent to find a way to embrace them the way we used to?

St Patrick's Day is sadly missed, because like the festival celebrations, it brings out the best of the culture with emphasis on the Anglo-Irish-African cuisine, a legacy of our heritage. Wearing the national dress and celebrating the national bird (the oriole) and the national flower (the heliconia, known as bird of paradise) are memories that will remain in our minds unless we create an atmosphere away from Montserrat where the culture is still relevant. Goat water, salt fish, Johnny cake, duckna, ginger beer, and sorrell—all are mouth watering and enticing to the palate and sorely missed. But surely we can cook those in England? Many would argue that it is not the same, because there is no coal pot and no wood fire for the goat water, no chainy bush for the duckna, and the breadfruit is hard to find and expensive. The colourful troupes on the streets dancing to the beat of brass band music mimic the festival celebrations. St Patrick's Day is celebrated in England, and some Montserratians do participate, but it is never the same away from home. No wonder folk are mourning the loss and take no interest in the various celebrations held in England. Things have certainly changed culturally, and the questions at the back of our minds which have generated much discussion are about the loss of the Montserrat culture.

The island of Montserrat has all this, but there is still concern that it could be losing its traditions to other cultures. I had a difficult conversation with a local young man living in Montserrat. He tried to convince me on the phone that it is people of our generation living in England who create issues related to cultural stagnancy, because we do not pass it on to our children. My first response to this was that perhaps he was speaking from a personal perspective, despite not living in England. My second thought was that given that we are from the same peer group, there must be some truth in what he is saying, since a number of the next generation are still asking questions about the culture. Then again, he appeared to be speaking on behalf of the Diaspora, and to this end I cannot but discount his allegations as a bit of self-served guilt.

It is hardly possible to speak on behalf of the entire Montserrat Diaspora, but there is obvious evidence on some of the social networking sites that people are keen to preserve the Montserrat culture the way it was prior to 1995. Alas, there are a number of lessons to learn, and we must create awareness that culture is not necessarily taught in a formal way, but it is in fact passed down from generation to generation as a matter of course. Therefore it is the responsibility of every single person of Montserrat origin to pass on the culture so that it doesn't deviate too far from what it actually is. Just as it is said that children live what they learn, I add 'hear and see'. The continuous practices of a people are passed on indirectly in most instances, through passive acquisition.

Culture should not necessarily be seen as a lesson one learns formally. It is certainly unlike any module in school, which is picked up and carried on through real intent. Further, it might be useful to clarify culture in context and the loss or gain associated with it. Can one really lose one's culture? Could it be the context of culture of which we are so concerned? From childhood to present times, I have seen culture change over time, in keeping with the development of Montserrat and people's exposure to different environments and other cultures.

Over time we have spoken or heard people speak of the influences of the subcultures of places such as neighbouring Antigua and the United States of America, impacting negatively on the youth of Montserrat, who tend to emulate what they see on TV more than anything else. Access to cable television and satellite dishes from the '80s onward is cited as the factors that further reinforced what was considered to be the negative effects of the subcultures in Montserrat. Just as the '80s appear to have gone by quickly, so also were the days of playing cricket in the road with a coconut bat, or marbles in the dirt yard, or hide and seek in the bushes. Cinema was not a big option, especially for folks in the country areas, since the island only had one, which was placed centrally in the now destroyed capital of Plymouth. It was the indoors television screen that captured the audience of young and mature folk alike.

Public outcries make no difference because change is synonymous with development. Over time the Montserrat culture has evolved into what it is now, and yet we continue to try to manipulate it into remaining stagnant—a battle that cannot be won, an argument many will dispute but never prove wrong. I read an interesting account by a writer who was brave enough to refer to the culture we are now struggling to maintain as a mere illusion, because culture appears to be evolving constantly. Could it be that what we really seek to hold on to so desperately is based on nothing but an illusion? After all is said and done, from all accounts the real culture of Montserrat is based on past bloodshed, wars, plantations, and slavery. The stripping of African cultures and the adoption of Irish names, values, and customs is certainly where it all began, and it is now only evidenced by a few ambitious authors' attempts to capture the world of our ancestors in a few history books. I am still uncertain who I descended from; my family tree took me as far as the Dominican Republic but gave no real insight into my obvious Irish or English connections. Of Africa I have no knowledge of my relations.

When all is said and done, is it too late to save the Montserrat culture? Is there a way of saving the culture we value so much? If the culture can be saved or preserved, who will take the lead? Who will pass on what we really are as a people—our likes, dislikes cuisine, dances, and folklore? Will the 'original' Montserratians be just a memory in the next hundred years, with the only true memory a few skeletons and some pottery in a grave? I can imagine a few overzealous authors taking up the challenge years from now, trying to capture the way they think we were with mispronunciations of our dialect and poor choreography of our dances. If history were to repeat itself, would we, like the Caribs and Arawaks—the first known Montserrat folk—become extinct, only to be replaced by a new generation of people who may or may not have the interest or inclination to learn more about our culture?

Some documented evidence from books, the Internet, newspaper articles, and more are readily available and show that this generation of Montserratians was keen to leave a legacy behind. As a songwriter admonishes, 'I'm warning you, my friend, hold on to your property and leave it for your children.' Will we follow this advice so that our culture as we know it will not just be a memory, changed and distorted many times over? Could this be the time for leaders to formalise a plan to save the culture, and if so, what angle will it take? There are so many questions to ask that I could go on and on, but where are the answers? My heart like that of many others yearn for what Montserrat was, my country my home; which I have not seen for many years. Now known as a diaspora, is there still a place to call home, or is it just a tourist abode meant to be visited every so often, wondering who is standing on the street beside me or in the supermarket cashing next to me?

Though one can get carried away into feeling sorry for what has gone, what is likely to go, and what one wishes one could save, a small voice in my head is saying all is not lost, for there is still hope. This is a subject that has no end and will be captured later in this book, as folks continue to reveal the way they feel about Montserrat, the culture, and the people.

CHAPTER 3

Relationships and Culture

'I had no professional help to overcome my feelings of moving from Montserrat. If I was going through anything, I would phone my friends because they identified with me, and that made me feel better. Mixing with Montserratians at church also helped me.'

One of the greatest losses cited by a number of Montserrat folk is the close relationships that existed between relatives, the extended family, neighbours, and friends. Even expatriates were treated as family to some extent, because they played a very important role in the island's existence. Alas, every single member of a family did not migrate to the United Kingdom but went to various parts of the world, trying to find safety and a place where they would fit in and find suitable work and schooling. Large numbers also relocated to the Caribbean Islands and the United States of America, and smaller numbers can be found elsewhere in the world. Relatives ended up living in different cities, initially losing contact but later regaining communication via social networking sites.

Montserrat is made up of close-knit families, and some have even dared to say that most are related by blood. Whether friend or family, due to the size of the population most people are known to each other in some way, if not by name then at least by face, occupation, or interest. One can therefore imagine the effect of not seeing a familiar face or hearing known voices. People missed each other terribly for one reason or the other. Things were especially difficult during the first few years following the mass evacuation of 1997.

From time to time I have wondered why the migration of two-thirds of a population has not been given more recognition. The percentage of the population that left within a short time is surely quite unusual. Never mind that the total number of migrants was only approximately eight thousand, which in terms of mass migration would be laughable by the standards of many, given the population of larger countries. Still, this occurrence is of great significance for Montserrat folk, and over the years we have compensated for this loss by linking with each other on the all too familiar networking sites. The most significant link up appears to occur during the annual Montserrat Festival celebrations, which occur in December.

Relationships with non-Montserratians have their advantages and disadvantages, and as with most issues that affect human beings, the disadvantages are usually seen to outweigh the advantages. The impact is usually determined by the issue itself and the real or perceived victim. Issues such as prejudice and discrimination have been raised from time to time as having a negative impact on people's lives, but I have tried to write with caution around these subjects because they are mostly based on subjective views and as such are very difficult to prove factually. I have met different types of people during my journey, and most of my experiences have been both positive and negative. I have embraced the positive and tried to build a personal framework of reference which will provide strength when the not-so-positive occurs.

I have learnt from those that are downright negative and deliberate and used the experiences in reflection, to become a more positive person and set an example for others. Like many things in life, experiences can cause displeasure and even force one to retaliate in ways foreign to the personality, and understanding cause and effect is a good way to create a state of appropriate responses. I have worked and interacted with people of many races, of mixed cultures and personalities, and I have found some good friendships and helpful people. I have also found that one's approach to events often makes a difference in setting the stage for ongoing associations.

Interpersonal relationships including dating, courtship, and marriage have suffered to some extent as a result of migration following the erupting volcano. Montserrat folk as a people are not strangers to the experience of varied and mixed relationships. Migration to England cannot be totally blamed as the only cause of differences in relationships, but it has certainly made its contribution to split relationships among married and unmarried couples, caused by distance and other issues. Where one partner migrated to the United Kingdom and the other remained in Montserrat, the difficulty of maintaining a long-distance relationship takes its toll on one or both partners, resulting in varied outcomes.

The struggles of the lone woman with the children in England cannot be overlooked as a contributor to ongoing stress and even inability to cope. The partner who remains on island is often given the false impression that all is well, and many see the tiny financial support given by the state as enough to maintain a family, pay the rent, and buy food and clothes. Out of shame, many have not expressed the financial pressure they have been under during the early years and the difficulties experienced in making ends meet. Some will never talk of this, while others only discuss it in hushed tones. In an effort to make no demands on those back in Montserrat suffering through volcanic issues, the struggling partners in England improvise, as is expected.

Accounts have been given of either spouse moving to one common location or deciding to split permanently. Others turn a blind eye in denial or show little or no interest continuing with their separate lives, with no one the wiser as to what direction will create positive outcomes. For some, loneliness and hardships have resulted in reduced coping mechanisms, break-ups and lack of focus or reasoning. It has been often deemed easier to thrash out issues when both partners are in the same location; a solution is almost impossible when separated by time zones and oceans. Then there is the other issue of finding new interests and losing interest in the old and familiar, which is not unique to migration but is common among most human beings, whether they are living together or separated by distance and time.

Despite those common and ongoing experiences experienced by Montserratians at home and abroad, there are some types of relationships which fall outside the cultural norms and experiences of Montserrat folk at home. As pointed out in many discussions, these relationships could have occurred in Montserrat but would certainly not have been very prevalent. I will discuss a couple which I find very intriguing and not necessarily negative.

Go with the Flow Syndrome

*'I don't want to settle for less than I deserve. I want to get
married, have children and travel the world'*

'Go with the flow' is a type of relationship that sounds very catchy and
in fact appears to be a growing trend among both young and matured
folk. If anyone wants to understand it any better, all they need to do is
follow some of the popular soaps on television, which are quite insightful
on relationships in general. Forming committed relationships can be
very difficult and sometimes daunting in England; it is not uncommon
to hear a man say, 'Just go with the flow.' This means that he wants to
have some form of ongoing relationship with you, including intimacy, but
with no commitment. This is culturally unacceptable by many Montserrat
folk, who would prefer a lasting relationship that results in some form of
permanency.

When going with the flow, both persons can hold hands, kiss, meet
up, love, and spend quality time together, and in fact do most things
people in relationships do—but there is no 'us', just 'you' and 'I'. This
allows for no commitment among those involved.

Laura had the following experience—a story that is very similar to
others'. She was at a work party when her colleague, Will, walked up
and greeted her with a shy smile. Laura had seen him in the escalator
a few times and thought he was cute but a bit too quiet. She was a shy
person, and since migrating from Montserrat almost ten years earlier, she
hadn't dated anyone and often felt she had lost her flirtatious touch. On
greeting Will, her heart was beating in her chest with great intensity, and
she could hardly breathe. As Will held out his hands to shake hers, she
noticed that he had long, nicely shaped fingers, like that of a pianist. Laura
tried to control the shaking of her own hands. She really liked this guy,
who appeared to have everything going for him that interested her. He
had a fit, attractive body and was well groomed, with nice white teeth that
dazzled when he smiled. He was always smartly dressed, and he oozed
charm and good looks.

The only drawback was that he was about an inch shorter than her in
heels, but without the heels they were about the same height. She could
live with that, she thought, because everything else was perfect. Laura
was a beautiful girl with a cool, dark complexion that made people take a

second look, and she was very charming with dimples that sunk deep in her cheeks when she smiled. As chemistry went these two lovely people found they had a lot in common and started seeing each other.

Six months later after spending lots of time together and enjoying fun as a newly involved couple, Laura broached the subject of commitment. She realised that up to that point Will had not told her that he loved her, not even the time when she had earnestly poured out her heart to him. He had alluded to it cautiously once but appeared to be scared of being forthright. She had a sudden recall now that he had actually said he loved her at a time when she tried to end the relationship once before. As if he was scared, he had shifted uncomfortably and had said with downcast eyes, 'You know I love you, and you love me.' Then there was the other time when he had hinted they were not just having sex but actually in a relationship. 'You're so silly,' he had said. 'Does this look like casual sex to you?'

My heart went out to Laura, who was in obvious pain. She had been very naive and disadvantaged by Will, and it was clear to see the hurt and pain she was still experiencing. Guilty of awakening her emotional pain, I allowed her to cry and offered comforting words that helped sooth her obvious embarrassment at disclosing so much of herself. She appeared to have been the unsuspecting victim of a man so cunning that any innocent person would fall for his tricks. I was happy that I didn't know Will; her story may have affected my association with him after this. As it turned out, although he really liked her a lot, Will had no intention of having a committed relationship with Laura and was very blatant and cruel in his disclosure of intent.

When she did broach the subject of commitment, he told her right there and then, 'We're just friends. Have I ever given you the impression that we would be anything else?' Appearing oblivious to the impact of his words on innocent Laura, he continued. 'I do not want any woman, but if I did, you're nice and I would have chosen you. Why do women have to spoil everything? Girl, just go with the flow and enjoy yourself.' Will continued his onslaught by reminding Laura that she was in England and not little Montserrat. For the first time Laura began to realise what a selfish, egotistical person he was.

Laura hoped he would change his mind, so she continued with him for the next several months, having been with him for about two years. She kept coming back to the subject of commitment but always got the same response. Laura stopped seeing Will and was relieved that he made it easy for her to do so. He had repeatedly requested photos of her, to which she complied, but he never shared any of his and gave excuses of reasons why he couldn't send one by text. Laura knew he was lying and eventually got hold of one of his to prove a point. She kept this on her phone until her opportunity came to test him. She gave Will her phone one day when they met up, knowing full well he would search all her applications.

On finding the photo on the phone, Will practically went mad, running all over the house in his effort to delete it. Playing his game, Laura helped him to delete it in the end. He finally left, accusing her of not to be trusted. With a sigh of relief, Laura quietly watched him go and closed her door with finality. Laura was an honest girl with no ulterior motives, but Will was leaving himself open so he could see whomever he wished with no questions asked. In fact Laura knew nothing personal about him except his name and work place. He had never revealed his date of birth or the names of relatives.

He assured her that the best way to think of England was as a lonely place where a woman is respected for being a diva, meaning she was not being committed to any man. He suggested the way to do this was to let everyone know that she didn't need a man in her life and could do what she felt like. Will reinforced that this was trendy in England, where people accepted loneliness as a way of life and counted themselves lucky to have the type of relationship he was offering Laura.

Back in Montserrat loneliness was not a way of life and did not exist the way she was told it does in England; people often just stopped by for a chat or a bit of gossip. The people living around you were either relatives or friends, and if they were neither, you wouldn't know the difference unless you asked. Some young Montserrat folk I have spoken to have set boundaries around their relationships, hence protecting themselves from the type of psuedo-relationship in which Laura found herself.

Will was a West Indian born in Britain but not of Montserrat origin. Unfortunately I have not had any feedback from Montserrat men on this type of relationship, but I suspect not all would see it from a negative perspective. Some Montserrat men I spoke to continue the tradition of committing to a lady they had been seeing over a period of time, which would eventually result in marriage if she pushed for it. Others have adopted the more Western styles of dating. One non-Montserrat, British West Indian young man I spoke to supported the concept of 'go with the flow' relationships. He went as far as to reassure me that life was to be enjoyed, 'So why tie down yourself with someone because you've had fun with them?' The basis of such a relationship is that one has no basis for complaining even when disappointed.

The relationship turned out to be one of convenience only, so one either accepts it or move on. Despite this less than satisfactory twist to modern relationships, there have been many success stories of Montserrat folk having similar relationships to what would fit in with their cultural norms. Some have gotten to know other Montserratians while others continue to experience successful relationships with non-Montserratians. It's therefore not all doom and gloom for relationships in England, although there are major concerns.

The other side to finding appropriate and meaningful relationships in England is the vulnerability of unsuspecting young ladies from Montserrat who find themselves easy targets by nature of being British. There are scammers out there who look for innocent persons with British passports. These con artists have been shown on some media documentaries to court and marry unsuspecting women despite less than honourable intent. They pursue the passport, and once acquired they beat a hasty retreat out of the less than perfect relationship.

From the sound of things, although some have been caught out; most Montserrat ladies appear to be cautious and in control, resulting in only a small minority being caught in the trap. Further, recent British legislation has made it increasingly difficult for individuals to marry in order to obtain citizenship in England, which provides some protection for the unsuspecting.

Cougar

*'Too old for him or just right? Surely it is his choice. Or is it
just a case of the female version of cradle snatching?'*

Another type of relationship worth taking note of is the cougar diva. In Montserrat it would have been referred to as cradle snatching or robbing the cradle. The term 'cougar' has been bantered about recently by some of my country's people in relation to those older ladies among us who appear to be more comfortable in relationships with significantly younger men. Don't get me wrong the young men appear to enjoy the relationship too and there is no evidence of one sidedness. Of course it is difficult to tell whether this is circumstantial or not, or what the motivating factor is. Most of my women associates have a cut-off limit of around a six-year gap and merely shake their heads with a laugh at the thought of exploring someone outside that range.

Others find it funny and intriguing, and they are not reluctant to give it a go. My research revealed that to be deemed a cougar, the woman would have to be at least age thirty-five. Women of this age are not considered to be cougars unless their sexual partners are less than twenty-five years. The minimum acceptable age gap appears to be ten years. Those women who date men young enough to be their sons are sometimes labelled as cougars; a typical example would be a forty-something woman being involved with a man in his twenties. A woman over fifty years old could be involved with a thirty-something man. The label tends to be less significant when the man is over forty, as he is no longer seen as a vulnerable youth. In Montserrat this relationship was not a common one, if it even occurred. The opposite was true of the male version of the cougar and this catchy old song: 'Old man lek buddy tarm a wah ya do wid yung gyel' (Old man like buddy Tom, what are you doing with young girl.). This was popularly sung in humour to describe an older man with a very young girl.

The following story was told by a Montserrat lady who was caught in the cougar dilemma.

Sini stood at the door in shock as she listened to her niece Leah on the phone discussing some lady who was openly dating a man twenty years her junior. As Leah repeated the name 'cougar' on the phone, she suddenly realised she had an audience and turned around to look at Sini with raised eyebrows. Leah asked quietly, 'Have you been eavesdropping on my conversation?'

Sini answered with her own question. 'What is a cougar?'

Leah replied with a note of amazement, 'Don't you know what a cougar is? Are you for real? She is an older woman who dates a significantly younger man. Just like you and Leon are doing right now. Auntie, your boyfriend is two years younger than my boyfriend. You're just like Jay, who we were discussing on the phone; she is dating a boy so young that he could be her son, and she isn't bothered by what anyone thinks. When they are out together, people who know them stare at them all the time.'

Shocked at the blatantly cruel and direct answer, Sini walked out of the room and shut the door behind her. She could feel a headache coming on. 'I am a cougar,' she thought, 'or I will be when Leon has had the talk he has been begging to have for weeks now.' As she sat on her red leather sofa, she put her hand on her now throbbing temples and squeezed her eyes shut. She didn't hear Leah walk up to her chattering about the so-called cougar who was the latest interest of the gossiping community. Sini was lost in thoughts as she reflected on her life and the events of the last two years.

It had all started on a warm Sunday in London as she walked out of the executive meeting towards her car. Leon, whom she had complimented about the cologne he was wearing, came towards her smiling. He didn't go to his posh silver Mercedes, which was parked next to hers in the huge car park, but he came to hers instead.

She looked at him appreciatively and saw that his eyes mirrored hers. 'Hmm,' she thought, 'he likes me, and he's not a bad looker, either.' He definitely looked confident too, a combination difficult to find in her circle these days. Sini's eyes roved over Leon's body as he walked towards her. He had really white teeth and wasn't afraid to show them. She could tell he spent quality time in the gym.

'Can I have a ride?' The sound of Leon's deep voice brought her out of her reverie, and she looked him in the eyes and smiled.

'My pleasure!'

Sini opened her brand-new green Mercedes Sport from a distance with a neat flick of her keys. She was showing off for him now and didn't try to hide it. To think that this young man twenty years her junior was interested in her had her pulse racing. She walked quickly to the driver's side and entered the car, not giving Leon the opportunity to demonstrate his well-mannered decorum by opening the door for her. She had to establish her independence and didn't want him to think she was a granny. Her friends had called her a diva, and there was no way she was going to spoil that image today. As Leon's long legs eased into the car beside her, she looked at his big shoes in concentration, not giving away her thoughts.

It was difficult to tell his shoe size, because he was wearing shoes with a really long, pointed tip. There was no way his toes would be narrow enough to fit into that long point. In fact his feet reminded her of her childhood image of the fairy tale Rumpelstilstin. Sini had a really bad sense of humour and had to control herself from laughing out loud; there was no way she was going to spoil things before exploring what he had to offer.

Leon was saying something to her softly. 'Don't move,' he said as he leaned towards her still smiling. Sini sat still, trying to control her breathing. The kiss was soft and full of passion; her eyes were closed, and she just didn't want it to stop. Pulling away, she looked at Leon, who still had his eyes closed, and she said quietly, 'What was that for?'

Leon did not answer; he was overwhelmed with passion and struggled hard for control. 'Wow, I've never felt like this before. That is some kiss,' he remarked.

That was the start of an ongoing romance between Leon and Sini. They flirted endlessly, attended different events together, and talked long hours on the phone. There were so many things to enjoy together because they had lots in common. As with everything else, though, all good things must come to an end, and so it did the day Sini felt shame and embarrassment at being called a cougar. She knew she couldn't withstand being talked about in this way in the Montserrat community. How would she look people in the eye when this became common knowledge?

After listening to her niece, Sini ended her relationship with Leon but was still unsure if she had made the right decision. She no longer lived in Montserrat; she lived in a different culture, where the norms and expectations were certainly different. Despite this she felt obligated to be respectable in her behaviours. Gossip was a part of the Montserrat culture, and she couldn't do anything about that. Of course the gossip only lasted until something else came along, but then again Montserratians didn't forget things like that. When asked for my opinion on the issue, my response to her was that this had to be a call based on her moral values and what was ethically appropriate. After all, I was a born and bred Montserratian, and culturally our values were the same whether at home or abroad.

There are times when we take chances outside the norm, but there is something that always points us back to our roots and culture. I was told in no uncertain terms that my response did not help to clear the dilemma but was rather politically correct. Then again, should we or should we not allow the culture to dictate our relationship choices? This is some moral dilemma but not necessarily a new one, for which there is no clear answer. I have no prior knowledge of the cougar relationship occurring in post-migration Montserrat. This does not mean it never occurred, but needless to say if it did, it would have had to be very clandestine not to be gossiped about. Hiding any kind of relationship in Montserrat would be difficult if not impossible, because someone always knew or thought they knew what was going on. In no time the news would all over the island, and true or false, labels never went away.

The cultural reality is, if two people of the opposite sex are seen together socially, just casually a few times, the involvement label was immediately whispered around in a convincing manner. The effect was that some people chose to ignore the gossip and had close friendships with the opposite sex, while others became secretive in a place where there were no secrets anyway. This is not to say that every single Montserratian thinks this way; the interpretation of the otherwise innocent interaction is usually dependant on who saw whom. The freedom to see anyone and date openly in England has been embraced slowly but surely by Montserratians when it was realised there is no one looking over your shoulder. Most people in England, except for those bounded by certain cultures, formed relationships freely and were not afraid to hug and kiss their friends in greeting, be they of same or opposite sex.

There is no stigma attached to dating. Despite this, some hesitate to take their opposite sex friends around fellow Montserratians in England, for fear of being stigmatised. We cannot overlook the fact that there are a number us Montserratians who continue to make decisions based on the way things were back in Montserrat. We are always concerned about what Montserratians will say when they hear and how bad we will look. There are others, however, who are more than willing to take risks, make independent decisions, and learn from their mistakes as a result. Braving the disapproval of fellow country associates cannot be an easy decision to make, but experimenting with different types of relationships should not necessarily be discouraged because at the end of the day, each person's individual experience is unique and geared towards some form of fulfilment and growth.

There is a positive side to the cougar relationship, and it can in fact bring satisfaction to both parties. Some men may seek out an older woman as a matter of preference; the older woman makes that choice for similar reasons. It is important to emphasise that there is a cultural downside to overcoming what appears to be less than favourable relationship types which are of less prevalence in Montserrat. There is always an avenue for seeking advice where there is uncertainty or indecision about anything in

England, including relationships. There is one thing about the Montserrat culture that can constitute a huge hindrance to success in relationships. Montserratians do not like to share their business with other people, so despite having major relationship, job, and other stressful issues, people would prefer to deal with these in their own way rather than visit a counsellor.

In some instances seeking support can be seen as a sign of weakness, an inability to cope, or an admission that things are not working. A lack of trust affects our ability to open up to others about the things that affect us most. This is a real issue among Caribbean people in general, and it is seen even in the workplace where counselling is offered. Furthermore, I lived and worked in Montserrat prior to migrating, and I had the experience of supporting and offering support to people experiencing all sorts of problems. Relationship problems created the greatest taboo. Having completed courses on family counselling at the University of Tampa, Florida, followed by a workshop in St Lucia, I felt I was in a good position to offer counselling and support to those who needed it.

Additionally, two government psychologists with whom I was fortunate to work closely were made available to Montserratians following the volcanic activity. Despite this a large number of people known to be affected by stressful issues were not comfortable with accepting assistance when they needed it. Assurances of confidentiality did not provide motivation to accept counselling support. I am constrained by the need for confidentiality and so will not go into too many details about this, but I want to add that many who accepted support have expressed discomfort at revealing their entire story, and they emphasised their trust for me as an individual rather than for the service offered. The few who actually sought help were very reluctant to share their real problems, and often said they didn't want anyone 'in their business'.

Men were more likely to be open about relationship issues, but women were very cautious. Rather than talking things through with a view to gaining greater insight and exploring ways of making things work, many people have been known to try to manage things on their own. Many of the decisions made on the basis of other people's views often resulted in negative outcomes. Those who sought counselling made conscious efforts to work on clearly identified goals and had better outcomes. In Britain there are more opportunities available to access counselling support; it is very heartening to learn that a number of workplaces offer counselling for staff who experience stress, whether work related or not. There have been mixed reviews about the benefits of this service, but as with anything else, each individual review differs. I would always advocate for giving it a try despite the perception of others. It appears from all accounts that more Montserrat folk are now open to accepting support from counsellors recommended by general practitioners and other health care providers, but there are those who have maintained the 'Montserrat mentality' deeply rooted in our culture of not sharing their problems. They may go on indefinitely accepting unrealistic relationships that fail to satisfy them mentally and physically. The fear of opening up to others is a real, ongoing issue even for those of us living in the more enlightened and resourceful cultures of the United Kingdom. I must interject here that this discourse is by no means a criticism of the way the Montserrat folk are, but rather a realistic view point. Our response is a reflection of our culture.

CHAPTER 4

A Historic Hurricane

'Dem say di harikiane a head striat foo awe!'

At this point you may be wondering at the relevance of Hurricane Hugo within the context of this book. Its main purpose is to give some insight into the apparent resilience of Montserrat folk during natural disasters. Comparisons can be made between the way individuals managed during and after Hugo and during the volcanic eruptions. The other perspective could be that Hugo was the first major disaster experienced by the majority of Montserratians in this era, and as such it set the stage for the preparedness and planning strategies seen during and after the volcanic eruptions. Had the volcanic eruptions been our first experience of a major natural disaster, the outcome might have been much different. I therefore narrate an account of one household of the events leading up to, during, and after Hurricane Hugo, mainly for reflective purposes.

'Hurricane Hugo is making a beeline for Montserrat.' This was the news going around the island on a very hot September day. The national broadcasting station blasted out the news that Hurricane Hugo was set to hit the Leeward Islands at 10.00 p.m. that night. 'Everyone is asked to batten down windows and secure doors, because this is a category five hurricane and is expected to cause considerable damage. Residents are advised to stock up on tinned foods and dried goods such as biscuits, powdered milk, and corned beef.'

That day as the two sisters, Denise and Sayrah, went about their chores, they were not sure whether the announcer should be taken seriously. They had heard this kind of announcement year after year, and nothing had ever come of it. Some high winds and rain had made their way to the island from time to time, but mainly in the form of a heavy storm. The eye of the hurricane was always looking somewhere else; it had never actually come directly at Montserrat in the last forty years or so. Montserrat was thought to be so blessed that nothing horrible ever happened there. That was how it appeared to the two young ladies anyway.

Denise and Sayrah had heard their dad speak of hurricanes that had actually hit Montserrat directly, and he was taking this one seriously; there was no doubt about it as he gathered galvanised sheets of steel and plywood to secure the windows.

Suddenly there was a shout from within the house. 'Girls, go to town and get some tinned stuff and dry food from Rams Supermarket. You heard what the radio said; Hurricane Hugo is coming here, and it won't miss the island this time.'

The girls stopped what they were doing because they had detected a sense of urgency in their mom's voice; she was seriously concerned too. On their way to Rams, they noticed that a number of houses were already battened down with galvanise sheets and plywood. People were milling about everywhere, some coming from town with shopping and others hurriedly on their way to town to get supplies. The villages were buzzing with activity as people tried to get livestock and chicken locked up safely. It was as if the world was coming to an end, and people made last-minute preparations. The crowds in town were even worse, and the topic of conversation was only Hurricane Hugo. A monster of a storm the likes never seen by Montserrat was coming and only the Lord could help them if it didn't weaken at sea or turn back.

As they entered Rams Supermarket, the first thing the sisters noticed was the half-empty shelves and the tired-looking workers. The supermarket was full of people, and there was an atmosphere of anticipation and suspense. Some people appeared very anxious, especially the older folk, while the younger were excited about the prospect of experiencing a hurricane for the first time. The two girls picked out groceries, filling their baskets with dry and tinned goods as instructed. They then picked up a mop on a stick and joked with a doctor who was also shopping for goods. He said, 'I see you're preparing for the hurricane.'

Denise said, 'Well, we don't want to be like the foolish virgins in the Bible who didn't have enough oil for their lamps, so we are preparing. This mop will get rid of all the water.' They laughed together. Little did they know that the hurricane would take mop and all much later that evening.

As they knelt to pray prior to bed time later that evening, they prayed for the hurricane to find a different path, but if it didn't they asked God to keep them safe. The households remained jovial and light-heartedly joked about the hurricane as they waited for whatever the night would bring. A number of questions crossed their minds as they tried to find possible reasons why the hurricane wouldn't turn back. Despite their scepticism, they were hoping it would not hit the island. It was difficult to be optimistic because they had never experienced this level of preparation and urgency for any disaster on the island before. Their four-bedroom house was situated midway between Fairfield and Broderick's and was prepared for the worst. The strong aluminium shutters had been reinforced with plywood, and the structure looked very sturdy. They had oil for the lamps and candles and matches just in case the electricity went out.

There were loads of dry and tinned food in the house, and they had packed an overnight bag, just in case. Their other clothing and linen were tied up neatly in large bags, ready for a worst-case scenario. That night there were more people in the house than usual, as people took the announcers' advice and went to houses that were believed to be strong enough to withstand a hurricane. A visiting preacher friend from Dominica was among those in the house, and it gave the girls a sense of security: they had a man of God on hand to pray for the storm to stop. According to a song, 'The wind and the wave shall obey his will, peace be still.'

After a while they realised that it was eerily still and silent outside; not a tree or leaf appeared to stir. Denise wasn't sure if this was because their senses were enhanced with anticipation and the waiting, but they had been told what to expect later, and every detail and sound outside was seen as a sign. It was going to be a long night, and no one felt sleepy. They sat and waited for whatever the night would bring.

Denise had seen the effects of a major hurricane before, and it wasn't pretty. 'Wild Gilbert' (Hurricane Gilbert) had hit Jamaica the year before, in 1988. She had gone to Jamaica to study to complete clinical observations as part of her nursing course, about a month after the hurricane had hit. It had been a shock to see debris all over the place and trees uprooted, twisted, and broken. The devastation had been immense and like nothing she had seen before. She hoped that Hugo would not wreak that kind of havoc on beautiful Montserrat. She knew it would be far too much for the island to withstand, but she took comfort in the fact that a large number of houses she had seen destroyed in Papeen, Jamaica, close to the University of the West Indies (UWI) Hospital where she had been assigned, were mainly built from galvanised steel and wood. Houses built similarly to those on Montserrat were of concrete and had sustained less structural damage in general. The damage was mainly to roofs and some windows. There were hardly any galvanised houses in Montserrat, and only a few wooden ones, so most people should be all right. Furthermore, Gilbert had been known to be one of the strongest hurricanes ever to hit the Caribbean Islands. The odds were that Hugo's damage shouldn't be as severe.

All of a sudden the occupants of the house in Fairfield realised the wind had picked up outside. They rushed to the window for a look but realised they couldn't see anything because the shutters wouldn't open after being boarded up. They had nothing better to do but to sit it out and pray for safety for themselves and for the nation. To pass the time they decided to tell jumbie stories, which never failed to bring fear and tears no matter how many times they listened to the narrator, who embellished the story for effect.

As the night wore on and the wind picked up, they could hear the storm increasing in intensity, making whistling sounds mingled with what seemed like the howl of an angry animal on the loose. ZJB Radio was giving constant updates on Hurricane Hugo: winds were heading towards Montserrat at a furious 160 miles per hour. There appeared to be no escape tonight, as it was definitely making a beeline for Montserrat and some nearby islands. Hugo was coming hard and fast, with its menacing tempo of continuous pounding and howling like madness.

The forecast came on again from the announcer on ZJB Radio, and they could hear the heightened tone of his bated excitement—or was it a case of fear? Guadeloupe had been hit, and Hugo was heading fast towards Montserrat, although from the sounds of things it was here already. It was furious in its anxiety to smash the island and continue on its path to creating more havoc before it lost strength. It had weakened as it hit land but was still bringing sustained winds of 140 miles per hour. The storm continued outside for some time, and then suddenly it was here in full force, swooping, twirling, twisting, and gyrating in a way only a hurricane can. It felt as if it was tearing viciously at the roof from all angles. Then with one great swoop, the roof in the house gave up its struggle to remain intact and vanished into the dark night. The household didn't see it go because most of the ceiling was still intact. The occupants could see the storm outside roving about swiftly in the darkness, tossing about madly in a vicious state of unrest.

By this time Hugo was like a massive monster on the loose, tossing about torrents of water mixed with debris from uprooted trees and bits and pieces of people's houses. It just took anything that bended unresistingly to its will. After what appeared to be an eternity, they realised with a sense of relief that the winds had stopped, and it was still pitch dark but calm outside. Someone got up and headed towards the intact door. In one accord there was a shout from the other occupants: 'No! Don't open the door! This is just the eye of the storm—it's not over yet.'

It would only be a matter of moments before Hugo returned in full force to continue its onslaught and destruction. It was quite obvious to them that anyone caught outside in the open would be lifted up like 'Mary Poppins' and taken far away—or be seriously harmed by flying debris. The people in the house tied rope to the ceiling in the hopes of holding it down during the next blast of wind.

Suddenly the wind started up again with its mournful howling sound and vicious pounding. Then Hugo swooped in again, this time picking up the ceiling, rope and all, tossing it far away, never to be seen again. The pull was so strong that even rope held by six pairs of hands disappeared with an ease that was difficult to describe. In one accord the occupants of the house rushed into the back bedroom for refuge; water was everywhere, but a part of the ceiling there had remained intact. Five of them clambered onto the double bed, and in the blur of events it was thought that they were holding the mattress over their heads for cover. This wouldn't work though. There just wasn't enough cover for them all, and the mattress got heavier and heavier with the rain water pouring from the skies.

Denise ran into the other corner bedroom on the south side of the house and hid in the clothes closet; it was built into the wall and made of very strong wood. She felt safer in there, where the sound from outside was muted and everything was dry. The hurricane's ferocity seemed to go on forever, until eventually the winds calmed down bit by bit. The place was no longer pitch black but greyish. Dawn was here, and they realised that it was close to daybreak and that they needed to make their getaway from the house now. They couldn't hear ZJB anymore and weren't sure what was going on. The entire roof was gone, but the walls and most windows and doors were still intact. The plywood had been torn off the window on the north side and the front of the house, and the shutters were twisted and damaged. The shutters on the kitchen door was also twisted but still in place. They were all alive, but there was no time to dwell on this because they were still scared and unsure of what to do next. As the group tumbled outside, they were amazed and shocked at the devastation around them. All the houses were still standing, but most were roofless and had various types of damage. Cable and electric wires lay everywhere, with poles partially broken and held in place by the cables or just lying flat on the ground.

The group were not sure where to go, and there was no functioning phone from which to call. No individual was anywhere to be seen, and for the time being Fairfield and Broderick's had become totally deserted. They were not sure where to go and how to get out of the village, through the twisted electric wires and lamp poles lying dangerously in the roads and pathways. Then they remembered that a contractor who had recently moved into the neighbourhood lived just down the hillside in a two-storey house with a concrete roof. They decided to go there for shelter. The house was only five minutes away, but it appeared to take almost forever to get there as they struggled among the debris.

Water was running everywhere and they had a child with them. Their mom found it difficult to walk and had to be supported and half carried, because just a few months ago she had sustained a stroke that left her weak on the left side. As they started down the hillside towards their point of refuge, they were sad, not knowing if any of their neighbours or loved ones had been injured. Many of the houses they could see, even those over at Amersham and Fort Barrington, appeared roofless.

As a mercy of mercies, they approached the one house that was fully intact and realised it was overflowing with village people. Some neighbours had taken refuge there during the night, and others had come in the morning when the storm had died down. Fortunately no one from Fairfield or Broderick's had been injured during the storm. The damage to the island cost millions; almost every house had sustained some damage. Jetty, the deep water harbour, was damaged, and so were churches and schools. A number of individuals had been injured as well. The clean-up relief came from many charitable organisations and countries. The islanders had not seen or eaten so much corned beef before or after Hugo. Soldiers came and rebuilt the island, and people built bigger houses from insurance money they had received. Being the resilient people they were, it was business as usual and in no time people had continued with their lives. Montserrat bounced back to normal, and the island soon regained its natural beauty.

There was no major disruption of culture, no mass migration of people or unsafe zones on the island. Some lives were enhanced as relatives overseas provided support. Insured properties were rebuilt in no time, and the trend across the island was the construction of larger houses designed to better withstand future hurricanes. There were no reports of major disruptions in relationships as a result of the hurricane. Some children were sent to various countries for short periods of schooling, but they returned when the island settled back into its normal routine. No mass evacuations or relocations resulted. Hugo's visit created massive destruction and damage that resulted in costly repair bills, but the return to normal was quick and almost uneventful in comparison to the disruption caused by the volcano. The island saw an influx of migrants from neighbouring islands following the hurricane, but there was no real fear of the negative impact their presence would have on the Montserrat culture. The Montserrat population itself had not been greatly affected, and people felt in control and did not have to safeguard the culture.

CHAPTER 5

Challenges and Successes

My decision to write this particular passage of such a personal nature was quite tentative, and it took a huge dose of measured bravery, which I honestly confess I do not have as a rule. I feel as if I am exposing myself to the world but will cautiously do this anyway. Relocating to England was a hard decision for me to make, especially from a career perspective. I did not know what to expect because I hadn't taken time to ask any friends or relative for accounts of what it would be like in the British working community. I had long gathered from snippets of conversation here and there that working with diversity was not necessarily straightforward and could have a negative or positive impact on individuals. It was also evident that personality, attitude, and tolerance played a big role in determining one's development away from familiar environments.

Despite a mixed overview of the way things were perceived to be by many, I arrived in England with an untainted and unspoilt frame of mind, determined to make no judgements. My first attempt at finding work, on advice by another migrant Montserrat relative, was to register with an agency. Registration was easy then, and I completed the application form in a matter of minutes. Because no CRB checks were required except for my personal identification number with the United Kingdom Central Council (UKCC) and my certificates of qualification, I was soon on my way to experiencing working in England.

My first assignment was at a nursing home in Reigate, Surrey, situated in an upper middle class area. The inmates were all white, and despite what I perceive to have been my initial awkwardness, I was encouraged to take on a full-time role in a semi-senior position. Surprisingly I was not overwhelmed or intimidated in anyway by the fact that I was the only person from an ethnic minority within that employ. Every single person, from management to employee, was white, but that didn't bother me in the least, and they didn't appear bothered by it either. Until I made the decision to write this passage, I never questioned the apparent acceptance of me as a person and a professional seeking work in England. I did not make any attempts to please but instead was plain, open, and honest, giving the best of myself as I provided care at the usual high standard that I would back in Montserrat.

The thing about being in my profession is that you are either a natural at what you do, asking for nothing in return except the agreed remuneration, or you are not good at the job and struggle from beginning to end. I have no negative recall of being treated less than anyone else within that employment, and was totally unaware of our differences then. I can only say that I was treated very well and will always remember the good experiences I had. Eventually I had to leave my first job despite the offer of a more permanent position, a room to stay in overnight (when working late) and transport allowance. (I lived in Hackney, which was two and a half hours travel by public transport at that time.)

The quality of public transport could have improved over time, hence reducing the travel times. Given that it was autumn, the cold weather had started to set in, and I felt every bit of the chill in my bones. I was still unaccustomed to cold weather, so it was no joy getting out to catch buses, trains, and then a cab to get to my destination very early in the mornings. The nights were even worse for me, since the Reigate train station was pretty much isolated at 11.00 p.m., causing me great discomfort and the occasional anxiety as I stood there waiting alone on the platform. The cars of the train were often empty, and I would sit for the hour or so it took to get to Victoria Station, always praying silently for safety. I knew I couldn't do this route indefinitely, hence my decision to seek something closer to home.

The agency was quite good and soon found me a locum job more locally, to care for what is known as winter pressures. This job offered a totally different experience for me for a number of reasons. I had moved from a good working experience where I was treated well into a less than ideal job. It was now winter and very cold. I was chilled to the bone, and my extremities numbed easily. Still, I had a family to support and had no choice but to get out there and work. Let me just say here that I was on benefits, which embarrassed me to no end. The decision to find work was entirely mine; no one forced me. I could have remained on benefits like others and tried to manage with the handouts. Personally, having handouts was demoralising, and I just went out there and did what I did best—work for my living.

Months and years later, as temperatures changed, I was to learn what real cold was, and I realised that I was simply intolerant to the cold. Assigned to work as an E grade, as agreed by the agency, I turned up for work on the first day. I was based a bus ride away from my flat, and it took me about ten minutes to get there. Given that the job location was somewhere in central London, in Hackney, it was no surprise that the ethnic component was multicultural and very different to that of my first job. What was surprising was the negative treatment I received this time around.

The manager's response to me was different to that of the manager at the previous job placement. This came as an ultimate shock and made me wonder years later whether the basis for the way I was treated was due to some social and historical experience she had had in the past. We were from the same ethnic background, although not the same country, and I confess I was expecting to be treated much better by 'my own kind'. I did not understand her frustration, which had nothing to do with my performance on the job. It all stemmed from her disappointment that I did not own a car. According to the manager, she had requested the job holder to be the owner and driver of a car, with a valid UK driver's licence. I did not fit into this category, having only been in the country for just over three months. I had a provisional driver's license then, but of course that wouldn't do.

Still, it was her response to this dilemma that created the most discomfort for me. Intentional or not, I was allocated to patients who lived distances apart, and it would take me up to an hour to get from one location to another. It was out of my control, and the time of travel depended on how quickly the buses were running. This was when bus lanes were not yet a reality, resulting in congestion that caused long travel delays. I never idled between clients, and anyone who knows my working pattern would also know that I work unceasingly when on the job. Ironically there were days when I got to my second allocation, having cared for the first patient who lived a distance away, only to be greeted with an ominous message awaiting me: 'Call the manager.' Heart pounding with anxiety, I would make the call and listen to the ranting and raving about being late getting to location B, and then I'd receive her usual tirade about requesting a car driver from the agency. Being very polite and humble by nature, I kept silent as I tried to make the job work. I eventually burst at the seams with feeling that I didn't deserve this unaccustomed type of treatment, and I decided to change my agency. This was when I first experienced discrimination and disappointment. I hasten to say that I cannot recall being treated this way since.

After finding a new agency, I was allocated another job, this time as a locum district nurse, which gave me a totally different perspective of working in London. The manager here was again of a similar ethnicity to me, but the way she treated me on the job was more of a nurturing nature. I did not lack experience generally, but where I did, a member of the staff provided the necessary support. Whereas the previous job made me feel undervalued, awkward, and out of place, this job had the opposite effect. My experience and confidence grew to the point where I felt I was ready for a more permanent job.

By May 1998, almost a year after migrating to England, I had secured my first permanent job in a London teaching hospital. I had dreaded this moment, as my orientation had been more community based since qualifying as a registered nurse in Montserrat. Further, my last job in Montserrat had been the coordination of mental health services on the island, which was community based. There was no mental institution in Montserrat and no psychiatrist, except one who visited the island quarterly. This meant that my responsibilities were wide and varied. I functioned at a very high level in that role, including diagnosing and making recommendations for patients in the general hospital, prisons, and community.

Providing education both individually and through the media, counselling and stress management and group sessions also followed. Administering direct patient bedside care had not been part of my job profile for many years, and it was difficult to imagine myself in that role again. Despite this I decided that to survive, I just had to jump in at the deep end. I had decided before travelling to England that I would not work in mental health away from Montserrat but would explore new career prospects.

With this in mind I had interviewed for two jobs in the same week and at the same hospital. I was successful at both and made a choice of the one for which I thought I would be most suitable. I made a good choice, and the support I received from colleagues during my time there was commendable. The employees were of mixed ethnicity and cultural backgrounds, but that was only evident by the colour of their skin. The working relationship from each one mirrored the other. I am not sure why this was so; it may have been as a result of the leadership, the management, the environment, and the location—or perhaps it was just a phenomenon where individuals of similar personalities met on mutual grounds.

Moving into the hospital setting as a way of making progress was something of a paradox. I had gained headway in securing a permanent job but had in fact taken on a lesser grade. The ethos of nursing in England is that if you were trained elsewhere, then on starting off in a permanent job, you must start at the bottom of the ladder. In this case the bottom was what was known as a grade D then (now called band five with the introduction of Agenda for Change). I had previously worked as a grade E with the agency and now resigned myself to less pay and a lower job status. This by no means demotivated me—it made me more determined to progress as fast as possible to what I thought to be an equivalent grade of what I was in Montserrat. One of the interview panellists had actually suggested that she could see me being promoted up two grades within six months.

I did not apply for my first promotion until four years later; I used the time to study for my first degree, a bachelors of science in health studies. No one had to tell me that I needed to better understand the British health care system, and especially the complex National Health Service (NHS), in order to progress. Therefore when funding for tertiary education was offered by the British government to the Montserrat migrants in 1998, I successfully applied for funding and a place at a university in London, where I gained a second-class honours degree.

As blessed as I was at that time, the hospital I worked at offered an opportunity to study for my master's degree in nursing, a challenge I gratefully accepted. At that time there was a lot of noise by organisations about investing in people, and I was happy to benefit from this. With funding in hand and a place at a different London university, I started the course but had to abort shortly after it started, to return to Montserrat. After a brief period of eighteen months in Montserrat, I returned to England back at square one. I had no job and had to start the job search process again. This was my first experience with real poverty. I had no money for rent and taxes. I had been sending money from Montserrat to pay for these all along, but there was nothing left now that I was here. For an entire month I survived on a hundred pounds only. I was never a big spender, so no one noticed the difference, and I still went around with a bright smile on my face, never asking for loans or handouts. My preacher offered me a loan of five hundred pounds with no pay-back date, but being me I promptly refused on the basis that I would ask for it when I got desperate. Poor as I was, I never did ask, and I managed on the bare minimum.

I applied for job seekers allowance in the interim but was told I was not eligible for this. There was no logical explanation for that response because I had made the relevant contributions for more than three years. With a heavy heart I applied for temporary work with the staff bank, at the hospital I had worked for before. I was immediately given work and continued there for the next seven months, after which I found a permanent job in a specialist area that I thought I would actually like despite my inexperience with that speciality. This time I successfully applied for a job at a higher grade, having already gained the knowledge and skills necessary to enable me for a higher level of functioning. I later left that job to become a trainee specialist in neurology.

Once settled I successfully reapplied to pursue the masters degree programme I had to leave before. Since then I've had job offers at a higher band but took up none of the offers as a result of issues of location, distance, and travel. Despite those offers, the realisation at this point in my career is that getting beyond specialist nurse at band seven in my particular field is a very challenging thing, and posts beyond this band are very limited. I recognised this while completing a project management module as part of my master's degree, when I attempted to redesign a new post to offer that opportunity. At the time the project made sense, and with my leadership training behind me, I felt more than ready for this.

I was soon brought back down to earth at the realisation that even when the project is your own, there is a lot of competition out there. The project did not go through in the end, but I was able to pass the project management module through critical analysis of the project itself.

On Reflection

I have learnt that the only way to succeed in life is to reflect on the things that went well and those that didn't go so well, with a view towards creating awareness for future reference. One of the things that worked for me was being able to manage myself. I was aware of what I wanted and was able to assess myself along the way, which took much thought, effort, discipline, and motivation—a challenge which helped me remain focussed at all times. It is certainly not easy to remain motivated when things are not going right in one's life, or appear out of sync with the way one planned the goals and envisioned the outcomes. Most people find that they are able to muster the initial interest in a project and remain motivated when there is continued success. Needless to say, the opposite is true when things don't go to plan; it becomes very easy to give up and lose focus when the going gets rough. My self-awareness has played an important role in understanding my personal feelings about things and issues as I went through different experiences.

As such I have had my share of successes and failures. It was important for me to understand what success means to me as an individual as well as how failure makes me feel. Progress could not have occurred had I sat and wait for it to happen, but rather when I set goals, improve educational status, and shared with others that set a motion in place for continued mobilisation. I have also found that the more I teach, the more knowledgeable I become. To teach, one has to do the relevant research, understand the subject, and find the correct method to present it to learners. Therefore one is not only learning by memorising but through strategy, understanding, and creativity.

Setting career goals has certainly helped me along the way in addition to self development through education and learning. Simple reflection on where I want to be in five years and setting out clear strategies to get there were the first steps to my aim at success. I have been asked from time to time, 'When last did you take a break from study?' My answer is never for I view life as a continuous learning process, a journey that never ends. When one is not learning formally, one is learning informally. Furthermore, in England continual professional development is one of the criteria for the job.

I must confess that the aspect of my existence and progress in England that gets the least attention is my personal and social life. I have found that the small bit of time I spend doing the things I enjoy are very beneficial to my well-being. The problem here is that distance, season, and opportunity create difficulties, which may be overcome if more attention were given to planning leisure activities. Despite having to swallow my pride and start at the bottom of the career ladder, I have used strategies which ensured that I achieve the successes that I identified at the beginning. A combination of humility, honesty, and hard work has enabled me to deal with the challenges as they come along. I recognise that I will not be successful at all times, nor succeed at every interview I attempt; however perseverance will guarantee future opportunities. The art of frequent reflections and self-awareness is the key to ongoing progress and the knowledge that success has different meanings for individuals. Finally real success for me doesn't mean necessarily having a top job or loads of money; but rather having opportunities to take steps forward no matter how tiny they may be.

CHAPTER 6

Despite the Odds

'I would like to make life better for myself and fit in as a British citizen.' My future plan is to complete my studies, find a good job, and hopefully one day buy a house in the UK so that I can finally set up a home away from home.'

For Montserratians, living in England and trying to integrate into the various subcultures is certainly a mixture of blessings and challenges, what with trying to survive among the hundreds of different cultures within the melting pot of London, while struggling to maintain our own culture and traditions. Many Montserratians, especially the young, have quickly blended in with the other cultures of London very easily, but others (especially the older and more matured) have retained their identities and cultures completely. The Montserrat contribution has somewhat enhanced the richness and uniqueness of London itself as a melting pot with its mix of many nations of different customs and traditions.

The range of music, food, language, and dress tells a story that requires no narration. It is for this very reason that Montserratians have been able to blend smoothly into the welcoming arms of cosmopolitan London. In my opinion there's hardly any common British type to be found in London, unlike other cities outside the capital. Most communities outside London are clearly identified through the maintenance of their traditions and cultures. For Brits it is often difficult for others to differentiate Montserrat culture and traditions from other Caribbean immigrants; we are just seen as Afro Caribbeans and often have to make a clear distinction of our identity to others less knowledgeable of our customs. There have been tales of difficulty communicating with others because some expressions are often misunderstood by those less familiar with the Montserrat culture and language.

Despite this most Montserratians have learnt to adapt to the differences and challenges, taking no offence at misinterpretations and misunderstandings related to their language. The famous Notting Hill Carnival, held in London, is a much bigger version of the Montserrat festival Jouvert Jump Up and is also shared and enjoyed by Montserratians who often form their own bands and troupes to draw crowds of similar tastes and cultures.

Other cities outside London have smaller versions of carnivals, and size being no issue, Montserrat folk enjoys these just the same. Despite the number of entertaining events which create both differences and similarities to the things Montserrat folk enjoy, some folks have fit in without actually losing who they are, and others have just gone with the flow and put aside their cultural identities to blend in. There is no right or wrong about this; each individual will determine what circumstance would suit him or her best.

I've often been asked about my survival in England on a number of occasions by persons who themselves are faltering in their will to remain unspoilt or unchanged culturally and traditionally. It is no doubt a difficult task; as with most things, it is easier to blend in than to stand out. I cannot say I have remained unchanged, and I daren't think of using the term unspoilt, but I can attempt to give an account of how I deal with the ongoing challenges related to adjustment in England. I wish to note here that the challenges I experience, and the strategies used to overcome them, are by no means unique or novel but are also shared by others. The biggest challenge reported to date results from the inability to socialise with fellow Montserratians mainly due to time limitations, work pressures, and other commitments.

As I was preparing a presentation for an upcoming ladies retreat in Chesham, I thought of my position as a Montserratian in London and the road I have travelled. The insight for the presentation came from my experiences, goals, aspirations, achievements, and challenges along the way. I decided to share the contents of that presentation as a motivator for all Montserratians at home and abroad in this book.

I must caution that the emphasis of this chapter is not to preach or teach, as it may appear to some, but rather to motivate people to use the greatest resource ever given to man to their advantage. I hope I am correct in thinking the majority of us Montserratians still are, or claim to be, Christians. Denominationally we might focus on different elements of the Word, but this chapter is not about denominations or religions; rather it offers insight into the support and strength I've found through the use of scriptural example. In life there is no doubt that we need to find methods of sustainability in everything we do. England is a very complex and challenging place to live no matter who you are, but especially if you are from a small, undeveloped country with no traffic lights, road signs, and the like. As such there are areas of frustration that are quite foreign and not part of the experience on the island of Montserrat. The distractions in England are numerous, but not necessarily in a negative way, and if one is not careful, it is very easy to lose oneself in a world of work, entertainment, competition, and achievements.

Spirituality and the ultimate belief in a superior spiritual being has always been an important facet of the Montserrat culture. However, it appears that many a Montserratian in England no longer find it pertinent to go to church. A large number of those I speak to believe in a superior being, and quite a few admit to being Christians. The point I am trying to make here, though, is that as a Montserratian in England, it is important to have that strong belief in God, which in the past has seen us through some of the major difficulties that we encountered. For many who migrated from Montserrat, it is the spirituality of our forefathers that has kept us going through thick and thin in modern England. During Hurricane Hugo and the volcanic eruptions, it was a strong belief in God that brought the faith to carry on when all appeared lost.

When life gets difficult, it is that faith by the grace of God that brings us back from the edge, giving us the strength to persevere. Many of us have had our share of successes and failures, some to greater extents than others. It is very impossible to think of anyone who's never experienced a failure at some point. Often people make plans with no thought that the outcome might not necessarily be what was anticipated. When plans do fail, some try to find explanations of why they failed, and some blame others or just give up, becoming angry. Those of us who have moved to England and other countries have a lot to learn from scriptural examples. Had it not been for the will of God and the partnership we have with Him, our hopes of stability and survival would have been very dim.

Growing in Partnership with God

We can take some good examples from biblical characters even if we are not Christians. Matthew 10:1-2 shows where Jesus called his twelve chosen disciples to him so that he could instruct them according to his will. He was sending them on a journey and gave them authority to carry out a number of tasks. Jesus's plan for his disciples was very specific, as we will see later in this chapter. What does all this have to do with us? Despite the fact that He is no longer present in flesh, we've been blessed with the power of prayer, so we can ask for God's guidance in planning our progress. Just as it is important to pray to God for His guidance, it is equally essential to understand His instructions.

The only way to gain clarity about what God wants from us is to take time to ask the Lord what direction we should take in our lives. Once we are satisfied in our hearts of what He wants from us, we need to make our plans following His guidance and direction. By listening to the Lord in prayer, we can further align ourselves with His specific purposes for our lives and therefore have greater success in reaching the goals He gives us. On a number of occasions I have met a young lady who often refers to her everyday relationship with God in a reassuring way. She has not changed her spiritual approach to life despite living in metropolitan England. The other day she said, 'God sent me a boyfriend, so I'm happy.' This was after living on her own for more than ten years; she had been patient and waited for the right moment and hopefully the right person.

As outlined in the book of Matthew, God always gives very clear instructions to His people so there is no confusion over what He wants them to do. We should never doubt that He will give us clear instructions when we ask for it. He has demonstrated His will in so many different ways. If the young lady had taken on any guy that came her way without following guidance and instruction, she could have had many regrets, but she waited until it was right.

A further look at another type of reliance of guidance is again from scripture. Jesus sent out his twelve disciples with the following set of instructions, and just look at how specific his instructions were. 'You must not go among the Gentiles or enter any town of the Samaritans. Instead go to the lost sheep of Israel and as you go, preach the following message: "The kingdom of heaven is near." He further instructed, 'Freely you have received, freely you should give . . . . Do not take with you any gold or silver or copper in your belts; take no bag for the journey, and no extra items of clothing, or sandals or a staff; for the worker is worth his keep.' I must admit that some of these instructions would be very hard to follow, for as humans we would surely worry about what to wear, where to find money to buy food, et cetera. Imagine the situation Montserrat folk travelling to England found themselves in during 1997 and 1998. A number of individuals had no clue what they were coming to, or where they would live, eat, or sleep, but they put their trust somewhere and came through faith. In the same way it is important to continue trusting in God to help us along the way now that we are settled and face different challenges. It cannot be overemphasised how important it is for our goals, plans, and instructions to come directly out of our time in prayer. Never forget that we can go to Him in prayer with confidence, asking for His strength and grace to achieve our goals. Most of all we need to be sure that our plans are also God's will—hence the importance of prayer and communication with Him.

Life is never as straightforward as we would like it to be, and that fact sometimes leaves us feeling frustrated and demotivated. Although some people are very good at dealing with this frustration, others may give up or give in and become depressed, even isolating themselves from others. Additionally we may blame others for our lack of success and setbacks in life, with no regard or thought for the simple fact that it could be God's will that our plans did not reach fruition at this particular time. Whatever the reason that many plans are not realised or as successful as it was pictured they would be; it is important to communicate about this and give Him the opportunity to direct or redirect us as He wishes. As humans we often require an explanation for things that don't go to plan, but God does not work this way simply because He knows what is best for us.

It often helps to delve into the scriptures to see how setbacks and challenges were dealt with. In the book of Romans, Paul made a plan to visit some churches but had a number of challenges on the way. Paul's setbacks came not only from people around him, but he was also restricted by God's sovereign plans. After being kept by the Holy Spirit from preaching in the province of Asia, Paul and his companions travelled throughout the region of Phrygia and Galatia instead. He engaged himself in other useful projects and did not sit back and give up because his original plan was foiled. Paul still had work to do, for he had a plan. He didn't stop his work completely, sit back, do nothing, and feel sorry for himself and blame others—this would have been unproductive. Instead we are shown how through persistent prayer he remained responsive to the Holy Spirit's promptings. He was therefore able to redirect his goals in order to align his plans with God's greater purposes. Note also that despite his setbacks and change of goals, he still intended to complete his original plan. Therefore he wrote to the church in Rome reassuring that his timing had changed, 'But I hope to stay a while with you, if the Lord permits.' That is truly persevering despite the odds.

If you really want something, you are motivated to go for it no matter what. If it looks impossible, put it to rest for a while and pray, looking out for the right time when He gives the okay to go ahead. Paul could have given up and refused to do anything else while he waited to carry out the original plan, but of course he did not. It is often easier to give up than to persevere, but when pursued there is a sense of achievement and self-worth that usually cannot be replaced. It is important to tell ourselves from the beginning that it is worth persevering to the end once we've started. Also, not being successful the first time around is not an indicator that others are against us, but merely that we need to try harder with a positive attitude.

This is the only attitude that will suffice through trying and difficult times. In addition to God's sovereign plans for us, there are a number of reasons why we may not achieve our goals. For some of us, we hold ourselves back when we start focussing on our long list of unrealized goals in our past. This becomes a hindrance when we start believing that the achievement of our goals isn't possible, and we think, 'I am never successful anyway; nobody likes me.' Don't be tempted to give in to subliminal messages or psychological influences from people who know how to play the demotivational game. Be mindful that when living in places such as England and other big cities, one has to recognise the ongoing competitions and challenges. It is not necessarily personal, but just the way things are, based on the environment and the culture. Therefore we must be prepared and cannot afford to be defeated before we even begin. That attitude can lead to more failure! When we focus on past failures, we lose sight of the fact that we can achieve goals. We slink away with our 'tails tucked between our legs', resigned to failure. This often happens when we do not have faith in what we are doing and in our abilities.

I had an experience with a young lady who was the best friend of a bride but did not know what she would say when called upon to give a speech at the reception. Not religious or spiritual at all, she wanted to give advice to the newlyweds, but as a single person she had no confidence in herself to say the right thing. She was also reluctant to use scripture for support because she was not known to be religious. After all, she had never been married and hardly attended church services, so how could she give marriage advice? Yet she wanted to her speech to be serious and full of wisdom. After much thought and reflection and some guidance and support, it was agreed that there was great benefit to using scripture as a source of wisdom and guide.

This was so touching that I got permission to add the speech here as a source of motivation. Through God's intervention, this is what she had to say at the reception.

Dear K & D,

See! Your winter is past; the single days are over at last. I've pondered and wondered what to say to you, my dearest friends, on this your wedding day.

Believe me, this short discourse took months and months of leafing through the recesses of my brain, when this 'aha' moment on me suddenly descend as flashes of the Bible's inherent resource burned through my brain like a living flame.

And so I found the words that with you should remain, sealed in the nucleus of your heart, from this your wedding day and thereafter. The only true words of wisdom; that can really suffice, as the essential advice for friends, as special to me as you.

Step 1

For now that you and D have made your choice, keep reflecting on these words of wisdom, your very supplement, and think on them day and night. As God's chosen people, holy and dearly loved, clothe yourselves with compassion, kindness, humility, gentleness, and patience, Bear with each other, forgive whatever grievances you may have against one another. Forgive as the Lord forgave you. Remember above all the virtues to put on love: love one another, love binds all virtues together in perfect unity, without love you have nothing.

Love is harmonious, forgiving, understanding; love is a beautiful thing; love is a gift from God; and love will overcome all difficulties. Pray for peace and joy, and let the peace of Christ rule in your hearts, since you are now members of one body. In all be thankful, be grateful, and whatever you do or say throughout your marriage, do it through the glory of God.

Step 2

When I read this line in the Song of Solomon, though not given to idle sentiment, a tear fell from my eyes. Sorry, K, I see that look in your eyes, but come on, this is no time to cry. Turn around, look each other in the eye. D, place K like a seal over your heart; like a seal on your arm. Just think—if one were to give all the wealth of his house for love, it would be utterly scorned. And so, D, at the end of this day we will listen keenly just to hear you say those magic words, 'Arise, my darling, my beautiful one, come with me, for K is yours and you're hers forever, to love and to cherish from this day.'

With the support of Bible scriptures, the most encouraging things were said on that day through the right guidance. Her friend has also set herself up in a good position to provide support in the future by casual reference to the poem she wrote to the couple. We are therefore advised against deception: 'Do not to be deceived, God is not mocked; for whatever a man sows, that he will also reap.' Whatever you need or desire, find scriptures relating to that issue. Then plant those scriptures inside your heart and mind in abundance by studying and praying about them. Reading the Bible regularly is something adopted by some folk, and the increased reliance on spiritual support can be seen by the number of people, adding a thought for the day or a Bible verse to their profiles on social networking sites. Folk have not hesitated to comment or click a 'like' button to show their support of the scriptures posted.

You do not need to walk around with a huge Bible anymore, because whole Bible applications are now downloadable to portable devices. If you invest in the right things and persevere by following God's instructions, the seeds of your plans will grow and produce a harvest of what you need or desire. For 'little is much when God is in it', and we really aught to remember that.

CHAPTER 7

The Memorial

'Diaspora? What diaspora?' 'It was the memorial of the icons that did it for me. Acceptance had come at last and reality set in. The new identity which we appear to have no choice but to accept; diaspora was the new name for Montserrat in England. As I walked into St Mark's Church at Dalston, Kingsland, my eyes hungrily searched the large, dimly lit building for familiar faces. The dim lights could have been purposeful for the occasion, or perhaps just a way of drawing attention to the beautiful stained glass windows. The original church, built around 1864, is said to have the capacity to house about 1800-2000 people. The church is the biggest I have seen, which made it difficult to even estimate how many of us were present. Set a few yards from Ridley Road Market, there were convenient parking bays for those who used private vehicles to get to the venue. Public transport was very accessible; the area boasted a number of buses, both Double Decker and bendy buses. There were two train stations in close proximity to St Mark's: Dalston Kingsland, situated a five-minute walk away, and the more recent Dalston Junction at about ten minutes walking distance. The location was ideal for this occasion for those reasons, among others.

As I walked to my car I looked at my watch and realised I was going to be late. My friend was calling as I drove off, but I couldn't answer the phone. That would be the ultimate crime, to talk on the phone while driving, and the penalty I would incur was not only financial but would result in points on my licence. I was worried about breaking the law, although the previous seven points I had incurred from 2004 to the present had now been cleared. I know what you must be thinking, 'frequent offender', but I can assure you I'm not. I would rather say I am a victim of circumstances, such as running the traffic light at 0.009 of a second too late. Can't picture that? Well neither can I, and I wasn't drunk on that New Year's Day, for I'm a teetotaller if ever there was one. I can't even blame the lack of traffic lights and cameras in Montserrat, where I drove for most of my adult life; I had been driving in England for a long time, so I should have stopped when the light was about to turn amber.

On the very day of the memorial there was a Jewish festival hampering my progress in traffic as I tried to get to the church. If I couldn't be early, then I'd settle for fashionably late. Today it took me three times longer than usual to get there. Amidst the delays and buildup of tension driven by my lateness, I decided to switch to more pleasant thoughts to reduce the accompanying stress. I thought of the old familiar faces I would encounter that day, where we had come from, and what we had become. *Diaspora*! Did we even belong anywhere? Was there actually still a place called home in the Caribbean, or were we now considered outcasts, mere visitors seeking shelter for a short visit to what used to be our homeland?

From a more personal perspective, a number of thoughts crossed my mind. 'Can I still call home, home, or will I be just a stranger in paradise? As the calypsonian so nicely put it, 'Will I be just a tourist in my own country?'

Would I be remembered and if so what, if anything, would I be remembered for? The recent use of the term 'diaspora' has been thrown around loosely to describe Montserrat folk who were forced to leave Montserrat from 1995 onward. This group of people to which I belong is not the first set of representative Montserrat diaspora to England. Montserrat folk have been migrating to England in large numbers since the '50s and at some point were said to have formed the largest group of Caribbean migrants in England. Let us not forget that what actually set this new group apart from the other migrant groups are the circumstances which brought them to England. I feel the need to reinforce that we did not want to leave Montserrat, and once forced to leave; our intention was always to return to the homeland.

I may be digressing a bit, but I'm certainly aware that there is still this need to define the meaning of diaspora since it appears a large number of people are still not sure what the term actually means. Some may see it as a bad term when used to describe our current status outside Montserrat. I therefore thought it pertinent to have a short discourse on some of the thoughts around the term within the Montserrat context. The Encarta

Online Dictionary definition is as follows: 'the scattering of language, culture, or people; dispersion of people, language, or culture'. Needless to say all of the definition categorically describes the current Montserrat situation.

As I used Google to scout around for appropriate information to share regarding this definition, I felt it was indeed befitting as I looked at the terms 'dispersion', 'culture scattering', and language. Back at St Mark's Church, my eyes travelled around the room on 20 March 2011 and came to rest on our very own doctor, whom I hadn't seen for many years. Unlike most he appeared to be enjoying the best of both worlds as he travelled back and forth from England to the Caribbean, running his medical service like it was an 'office in the sky'. For him the benefits would be twofold, as one can imagine. Still, how many would want to wear his shoes with all that constant travelling?

After a brief catch-up and exchange of business cards, my friend and I moved on up the aisle of the old Victorian church as we continued to scan the seats for familiar faces. The dim lights, though appropriate for the sobriety of the occasion, made everyone look darker than usual. We craved to see those we hadn't seen for five, ten, fifteen years or more, and we satisfied ourselves with recognition of the few who were sitting in close proximity to the aisle. The ceremony itself was quite simple but fitting, and I can only think that maybe subconsciously I was expecting a bit more pomp and ceremony for such iconic figures as John 'Bassy' Osborne, our past chief minister and longest serving politician in Montserrat and possibly the Caribbean. The other icon a representation of soca Caribbean and international was none other than the Mighty Arrow. The other two individuals, Rapa Mead and Noel Dada Tuitt, were of no less significance; they fulfilled important roles in Montserrat and were appreciated by many. The real purpose of this discourse is not to publish all the names, for fear of causing monotony, but rather to impress upon the reader the emotions experienced as a member of the Montserrat diaspora. I must also explain that I am by no means criticising the organisation or presentations of the memorial service, as I think simple is sometimes the best way to go.

Contributions were appropriately presented by a mix of the Montserrat Diaspora and some nationals still living in Montserrat. Jeanette Arnold, a member of the diaspora from another era of migrant Montserratians, also made an appropriate presentation. She is currently serving as a chair of the London Health Commission. Introducing herself as the niece of Sir Howard Fergus, she adequately read a dedication written by the living iconic figure himself to another icon, John A Osborne. The Alliougana singers put on a good show as usual and couldn't be faulted in any way. Hearing the blend of Montserrat voices singing melodiously in a unified blend of familiar pronunciation was wonderful. The ceremony ran its course, and then it was time to socialise and catch up with Montserrat folk, which for me was the most significant reason for being present that evening. No refreshment was offered, but no one commented on it. There was a feeling of satisfaction with talking to each other. Needless to say, as people get older, the memory also deteriorates and facial structures change. A couple of people I had known since childhood and still recognised took me aback because they couldn't remember who I was, which for me was sad. One lady, who hailed from the same area as I did, asked, 'Are you the sister of the nurse?'

Someone said, 'She *is* the nurse.'

She replied, 'Everyone looks so good, and I expected you to look white by now, as you were already clear.'

I humorously remarked, 'Ah, but I am so pale I can hardly recognise myself. Oh how I need some Montserrat sunshine.'

Although it was amusing the way she had unknowingly mixed me up, it certainly wasn't funny when your own people forgot you. Is that what happened to members of the diaspora overtime? We were scattered far and wide, only to become a vague memory to those we once knew? This was certainly a bit much to take in, but one could only imagine that in the next five years or so, some familiar faces would be even more unrecognisable.

In times past at my jobs in England, on hearing the combination of certain first and last names, I would easily identify a person as Montserratian without seeing his or her face. More recently the combinations, especially of the more traditional names such as Mary or William, are more obviously carried by Irish or English folk. The reality is that one can no longer assume that a name is only associated with Montserrat or a specific Caribbean island anymore; it can belong to anyone, and anyway, most of the Montserrat names as we know them are actually of Anglo-Irish origin.

Another area of concern is the occasional return of the migrants as permanent residents. The question has been asked by many who have been directly affected by issues related to permanent re-relocation to the island of Montserrat. Some question whether they are allowed the same rights as those Montserrat folk who never left the island. My personal experience was that on migration, a redundancy package was offered with the promise of an open arm welcome on return, a job, and a sense of belonging in every way. Like many this could have been a misunderstanding on which I now find I do not have the authority to make a judgement.

After completing my first degree in health studies at the University of North London in England, I returned to Montserrat four years after migrating. When seeking employment, I was told that my old job was vacant and was still available if I wanted it, so I took it with the intention of looking for another that suited my new qualifications and experience. I wasn't successful in securing a different post despite making my intentions known. I am not sure what the real reasons were and did not take it personally or make a judgement of the situation. Others had a different view and thought the successful applicant for the job would be one who had never left Montserrat. That was not the first or last time I have heard this comment, but again find myself in no position to make a judgement on it.

Housing was not an issue because I was able to find different types of accommodation when needed. Properties were rather expensive, and people were selling their lands at a very high cost. Several auctions were held for properties that had been reclaimed by the government, but they too were costly. My relationship with Montserrat folk, including those I knew before, showed no significant change, and I felt quite at home, as if I had not left for long. The cost of living was very high; a result of the migration of two-thirds of the population. Despite this folks went about their business looking relaxed and comfortable. It was difficult to tell that the volcano was still burning in the background, though the occasional pyroclastic flow and ash fall occurred from time to time.

The one important difference to note was that I did not consider myself as a member of the diaspora then. I was a true, born and bred Montserratian who had returned to my rightful place in the world, the land of my birth. Still, not being able to find anything suitable and not wanting to be tied down in my current field of work, I packed up and returned to England. My disillusionment with the job prospects in Montserrat triggered the move that time. I had no job to return to in England, for I had given that up whilst in Montserrat. It would only be a short time before I got another job in England on return. The feedback from other members of the diaspora suggests that others individual experiences have not been as favourable as my account. In fact there have been some public outcries from several members based in various parts of the world. They were concerned at being treated as visiting tourists in their own land.

The results of the Montserrat festival competitions of December 2010, such as the Calypso shows and Festival Queen Pageants, have left questions of whether Montserrat folk living in other countries are being judged fairly. The general consensus for one of the competitions was that the diaspora should have had a better position. It was difficult to form a personal opinion on this despite viewing the entire competition via live streaming on the Internet. It is always difficult to judge things from a distance. There appear to be some thoughts that the diaspora members were never allowed to win in Montserrat, even when their performance was proven to be the best. Of course this claim is a subjective one and would be very difficult to prove, especially when there were multiple judges.

Those affected appear to be saddened by the perception that members of the diaspora have been somehow cheated out of winning a crown. I can imagine some scuffing at these accusations, but I certainly think that there should be a way of addressing the issue. Whether there be any truth in this is not the real issue here; maybe this is the time to rethink the judging techniques and criteria to allow for equal opportunities. The change should allow for a more diversified strategy like those we see in larger countries, where the audience or the viewing public is allowed to contribute as judges.

The question here would be whether Montserrat is ready for this forward move, or whether it prefers to remain safety entrenched in its traditional style of using a panel of handpicked, well-known judges whose selection strategies appear to frustrate many. There is no easy answer to this question, and it sounds as if the diaspora feel powerless to intervene. Whatever happened to the promises that suggest the diaspora could return whenever they are ready to invest in the country? One would have thought that the now more exposed and in some cases highly educated diaspora would have been given the opportunity to help rebuild the country.

Take the nurses, for example: not only have they enhanced themselves academically, but they have gained new skills and immense experiences. How is it, then, that their offer of voluntary assistance to the island is not being taken? Do they pose a threat to the island's health or the nursing fraternity? I should think not. Some may argue that a number of nurses on Montserrat are now more qualified than they were fourteen years ago and some are known to hold a master's degree; which is great because academically they can hold their own among the rest of the world. However do they have the wealth of experience of the various nurses who are working in highly specialised areas, or would this be a simple case of cutting off the nose to spite the face? The answer to these questions is anyone's guess.

Another cause of discontent among the Montserrat Diaspora, on returning for holidays, is the annoyance of being referred to as being British in a less than polite manner. Not that being British is a bad thing; in fact we are all British according to our passports. It is generally thought that the English accent is what accounts for this negative tone when describing a Montserratian living in England. Many have expressed feelings of being made to feel as an outsider or being put in their place by the tone used by fellow islanders. Again there is a need to reinforce that had circumstances been different, such as the island being large enough and equipped to deal with the entire migrant population, then less people would have left. It was certainly not a case of Montserratians jumping off the sinking ship, as some like to believe. At most it should be seen as a situation which occurred as a means of survival, merely a means to an end. Let us not forget that the secondary school in Salem couldn't accommodate all of the children from around the country, and there weren't enough primary or nursery schools in the north. What of those people living in shelters which had only one toilet and no privacy? Aren't people still living in shelters, even today fifteen years later? What of the lack of jobs? Let's try some positive thinking and forget about penalising the diaspora for trying to survive. Just in case people are wondering, I can assure you that most individuals who left Montserrat did not have an easy life wherever they went; they've struggled hard to survive outside Montserrat, and many are still struggling. It is no wonder that people are hurt at being made to feel they have given up their birth right and have committed a crime for doing so. Montserrat will always be home to all of us, no matter what.

On the question of job opportunities for folks who have returned to Montserrat, there has been mixed feedback, and one individual who had previously migrated and then returned home stated that she was made to feel as if she was being punished for leaving. The general feedback is that on seeking employment appropriate to qualifications, the returnees have not been treated the same as the Montserratians who never left. The feedback has been that the jobs they are qualified for are often offered to a less qualified individual who never left. Here again this allegation would be difficult to prove on the basis of a few individuals' subjective accounts, which are not necessarily backed by documented evidence. If there be any accuracy in such accounts, then the ongoing talks of encouraging the diaspora to return would be likened to paying lip service and not meant to be taken seriously. Those who wish to return would find this very disappointing.

There are some interesting, ongoing debates that Montserratians at home and abroad resent the presence of other nationals living on Montserrat. There has been much murmuring of the influence of these people on the Montserrat culture. It is obvious that the very small population of residents in Montserrat cannot stand alone during the rebuilding of the island; the issue of economical support simply cannot be overlooked. Therefore one would expect that the purpose and presence of other folk on Montserrat could be seen as a positive one. Still, one cannot discount the subjective views of those affected in one way or another. The resentment from those living outside Montserrat may very well stem from the change of crime culture on the island rather than the migrants themselves. Up until the late '90s, Montserrat was said to have a virtually crime-free culture, but the reports coming from the homeland suggest there has been a dramatic change in the type and severity of crimes in recent times. It is expected that this would be of concern to a people who were previously proud about being able to leave car doors open with shopping bags in full view on the seat, and even sleeping at home with doors unlocked.

This brings us to the question of preserving the Montserrat culture. Is this possible, and if so, how? Is there really such a thing as preserving culture? The blend of cultures in Montserrat will certainly create subcultures, which can ultimately result in a shift from the way the Montserrat culture was perceived. One can imagine why the diaspora would be concerned. Although not clearly articulated by many, a large number of Montserratians look forward to returning to Montserrat at the height of the annual festivities in December to enjoy its unspoilt beauty. The driving force behind this is the culture, the way Montserrat used to be. The cuisine, goat water, Johnny cake, and salt fish. The language, familiar faces, music, dances folkways and masquerades. It is no wonder individuals are concerned that things are changing; the very thing they treasure is disappearing into something unfamiliar and unwelcome. These sentiments have been expressed over and over, and I see how difficult it is to be objective on this subject. We should not be too hard on the feelings of resentment expressed by the diaspora and others. Instead we need to find a way of ensuring that the new Montserrat works for everyone without losing too much of who and what we are. The only way forward may be forming supportive networks that embrace change in a positive way and that enable and empower all Montserratians far and near to accept the positive aspects of cultural diversity. Finding a way to secure that which we hold dear is a task in itself, and it needs addressing before it is too late.

One can't help but wonder if a memorial of sorts, arranged to celebrate the way Montserrat used to be before the volcano erupted, would serve the purpose of bringing closure to one era while signalling the beginning of a new one. Imagine a blend of cultures of people of various backgrounds sharing similar interests and coming together in unity despite their differences. As I write this, I am thinking that maybe this is what December 2012 is all about, and even while we moan and complain, the planners are trying to address these issues.

Victims of Change or Change Agents?

Change has been with us for quite a while. A long time for many but for others it is just a mere sign of things to come. After fifteen years, it is still uncertain where we are heading and what we are evolving into. It is no easy feat to acknowledge that one has been a victim of change, yet one may be unable to make an implicit or explicit claim to shaping things. Most people would prefer to be known or remembered for being the agents of change if at all possible; if they had a choice, they would prefer to be known for manipulating things rather than being manipulated. The challenges of the ever changing relationships, adaptations to new and unfamiliar environments and technology, career pathways, and new surroundings continue to keep us in a state of constant evolution.

Just as the earth turns on its axis, constantly experiencing new environments and coming into contact with whatever is blown in its path, so too the Montserrat people have remained in a state of constant learning and evolving. It would have been surprising had everyone accepted this constant change as a positive thing. Whether this is good or bad is irrelevant because individuals going through involuntary cultural changes seldom evaluate the benefits during the process unless they are forced to.

The irony of all this is that when similar changes occur as a result of intentional decision, making the evaluation of its benefits tends to be more organised—and even manipulated for the anticipated outcome of the individual. In forced migration the exact opposite might be true of the majority of individuals, and especially for the older and younger of the society, as well as the complacent. The dissatisfaction of not having control over some aspects of change ultimately puts us in the dangerous territory of the victim. Rather than asking the important question of 'How can I benefit from this change?' we moan about how we've been left out and things are not going the way we anticipated. We could sit and complain about how the changes have disrupted the life we once knew and the negative impact on our culture, relationships, and careers, but this will certainly not solve the problem. The question of 'What can I do to make it work for me?' often comes when someone puts it into our heads, or when it is too late and we are at the point of narrating the negative impact of the changes around us and what was lost rather than gained.

I do think survival is about grabbing hold of change and making it work, whether we are in Montserrat or England or some other country. Whether it is related to other nationals migrating into Montserrat or Montserratians migrating to another country, change is inevitable, and we would be better placed to embrace it and make it work for us. Still, it is acceptable that there are aspects of change that one would ideally reject because it affects our value systems, beliefs, and individual preferences. Driven by conscious risk assessments, the decision to accept or reject change will hopefully put us in a better position rather than sitting with our plates empty, waiting for our ideal recipes for progress and success to be served. Are we too laid back as a people?

To opt for no change is not necessarily conducive to preserving the culture, as some misguided individuals would like us to believe. In fact I think this reeks of stagnation at its most destructive, for where there is no progress or change, there is no development. Development is necessary for social and economic growth, and it really doesn't matter whether you are in a small island or a metropolitan country.

If one were to argue for the preservation of culture, then there are cases of certain indigenous peoples in the world whose cultures have been preserved over the years, and they are ultimately placed in reserved areas for that specific purpose. It might be useful to look up the Caribs in Dominica and the indigenous people of Australia as folk who might fit into this category. Being considered as unique is not a bad thing but we are certainly not indigenous in any way, even with our claim to an Anglo-Afro-Irish mixed heritage with its influence on our cuisine, music, names, and people. We as Montserrat folk have been evolving over time, and in fact our DNA might be the only way to prove who we really are, thus determining which culture we ultimately preserve as our own. Are we more African than Irish, or is it just a makeup of a number of unidentified DNA?

Don't get me wrong, I do think it is important to preserve the good things about our society, the things that make us Montserratian—but certainly not at the risk of remaining stagnant or economically depressed. From the look of things, it appears as if we do need productive migrants in Montserrat to contribute to the economic growth of the island.

A discussion I had with a fellow Montserratian the other day made me do a bit of introspection. Many Montserrat folk often appear to become victims of their own generosity, resulting in feelings of being used and disadvantaged. Yet they continue to give, complain, and then give again, asking and receiving little or nothing in return. My discussion was with one of the most giving human beings I know. As a very skilled Montserratian, he is often asked for favours to assist in some odd job or the other.

Not being of a mercenary nature, he assists individuals willingly and asks for nothing in return. As far as he is concerned, giving assistance to his people is an act of generosity which he does out of the kindness of his heart. Having given to those in need for years, he was caught by surprise when he needed assistance and received none. He explained that he was tired because he had a lot of work to do. Those close to him had commented on how he had been busy lately and looked very tired recently, but yet they offered no assistance. He updated those individuals who asked about the amount of work he was undertaking on his own and explained that it needed input from a number of hands.

The generous man's friends still offered no assistance. He was rather upset and disillusioned at what he considered to be the selfishness of those he had helped in the past. When asked if he had directly requested help from his associates, he retorted that he shouldn't have to ask, as he often assisted without being asked and expected that attitude to be reciprocated. In the past I often heard visitors to Montserrat, and those coming into contact with Montserratians, say how helpful we are as a people, even describing us as nice.

Being located away from Montserrat has not changed this aspect of many of us, but it has highlighted how people continue to take without giving anything in return. This realisation would hit suddenly, at a time when one needs assistance most. The usual advice is 'Don't be weary in well doing', a scripture aptly used to encourage those who feel used. Back in Montserrat before the culture started changing, folks would have a 'maroon' when there was a lot of work to do, such as building a house. It was normal for individuals from different areas both near and far to work freely to complete the foundation and the roof. The lady of the house would cook a large amount of food and provide alcohol for the workers. This was an ongoing process, and folk would take turns to assist each other when they had work to do; food and liquor was enough motivation to get them going. Then things gradually changed over time, and individuals started requesting payments for jobs. The togetherness eventually dissipated and then disappeared.

The experience of giving a lot without receiving anything in return may result in some people reducing the amount of assistance they give, while others may consider reciprocating the negative approach to generosity. Despite this, we have been taught the importance of giving without necessarily expecting anything in return. Is there such a thing as giving without wanting something in return? I dare say such a paradox raises our consciousness that to give without receiving can leave us feeling unreplenished and unrestored. Just as the earth needs replenishing and regenerating, in the same way individuals have similar needs, which if not met can leave a void that ultimately reduces satisfaction levels. Many may argue that it is better to give than to receive, but let's face it—at some point we need to experience the joy of receiving as well as that of giving.

The term 'too much information' is something else to be considered regarding its impact and implications for Montserrat folk living abroad. A number of individuals have expressed concerns that when asked simple questions, many of us would give a full history rather than just giving a simple straightforward answer. In this case it didn't matter if the question asked was about Dick's shoes. We would also hear about his toe right up to his head, and then his children, mother, and the rest of his ancestors. After this Dick becomes an open book, and if he is in certain places, he may even hear aspects of his history of which he thought no one knew.

To his dismay, he may later hear bits dropped into conversations or be told directly what was said about him. This is not a new issue, and some nationals would generally imply that this is what they expect from certain individuals anyway. Even if this is the way some folks are, we need to stop and think of the consequences of this act. Then again, is it all about the culture and the way people really are? Do we need to be mindful of how much we reveal to people? If asked 'Do you know June?' Shouldn't the answer be yes or no? There is no reason to give a full history of who her relatives are and what she did way back in the past. A number of individuals have expressed concerns on the way information is shared and its implications. Is this part of the culture? I guess we know the answer to that question.

Do we then stop giving if we are not receiving without asking? That's not what I am saying at all. Rather, there is a need to look at what and how much we are giving, and then determine if it is too much and its effects on others. For the recipient, it could be a burden if too much information is given. To the person who doesn't mean well, you've just given ammunition to the detriment of another. Learning a new way of passing on only the information sought would certainly be beneficial to all involved and may reduce feelings of being inundated by too much information. The undeserving or less generous, if there is ever such a person, could certainly be encouraged to find a way to give something back and hence become more deserving of generosity. On the island of Montserrat, we often grumble about our dissatisfaction with people taking over, but yet we continue to give them everything they ask for and more to support the so-called takeover process.

Does this make us the ultimate victims of our generosity? Or do we need to manage what we share in a more conscientious way that would then serve to protect self, culture, and heritage in order to survive? Maybe we are too stuck in our ways to evolve with other changing cultures, or maybe like the changes following the volcano, we will be forced to accept things that are thrust upon us and satisfy ourselves with complaining about them. A paradigm shift in our attitudes towards expectations, sharing, and giving would certainly support how we think of others and put us in control of the way we allow change to affects us.

CHAPTER 8

Tribute

Soca, soca! Feelin' hot hot hot! Gimme libit wah ya yet deh!
Coori arrow, coori!

The following poem was written in memory of the Mighty Arrow, one of the greatest iconic artists and singers of Montserrat. I have been listening to Arrow's melodious soca singing voice since childhood, and I continue to dance to many of his songs. Soca, a variation of calypso music, happens to be the type of music that a number of Montserratians enjoy dancing to. The first time I wrote of Arrow's music, in 2004 at a diversity barbecue held at my work place, the aim was to celebrate multiculturalism. Folks from many countries participated, and most were wearing their cultural or national dress. Clothed in national dress, I proudly lifting my voice as I mentioned the song that brought him international fame, 'Feeling Hot, Hot, Hot'. As I followed the trend of the condolences by Montserratians on Facebook on the day of his farewell on earth, words for the poem below flowed into my saddened thoughts.

They have written you down in history,
The first ever Montserrat artist,
To lift us internationally
With your melodious sound in the movies,
Chanting 'hot, hot, hot' and 'do you want to go home'.
Of course no one could do it better than that,
Even on YouTube, status confirmation,
Making it easy for us to Facebook a dedication.
You are now among the legends great;
Unforgettable, make no apology.
You brought us to fame internationally;
Now, the father almighty
Has taken you to rest eternally,
Forever in the saddened hearts of friends and family.
Your memory lives and shall remain,
Though, alas the dust
Covers your arrow-shaped,
Brightly coloured new home
From us, your body to secure
Six feet, not an inch more.
They've convinced us, dear Arrow,
It is but an inevitable prerequisite.
Preacher assures it's only temporary, this,
For your soul shall find eternal rest
As it returns to a place called paradise,
Where finally your rest, we pray,
Will be with the angels in heavenly bliss.
Continue singing in glory,
Moving to the beat,
Though it won't be hot hot hot,
For in heaven there can be no heat,
Else angels would beat a hasty retreat.
May God keep you safely in sweet peace,
In heaven where there is only joy and peace.

Written on 1/10/10

Celebrate Diversity

Embracing diversity is the element of survival in any melting pot! This is a simple poem of liberation, written in 2004 and inspired by a moment of homesickness for Montserrat. On this day diversity was celebrated at the workplace of a London hospital situated in a multicultural area of England. Employees and employers alike enjoyed a day of liberation while they shared their talents, customs, and traditions through music, food, cuisine, and national and cultural attire. It was a wonderful and memorable event.

Come celebrate your roots
Come celebrate your culture
Come celebrate the freedom
To show who you are
What you are
Wherever you are!
Whether you come from Europe or Asia
Or you come from mother Africa
Cradle cloth carefully wrapped
Carrying baby on your back
It really doesn't matter
If you come from the West Indies
Singing Hot Hot Hot
Like the Mighty Arrow from Montserrat
Liberate your talents
Show the world what you've got
Diversity demands celebration
Right here in Hackney
London's cultural melting pot
Ladies dressed up like beauty Queens
Robed in national attire
Celebrating diversity
Parading in yellow green and white,
Long greens sash some banner.
No peasant plantation symbol this

Just the Montserrat National attire
Feeling happy and free
In this far away country
Partial representation of tradition and culture
Variety of customs and nationality
That is real diversity!

Lest I Forget

By Alison Wells-Inyang

Alison was happy to share this poem that she wrote in 1996 when she left Montserrat following volcanic eruptions. She confessed writing it during one of her moments of homesickness.

Remind me of my homeland

My people
My culture
My history
Remind me lest I forget
Take me to memory lane
To recall my life that once was
Tell me of my native land
My beloved island
Where mountains climb to the heavens
Tell me of the ocean that licks at the ebony sand
Glistening in the golden ray of sunshine
Let me reminisce of my frolicking days
Carefree as the seagulls that glide through the air
Remind me of the days when fruit trees weep in distress as I robbed
them of their prized jewels
Remind me of the days when the sound of sweet steel pan music,
Have hips swinging to its beat
Miss Goosey prancing down the streets
Let me not forget the days
When the jumbies walk the streets,
When the story tellers found delight,

As voices ring out in ancestral folk songs,
Remind me of your people,
That held you in high esteem,
Boasting of your emerald beauty,
Nestled in the ocean blue,
A people who were your pride,
Yes
Remind me of my homeland,
Montserrat,
Imprint in my heart
Memories of yester year
Lest I forget

The Journey

By Alison Wells-Inyang

Another poem written by Alison telling of her journey from the motherland and the emotions leaving the island evoked. She was originally from Webbs. She has since settled into and adjusted to life in metropolitan London where she has a rewarding job and family. She has not parted from but rather embraces her spirituality as a focal point of her wellbeing.

The journey

Reluctantly I left my warm cocoon,
My birthright
A place that nurtured and protected me
Together we were one
We rode life tides,
Enjoyed its carefree pleasures
Rebuking the rebelliousness
That lurks within its path
We laughed
We loved
We cried
We shared
We felt free and wonderfully alive
We built a lifetime of sheer joy filled memories
But it was time to set me free
To explore another world
Another culture
You bid me farewell

Silently you prayed
My new journey would be a blessing.
I cried bitter tears at our departure
Knowing the distance that lies ahead
Between us
Not knowing if time would be cruel to us
Wondering when we would rediscover each other
To reminisce about the bygone days
But go I must
Until my love
My native land
My home
I too wish you God speed

Gone but Not Forgotten

Caught off-guard by the passing of another Montserrat icon while writing this book, the following poem popped into my mind. I thought it a good indicator that I should share it.

Bassy

You have now passed,
Leaving behind
All suffering at long last.
For you flags fly at half mast.
Now you're gone, leaving behind
A land once subject
To a unique leadership style.
Full of quotations,
You let it be known 'Studiation beat education',
A common phrase to your people,
No need for definition.
To Montserratians home and abroad,
The meaning well-known,
The usefulness of wisdom
Not necessarily outweighs.
Can't replace formal education,
Just very useful to man's survival.
May your soul rest in peace.
Now take a much deserved rest,
Longest serving Chief Minister,
Deserving of your accolade.
Hopefully now in a place
Reserved for those who are blessed,
That place of eternal rest.
Your riches you neither flaunt nor hide.
Shipping magnate, you found wealth
Travelling the high seas,
Riding time and tide,
Vision announced.
To all Montserratians, let it be known:

Aim high, car, house, and job,
Every household on island one to own.
Raised high, let your ambitions be known
Your legacy lives on beyond present time,
Encouragement to all creating a smile
As satisfaction dictates
Good national intention.
There was always for you another election.

Leading the country with style and passion,
Even your health's treachery
Would not dictate the need to step down
From the politics which ultimately your world defined.
A man of your word in any forum, it was well-known
You could certainly always hold your own.
Now leaving behind a legacy of equality
To a people bent on true democracy,
A promise to be kept in its entirety.
State and country now mourn you in true unity;
Wherever we are, we honour you in sincerity.
Though your passing is just one step
Behind the soca king, saluted internationally,
Bassy, you are well-known for longevity,
Now saluted with flags of many a nation and country;
You too are known outside the Montserrat locality.

Diaspora

This piece was written merely as an expression of what it must feel like to have no identity within one's own country. To be referred to as the Diaspora is not readily accepted by a number of Montserratians and it ultimately leaves some with a deep sense of no longer belonging. The emotional aspect of this idea sums up the feeling. The meaning of the occassion changes to that of catching up.

Diaspora this, diaspora that!
Don't call me diaspora,
Lest you aim to become an enemy!
Memorial of the icons finally did it for me—
Acceptance at last, simple reality.
New diaspora, the new we!
Raise a toast to accept invisible identity
Labelled! Belonging to no town or country,
Now define deprivation of liberty.
Choice is limited; no one asked.
Do you accept anonymity?

Therefore I respectfully reject diaspora
As a new name for Montserrat in England.
Better to call me black, lest I forget
True determinant of ethnicity.
Still searching for true identity,
Walking the aisle, staring hungrily.
What I could see!

Old Victorian church building,
Dimmed, light bulbs missing.
Searching for familiar faces;
Others mirrored my plight.
Familiar folks I had not laid sight on for years
Eyes wide open, fixed! Pupils adjusting, wide like a farthing,
Observing, greeting, smiling.
Today no cameras will be clicking!

Question mark on faces, fixed frown, eyebrows meeting,
Trying to leaf through memory.
Yet long or short term, I figure it's the connectivity
Who's diagnosing, lets face reality.
The beauty of old, eccentric architecture,
No time for admiring painted glass windows.
Set a few yards from Riddley Market,
Location, ideal destination:
St Mark's at Dalston Hackney.

Short distance from where the guys
Used to sit and reminisce.
Glass of rum, or is it just any spirit?
Glazed look on faces, some even dared to admit
Craving to light a split.
Missing Montserrat, they would never, ever admit.

Today location carefully chosen,
Offering convenient parking bays
For those cost would otherwise have broken.
This current Montserrat solemn outing,
A stage to meet those missing
I apologise so hard for staring!
So accept my apology, I bid you: I'm sorry, so very sorry.
Only my peers for whom I'm scouting,
Most likely place to find them:
In current company, not necessarily reminiscing.

Narddy Food a Sowar (For Old Time's Sake)

(Memories of a very old Montserrat folk song, by Miss
Annie Wells-Sutton of Webbs)

Who can resist addressing the things that displaced Montserratians use to remind them of back home? The song will not have any significance for most, but for some older folks it certainly will. Hence I felt it was worth adding.

According to Miss Annie, who also migrated to the United Kingdom in 1997, the song below tells a story about a man who had a wife and family but had kept another lady away from home. She feels it's significant because it somehow reminds one of a legacy handed down from the ancestors, where folks would work in a different area from where their families were located. This would sometimes result in the start of another family and the ultimate neglect of the first. Montserratian calypsos are noted for containing lyrics that encompass the latest gossip, and this one was no different. The author of this piece is unknown.

It also draws our attention of how things have changed over the years, as the culture evolves from one level to the next. One can imagine how this very simple song provided entertainment to people in the '50s, while today it is of no significance, and only a few would even remember it or the circumstances under which it was written. There is certainly flexibility within the guidelines, which determine our negotiation of cultural behaviours.

Narddy food a sowar
Narddy food a sowar
Narddy food a sowar

Narddy wouldn come yet um
Narddy wouldn come yet um
Narddy wouldn come yet um

Mi goo dung di road
Mi hear mi niam a carl
Mi hear mi niam a carl
O yea! Mi hear mi niam a carl

Wa mi ago do
Wa mi ago do
Wa mi ago do

Mi a go dung di road
Mi hear mi niam a carl
Mi hear mi nian a carl
Mi hear mi niam a carl

Wa mi a go do
Wa mi ago do
Wa mi ago do mam
Mi hear mi niam a carl

Lardy

(Another Version of the same song)

I sat with my mom one day teasing her about her name. Fondly known by her pet name culturally, 'Nanan', she now wants to be known by the official name on her birth certificate, Roseanne. It was funny how her name caused her to have an argument with a health care assistant at a hospital where she was being treated as an inpatient. The care worker knew her from back in Montserrat and addressed her as Nanan. Mom got very angry, telling her that her proper name was Roseanne. Apologising, the lady patiently explained to her that all her life she had known her as Nanan and was being respectable when she called her Miss Nanan. Not for anything will my mom accept that, and for all intents and purposes the only name she answers to is Roseanne or Rose.

Nonplussed at her not wanting to use her posh identity, I ended up listening to her reminisce about the Montserrat she knew long ago. She went through a number of old folk songs, which pulled at my heart strings as I recognised how homesick she was. Now almost eighty years old, it is unlikely that she will ever return to the Montserrat she once knew and love. I cannot even begin to imagine how this must feel. She sits in a room on her own most days, and she also goes to a day centre for socialisation purposes, but her age and health related issues means that there is a limit to what she can do. She also gave another version of the song above, which has no relevance to modern-day songs, but for people like her and others it is of great value.

I can imagine her smile as she reads her contribution to this book despite the song's lack of singificance for most.

Lardi wouldn' kip fan sout
Dem say
Sout nearga rab e dung
Di pickney dem a barl

O yo, Lardi cum hooam
O yo, Lardi cum hooam

Lardi food a sowar

Di wife a barl
O yea
Lardi cum hooam

Di pickney dem hungry
Di wife a barl
Lardi cum hooam

CHAPTER 9

Folk Stories: Keeping Culture Alive

Jack O'Lantern (Won a consolation prize for the creative writing competition in Montserrat, 2010.)
Jack e lantoon a come, run! Lookee up a mountin, you see de light?

Background

The jack o'lantern is a big part of the legends and myths of Montserrat culture. Many people have said they've seen the jack o'lantern, or '*jack e lantoon*', as it sounds in dialect. It is also described by a number of people as a ball of fire that travels very quickly through the sky. For others the imagination determined their perception of this creature's shape and form. Whatever it looked like, it is well-known as a mythical creature that folks are afraid of, especially children as the story shows below. People living in various parts of the island and other West Indian islands claim to have seen this creature on several occasions. Still, there was a lot of pretence at home from the parents of the children in the story, who taught them not to believe in the mythical creature.

A well-known Montserrat custom is that almost every child has a house name that is different from their birth certificate. The names of the three children in this story, Barba-Put, Boye-Boye, and Di-Di are pet-names also referred to as nick names. The names originally belonged to ancestors who were supposed to protect them. Barba-Put was always a very sick child and was not thriving very well. Her dad's late wife was thought to be responsible for this, because she was angry that the child hadn't been named for her. She brought the news in a dream that the child needed to be called Barba-Put. From that day onwards, the name Barba-Put stuck, until later on in life it was changed back to the lady's official name. This is all part of the cultural norm which in times past would be achieved with the help of a 'jumbie dance ceremony.' It was not ascertained if this naming method worked or if it was just coincidence that the illnesses got better. The name was not placed on the birth certificate.

Di-Di was not named for an ancestor; the name came from a very nice lady who owned the house in which she was born. It was felt that Di-Di had some of the characteristics of this lady, although she was not related. Boye-Boye was also named for an ancestor, and he was always a healthy, robust boy from birth; he appeared to have gotten the correct name. Boye-Boye is no longer known by this name, and only a few actually remember he was called this in the past.

In a strange way, since the Montserratians' arrival in England, a large number of young people and a few older ones refused to answer to their 'pet' or 'house names'. One reason could be that those names were no longer considered posh enough or appropriate for modern England. The other explanation could be that these names could confuse the British, who often need an explanation of the double naming system used back in Montserrat. Further, it is imperative that for official reasons people are fairly consistent with names and identity. A large number of those born in England have not been given the traditional house name and use their name on the birth certificate only.

The story is narrated in a light, entertaining manner and is based on a true story about the lives of the only family living in Broderick's at the base of Chances Peak Mountain in the 1970s. The two-floor estate house was surrounded by many acres of farmland and housed a paddock filled with cows, bulls, and calves. Other animals on the farm included sheep and goat imported from England by the government, and rabbits. Further afield were fruits unlimited: mangoes, guavas, manciport, sugar apples, soursop, and bananas, to name a few. A bit further up the mountain were the fresh-water springs of Spring Ghaut, and then there was Broderick's Mountain, where the famous mountain chicken lived prior to the volcanic eruptions. Ironically some of the island's mountain chicken was also tabbed for mass migration to save them from extinction after their natural habitat was destroyed. The first set travelled to the United Kingdom in 1999 and have just been returned 2010 for trial repatriation to Montserrat.

The Story

Well, I've never see anything like this. When you're young, you can be really foolish and ludicrous. Imagine this—I just looked up the word 'jack o'lantern' and found out the web definition for it. According to Wikipedia, it is a fungus, a large poisonous agaric with orange caps and narrow, clustered stalks; the gills are luminescent. Well, I never laughed so much. All this time I had it in my head that the jack o'lantern is an animal with similar characteristics, shape, and form of a reindeer, with two big, bold eyes that spewed fire. This animal in my imagination flies in the sky at nights. I grew up at Broderick's Mountain under Chances Peak, which had its fair share of fantasies and myths. My younger siblings, Boye-Boye, seven; Barba-Put, six and I Di-Di, ten; had some experiences that, if they had to be recalled, would make people wonder in amazement if they were for real. One night Boye-Boye, Barba-Put, and I sat at our favourite window seeing who could count the most fireflies. There were so many of them that we ended up in the hundreds.

All of a sudden Barba-Put said, 'Oh my goodness! Shh, stop that noise! Look! What's that?' By this time she was pointing a shaking finger in the direction of Mermaid Hole, just at the base of Chances Peak.

My body ran cold as I slowly turned my head and saw two huge, bulging eyes of fire gracefully rise up in the sky and then glide towards us in what appeared to be a taunting manner; as if to say, 'I am going to get one of you tonight.'

Mind you, to this day there has only been one house on the Broderick's Estate, and that was the one we lived in. That meant if some creature like the jack o'lantern came to human beings, it had to be either me, Barba-Put, or Boye-Boye. As these thoughts crossed my mind, time appeared to stand still. In the meantime the distance between the creature and us was decreasing as the creature kept moving towards us in slow motion.

The three of us by this time had started doing everything in unison. This was a routine; whenever we were scared or in trouble, we didn't have to speak but acted as if on automatic. Even if we wanted to, neither of us could have uttered a sound at that time. On that hot summer night, we stood still as if we were as frozen as the icicles in the Antarctic. Three heads, eyes wide like saucers, watched in awe, mesmerised as the jack o'lantern drew even closer, a huge monster gliding on its featherlike wings. All of a sudden it stopped about a metre away from the house, hovering in midair as if ready to pounce on us. Triple jeopardy—we made a mad dash for the bedrooms. We pushed and shoved each other, trying to squeeze through the narrow doorway at the same time. We knew the last one through could be caught by the creature, and no one wanted to be taken away.

As the pulling, pushing, and jostling in the doorway continued, I could hear my mother in the kitchen, where she was making johnny cake and salt fish for supper. She shouted, 'You all stop the nonsense right now! Don't make me come out there, otherwise you all will be sorry.' On Friday nights we often kept vigil, sneaking into the kitchen every few minutes to pinch a piece of hot johnny cake while Mom would say, 'Get out of the kitchen before you get burn, you hear me?' At the same time the wonderful aroma of freshly grated local Creole cocoa boiling in milk from our own cows, with a cinnamon stick and nutmeg; would be brewing and tempting us to defy Mom's warning to keep out the kitchen. I didn't like milking cows, so I always kept my distance, just in case cow knocked me down with its curved horns. The others liked to milk the cows and drink the milk fresh from their result. They sometimes add limes to make the milk curdle. I couldn't drink the milk unless it was boiled properly.

After tonight we weren't sure we would ever drink milk again, or even see a cow. The hustle now was about getting away from jack o'lantern together. The strange thing was that the creature never appeared to bother adults; it didn't matter how late at night they had to go out, assisting an animal giving birth or checking to see if we remembered to lock the gate. But just let Boye-Boye, Barba-Put, or me look outside, and the thing would be on the lookout way up in the hills, ready to pounce and gobble us up. We couldn't tell Mom or Dad when it started flying towards us on feathered wings, because they would just suck their teeth or stupes and say, 'Stop talking nonsense and go pray.' Pray? Well, tonight even if we wanted to pray, I for one couldn't even remember my name; never mind how to begin to pray.

All of a sudden we burst free of the door and fell flat on the floor, out of breath. The window was well behind us by now, but that didn't make a difference because we were not looking in that direction. If you looked in the creature's eye it would remember you and come back for you. We crawled under the bed in our parents' bedroom. Suddenly a bright light shone up through the floor board, right into our downturned faces. Momentarily the thought flashed through my mind that all of the poor shub shub, which lived in the soft, dry dirt under the floor, must be burnt up by now. I couldn't imagine the thought of that and my chest tightened 'til I almost couldn't breathe.

Just then we heard a long scream. What was that sound? A siren? But there were no sirens in Broderick's Mountain. Just the jack o'lantern, and the mermaid up at Mermaid Hole, at the base of Chances Peak. She sometimes left her cave to go up to the big, beautiful pond on Chances Peak. We often passed it on our way to the top, and it was beautiful with crystal clear waters that reflected the blue skies and showed one's image like a mirror. I would sometimes dip my feet in the cold water, look at my reflection, and imagine that I was a mermaid as well—a beautiful half fish, half human, young maiden with a fish tail instead of feet. But how did it walk out of its home at Mermaid Hole and climb up that peak, 1, 200 feet up the mountain for its swim? That was so surreal. Was it? So this menacing, jack o'lantern with its eyes of fire was under the floor boards, and we were under the bed, trying not to look down into the eyes of the creature. We were quivering like wet cats. Oh dear, what were we going to do? The screaming wouldn't stop, either. Who could be screeching like that, like some hyena out in the African jungle?

Suddenly something grabbed my leg and pulled me from under the bed. The screaming got louder. Then slap, slap; left cheek, right cheek. Abruptly the screaming stopped, and I came back to reality with a rude bump. My mother was standing in front of me, one hand on her hip and a pot spoon in the other. She bent over and peeked under the bed, saying, 'Come out here, come out from under there right now, you two.' Boye-Boye and Barba-Put slowly crawled out from under the bed and lifted up their faces, as if waiting for their slap too. The slaps didn't come because they had not been screaming, and I realised that the hideous sound had been coming from my own throat.

'Come with me,' said Mom sternly with a frown on her brows, and she marched us swiftly towards the door. Noticing our hesitation, she grabbed one of our hands each, two in one hand and one in the other. She marched us towards the door with a look of determination on her face, grumbling under her breath, 'This jack o'lantern nonsense must stop. I say it must stop right now.' We could always tell when she was annoyed, because she repeated everything.

I was sure she was hustling so she could get back to the johnny cake, salt fish, and cocoa tea. At the bottom of the steps, like a demented woman who wanted us to be eaten by that creature, she headed under the floor towards the bright ball of fire. As we got closer, we started whimpering like dogs in agony, and that made her more determined. All this time none of us had uttered a sound because the creature wasn't getting the opportunity to hear our voices. If it did hear us, we knew it would memorise the sound and return for the owner at some point. As we headed under the floor, the bright light started towards us, and at the same time Boye-Boye, Barba-Put, and I started to scream. And oh, did we have some strong vocal cords; they would be the envy of fire trucks. The screaming continued as we got close, but then we suddenly stopped in our tracks, our mouths wide open in shock. We looked at Mom beseechingly, as if to say, '*Pleeeeease, pleeeeease*, Mom, don't let it have us. We promise to be good, we promise never to be bad again!'

All the same, Mom continued to prod us forward, when all of a sudden the bright light of fire flashed in our faces, and there was Dad in front of us with a torch in hand, saying, 'I hope you've learnt your lesson. I am the jack o'lantern.'

He was joking, right? He couldn't fly. No way—there must have been a jack o'lantern out there somewhere.

I was sure Dad had frightened it away. We couldn't understand what game he was playing. To this day, when we counted fireflies, we were always careful not to look up at the mountain. Not at night, anyway.

One night when Aunty came to visit us, we heard the adults talking softly in the living room. Nosey kids that we were, we crept quietly behind the door and listened. Mom was in a heated exchange with Dad. Eyes wide, we turned in unison to look at each other and then eased closer to the door.

All of a sudden clumsy little Barba-Put fell through the unlocked door with a shrill scream. Boye-boye and I rushed in to help her up so that all of us would get into trouble together. We shared everything, didn't we?

Dad was livid. He raised his voice, lifted up his big shoulders, and bellowed at us. 'Ah wah ah you ah do in yah, eavesdrappus hear no good u demself. Ah you gout to in yah and no cum back antil mi say so. Angrily he kept going on and on telling us off.[3] Dat ah Disubediunce ah you hear

---

[3] What are you doing in here, those who eavesdrop hear no good of themselves. Get out and don't come back until I ask you to.

mi? Ah you look pan mi wuk yah. Pickney no hear wah marmie say drink peppa warta, lime an' sarl.[4]

Looking at Mom, he pointed a finger at her, saying, 'Dem pikney deh outu cantrual. If you no trian dem, you ago ban you belly an barl wumun, mark mi wurds.' Not waiting to hear anymore we sped out of the room like the Jack o'lantern was behind us. We knew that wasn't the last we would hear of our disobedience.

No jack e lantoon ago kech awi, nat now, nat eva an if e tek wan u a-wi e ah go hafu tek arl tree u a-we—togeda and dat no passible.

Carib Dream Wedding

(Written in fond memory of my grandmother, Miss 'Mon' of Molyneaux)

By the time she had gotten to bed late that night, Miss Mon had gone out like a light from extreme tiredness. That day had been an extremely busy one for her, as she had supervised two young men to climb the very tall and precarious coconut trees on the large plantation. It was about midnight, and Miss Mon was deep in the world of sleep but having a very restless night. Tossing and turning, she mumbled incomprehensively on and off in her sleep. She appeared to be communicating with someone or something, and she seemed perplexed at whatever was being communicated. At one point she folded her arms and shook her head vehemently and then suddenly threw her hands up in the air as if in resignation. She then settled quietly, her ears tipped up and chest heaving as if listening pensively to some kind of message. Time passed and all was quiet as Miss Mon's breathing eventually settled.

The calm didn't last long. Mumbling again in her sleep, she had a frown on her otherwise smooth brows as she asked some kind of a question. It sounded as if she was trying to say the word 'Carib' in a questioning

---

[4] That is disobedience, do you understand? Look at this calamity.Children who don't listen will come to no good.

manner. The restlessness and mumbling continued for some time until eventually beads of sweat could be seen on her brows.

The next day was market day in Plymouth, and her bountiful fruits and vegetables were in great demand. Her produce was always huge, healthy, and enjoyable by those who purchased them. She had some land up in Killicranky, where the soil was very fertile, yielding produce such as dasheen, eddoes, yam, sweet potatoes, and toolooma.[5]

There was a spring of clear, sweet-flowing, icy cold water which remained refreshing no matter how hot the day was. Just like the waters in Runaway Ghaut, having tasted it once, one just had to come back for more. This water was pure and uncontaminated because it bubbled up gently from deep within the inaccessible recesses of the hills. It was a certain source of hydration not only for humans but for the vegetables and provisions planted at its mineral-drenched wetness. Miss Mon had watched the young men picking the coconuts, cautioning that they had to be extremely careful. She had to ensure that they didn't fall, causing injury to themselves during the climb. Both young men were only about sixteen years old and had no consideration for safety issues. They were more about showing off their muscles and their climbing skills, bantering with each other as they laboriously took the final few feet to the top of the heavily laden coconut tree. Oblivious to Miss Mon's voice of caution, the young men took the last triumphant heave unto the cluttered heart of the tree.

Once again she shouted up to them, 'Pick the young ones first, and don't drop them on those cannons.' There were two small cannons situated close to the coconut trees, pointing out to sea. They rested on paved slabs not far from the trees the lads were climbing. The cannons had inscriptions which identified them as remnants of the wars between the English and French, which took place in the seventeenth and eighteenth centuries as they vied for the lush, picturesque island. The island initially owned by the English had been taken over by the French occupation for a short time, only to be reoccupied by the English. That was the last time the island had changed hands, as it continued to be British to this day. Still, the iron cannons remain scattered strategically on the island as a reminder of the colourful history and brief touch with war. With one

---

5   The arrowroot plant.

hand on her hip and the other shielding her eyes from the sun, Miss Mon watched the young men like a hawk. She was aware of her responsibility to the neighbours' sons and was not afraid to be firm with them. One mistake could result in a slip and that would be the end for either of them. She would do her best to ensure they acted sensibly and cautiously. Aware that young people often recognised danger only after they had been affected, Miss Mon kept her eyes trained on them throughout the entire process shouting encouragement now and then as a reminder they were being watched.

With great creativity the taller of the two neatly twisted a young coconut from where it was attached, placing it into the crocus bag he had tied around his waist. He had a very artistic way of picking the coconuts which made the job look very simply and fun. Stopping for a brief break, he shouted down to Miss Mon questioningly, 'Do you mind if I have one now?'

'Of course not,' replied Miss Mon, 'but be very careful now.'

With that the young lad pulled a sharp machete from his strong leather belt. With a quick flick of his wrist, he had cut off the green bottom bits of the young coconut, exposing the white meat. With his fingers he pulled off the thin flesh of the coconut and slipped it into his mouth, enjoying the rewards of his labour. He then raised the coconut to his lips and drank the juice noisily. Clear juices were running down his chin onto his tummy, but he wasn't bothered by that. The coconut water was sweet and filling. He lifted the machete and held the coconut in his palm away from his body, splitting it open and exposing the white flesh in its entirety. He finished the nutritious coconut meat with obvious relish, released a burp, and went to work again.

After picking the coconuts, they had cut off the bottom bits in preparation for taking them to the market and then tied them up in crocus bags. Miss Mon and the young men went off to Killikranky to harvest the provisions. The produce from this area was very big but easy to pluck from the ground, because the soil was soft and wet from the running springs. That day they had cut a number of bananas, plantains, and hi-t (hi-ti is similar to the banana and plantain but thicker around the middle with a thicker skin) as well. Loading up the donkey was very tricky because they had no saddle for it, but they managed somehow. At the end of all their hard work, they had caught two mountain chickens and cooked them up with yellow yam and dasheen sprout. They cooked on a wood fire created from dry twigs, and the finished product had a special enjoyability to it.

It didn't matter that the sauce was grey in colour; it was the taste that mattered. Sated, they washed and cut the roots off the provisions before setting off for home with their bags full of ground food for the market.

Marse Jo[6] had been out to sea that day, and when he returned with his catch of fish—including doctor fish, grouper, old wife, and snapper—he found the restless Miss Mon tossing and mumbling in her sleep. In the daytime Marse Jo managed the sugar plantation of a hundred workers. He was a good foreman who allowed the workers to take molasses home for their families. Grinding sugar cane was not an easy job; the huge iron machines took a lot of effort to work. The workers were loyal, though, and worked honestly for their money. Their bonus reward was the molasses, which meant they didn't have to buy sugar for their families. Marse Jo's family had also benefited from the molasses for many years, which could be the ultimate reason why the entire family had been suffering from diabetes for generations.

Grabbing hold of her shoulders with his big, strong hands, Marse Jo shook Miss Mon awake. Startled, she opened her eyes wide, staring ahead as if she was looking right through him. She remained that way for several minutes. Marse Jo sat looking at her in wonder, waiting for her to say something. Getting impatient, he touched her and said, 'Mon, are you saying something?' Staring ahead, Miss Mon shook her head and closed her eyes. Not knowing what to make of the whole thing Marse Joe slipped into bed beside her. In no time his snore filled the house. In the meantime Miss Mon lay beside him trying to make sense of the dream she just had. It had been so real that she didn't know how to discuss it with anyone, especially Marse Jo.

The next morning the household awoke, and Marse Jo noticed that Miss Mon was acting a bit unusual. She stood in front of the mirror for a long time, looking at her reflection as if she was actually seeing someone else. Marse Jo, who usually took forever to get dressed, was ready an hour before her and kept saying, 'Hurry up, woman. What is keeping you?' At her non-response, he tried his irresistible humour on her. 'You know, my dear Carib woman, chieftess, queenest, there is none like you. You have the natural beauty of a Carib African Irish queen. Look at those majestic

---

6   Master Jo

cheekbones and the hair down your back, as silky as a spider's web. There is no such beauty to behold anywhere in the world.'

He waited for her usual playful response, but it didn't appear, and Marse Jo was getting really concerned for her. He couldn't understand what was going on. He had left her in her usual good mood and gone fishing that day. Now he had returned to find that she had suddenly changed into a humourless human being whom he was now trying hard to understand.

Being a very patient man, Marse Jo continued with his one-sided humorous banter. 'My statuesque one with the body of a goddess and love to rival Venus, come tell your man the secret of your silence.'

Still not a word came from her lips. Miss Mon was not buying into his efforts, and his frustration was starting to show in his movements as he walked about sorting his stuff.

On their way to the market that day, Miss Mon was very quiet as she looked at the beautiful flora and fauna around them. At the market in Plymouth, her customers greeted her as usual and even commented on her quietness. She just smiled at them and said, 'Ah boy, only who feels it knows it.' Having sold all the produce quicker than usual that day, she left Marse Jo selling the fish and headed off to do her shopping. As she checked her shopping list, she picked up extra things she wanted to use. She wondered how she was going to explain them to Marse Jo. They had fourteen children to feed and couldn't afford to waste a penny. Thankfully they grew their own produce, and Marse Jo fished weekly so there was no hardship. Things were very good in their household, and the children were well cared for.

On their way home that evening, she managed a bit of small talk with Marse Jo, but he was still concerned. Nothing about her made sense at the moment. At home she busied herself in the kitchen making his favourite dumplings (or cartwheels as he jokingly called them) with stewed mutton. Marse Jo noticed she was using extra elbow grease to knead the dumplings but said nothing. He hoped his shaky tooth wouldn't fall out while he was eating. During the evening all appeared to be going well on the surface—until the children finished the washing up and went off to bed.

Lighting a candle, he sat on the easy chair and asked Miss Mon to bring the pants she was darning and sit beside him. Obligingly she came over, and they sat in silent camaraderie while he smoked his pipe. Marse Jo had a sweet tooth, and he went to get some vanilla fudge that Miss

Mon had made last week. Her fudge was amazingly light and fluffy, with a delicate flavour that made one want more. As he bit into the fudge, Marse Jo gave a loud shout as his loose tooth came away in his hand. Concerned and feeling guilty that it might have been loosened further by the cartwheels she had given him, Miss Mon jumped up to help. Holding his head in his hands, he remained quiet as he tried to manage the pain coming from his gums. In anguish he moaned at Miss Mon, 'Why don't you speak to me Mon? Why?'

Trying to get him over the pain, Miss Mon suddenly opened up and told Marse Jo the entire story of her dream with the Caribs. It turned out that she had visited a cave where she had encountered some Caribs sitting around a fire, dressed for a wedding ceremony. Unluckily for her, the Carib chief, who was nowhere in sight when she turned up, was about to get married to a girl who had suddenly fallen into the river on her way to the wedding. The canoe she was travelling in had capsized, and she couldn't swim but disappeared towards the rapids of the Great Alps waterfall in St Patrick's.

When Miss Mon, who looked a lot like the Carib bride to be, had turned up, the Caribs mistook her for the girl and proceeded with the wedding. Despite her protest she was prepared for the ceremony by young ladies who spoke over her in disgust, using a language she couldn't understand. They appeared to be annoyed at the Western clothes she was wearing. Finally they dressed her hair in flowers and put on a headdress of feathers. Miss Mon was fully dressed and was slapped on her arm to stop the noises she was making. She awaited her marriage to the chief.

The ceremony began with the clan making whooping noises of joy, much of which she couldn't understand. Then men beating goat-skin drums came out of nowhere and played music, to which ladies and men dressed in grass skirts danced ceremoniously. Others prepared an open fire and roasted a number of animals. The animals were fully intact—the skin and intestines were not removed prior to roasting.

No one spoke to her until a young man approached her; he was dressed up in what appeared to be the clothing of a chief. He came within an inch of her and looked deep into her eyes for a split second—and then let out a loud, wailing sound. It sounded to her like the howling of an injured lion. He then grabbed an arrow from one of his clansmen, stepped back, and aimed it directly at her. In fright Miss Mon started chattering, 'I told them . . . 'As if having second thoughts, the young man threw the bow and arrow to the ground, turning to an old Carib man with angry, questioning eyes. The old man, who was also a chief, spoke to the young man in Carib language, and the younger chief appeared to relax a bit.

The chief, satisfied at what was said, turned to Miss Mon once again, indicating that he wanted to speak to her. At first the chief started speaking in a low growl, and he kept repeating the same word over and over. It sounded as if he was saying bring something back and for whatever reason his fierceness became more pronounced as he advanced towards Miss Mon in a dance-like trance. As he got closer and closer, Miss Mon started to tremble in fear. Her heart hammered against her chest like it was trying to escape, and she knew she would rather do anything else than marry this creature. When he was about two feet away from her, the Carib chief stopped his growling and his advance. With a sigh of relief, Miss Mon turned to make her way out of there as quickly as she could. She hadn't turned as much as half a centimetre when a loud, rolling drumbeat suddenly sounded from her left. A large group of about twenty Carib ladies wearing grass skirts swooped out in a tribal dance. Immediately behind them were about twenty young men with triangular-shaped grass tied around their waist, just enough to cover their private parts.

As if turned to stone, Miss Mon watched them advance towards her with bows and arrows slung over their shoulders. They were followed closely by a flamboyantly dressed man in what appeared to be colourful peacock feathers. She believed him to be the top chief. He looked at her with piercing dark eyes as the huge goat he was riding came to a halt a few feet away from her. Miss Mon fleetingly wondered why he hadn't chosen a donkey instead. The rest of the group formed a semicircle around him and bowed. Miss Mon straightened up her shoulders without blinking, waiting expectantly for him to speak. He said nothing to her, so she supposed she was too low a mortal for him to communicate with. At the ripple of drums, the entire tribe, except the chief who had initially approached her and the head chief, started chanting and dancing.

After a prolonged period, they fell flat on their faces; then raised their faces up to the sun, which was blindingly hot. Each time the faces rose up to the sun, a loud sound came from somewhere among them. Several things were being said between drumbeat and the worshipping. It was a message that was being formulated for Miss Mon to take back to her people.

With relief Miss Mon poured the entire story of her strange dream to Marse Jo.[7] 'Oohh, Mase Jo,' she wailed in native Montserrat English, 'you no no wah dem tell me. Dem say de only way ah we ah go have peace a when we hooall wan jumbie dance, lissen to dem messige, an' do wah dem say. Now hear wah dem say.

'"Ah you tek warnin' foo ah you no see nutten yet." Marse Jo, woss deh fuh cum dem say, an di only way dem ah go stap, ah if ah we tek dem back. Dem say dat dem will settle fuh wan jumbie dance hearin', an dem warnt to see six young leardie and six young men in ah dem nashoonul dress, and six each nah grarse skuort, ah whine dem wearse to di beat oo di drum. Nat only dat, you see arl di funny tings ah goo arn dung yah, dem say dat mek dem sad and vex. Dem say dat di country ah go mash up and arl dat gat to stap right ooway. Tek heed eh! Marse Jo, dem no min tark nah no calbish cup. Dem shout um fan di kearve and ee echo roun an' cum back uhgen an uh gen.'

Marse Jo was amazed at this story and could now understand why so many emotions had shown on her face during her restless sleep. He hugged her tightly to calm her, saying, 'It's just a dream, Mon, a very bad dream—but it has some sense in it. Remember how they disturb the Carib archeological site up at Trants and took everything out of their village to the museum? That was not a smart move. People were not happy and told the archaeologist to put them back, but no one listened. These Caribs as we know them were Amerindians, and they lived here before us; in fact they could have been the first people to live on this island. They have one little spot called their village, and now they've been uprooted and placed in another dwelling place. Of course the ancestors are angry; it is no wonder you dreamt them. Quietly he looked into Miss Mon's eyes and said, 'Is that why you bought those things to set jumbie table, when Christmas is seven months away? I was wondering when I saw them, but now I understand. But it was just a dream you had Mon, just a dream, so

---

[7] Miss Mon's message in dialect is an instruction to take the Carib remains back to the village they were taken from: Trants. There is a warning that things will go wrong if this is not done, because the spirits are unhappy. The village of Trants, along with the island's airport, was destroyed by the volcanic eruption and is currently located in the unsafe zone.

you can relax now. Nothing else will happen—it's over now and remember you did nothing wrong so no one will harm you; it is over.'

Paragraph of Dialect to English version

Oh, Marse Jo, you don't know what they told me. Oh Marse Jo, they said that the only way we will have peace would be to hold a jumbie dance and follow the instructions. This is what they had to say: 'Heed this warning, for you have not seen anything yet. Marse Jo, it sounds like the worst is yet to come. And the only way to stop it happening is to take them back to their original place of rest. They said that they are happy to settle for a jumbie dance held by us. We need to listen to them, and this is the exact specification of what they want at the dance: six young ladies wearing the Montserrat national dress and six men wearing grass skirts. These young ladies and men should be whining (a fast swirling movement of the waist) their waist to the drum beats. Furthermore they want all the bad things happening here to stop, as it makes then angry. They say that the country is no longer any good, and things must change for the better. We must heed the warning. Marse Jo, they didn't say it in secret; they shouted it so loud that it echoed over and over again.

Island of Confidence

The story below narrates how a young Montserratian was able to fit in with relatives in the United States while using the opportunity to build her confidence during her holidays. It is common for not only Montserrat men but West Indians in general to have children with a number of women.

The story highlights Devora's experience growing up in Montserrat with a stepdad and the way she gained her confidence in New York City when she spent time with her dad and his children, her siblings. Despite not growing up with them, she was able to fit right in during her holidays and really looked forward to the time she spent with them in this metropolitan country of the United States. This ultimately helped to expand her social networks and exposed her to various subcultures, which she embraced without losing herself.

During Devora's childhood in the '70s, Montserrat boasted one cinema in the capital city, Plymouth, where most people looked forward to watching karate and kung fu on Friday nights. Some homes had televisions, but most children and young adults enjoyed a number of outdoor activities. It was the norm to see young people in the villages playing marbles, dodgeball, cricket, zig zag zagget with cherry seed (cashew seeds), and last person nah hooarl out (last person in the hole is out), to name a few.

There were the ring games, such as, 'Brown girl in the ring, the farmer in the dell, in and out the windows, show me your motions, tra la la la la and di goolie man house on fire, di goolie man run away, dem sen motor bike, dem sen bicycle to out di fire dung deh.'.

There were hand games such as 'Miss Mary': 'Miss Mary mack, mack, mack all dressed in black, black, black and when Susie was a baby, a baby, a baby; when Suzie was a baby, this is how she went ooh ah, ooh ooh ah.'

This was a good way of life, and the majority of people on the island were fit and strong from all the fresh air and sunshine the activities offered. People spent more time thinking and being creative; television and video games were not yet major distractions. From time to time fun fairs came to Montserrat and offered a different type of entertainment from the mundane. Despite being quite small with no international airport, Montserrat enjoyed various aspects of entertainment just like those living in the cities.

Excitement buzzed in the air again, and Devora noticed the flyers that had gone up overnight on lamp posts, on buildings, and everywhere. The holidays were coming, and all the kids had one thing in mind: Coney Island was coming to Montserrat. Next door John and Dana were going to the fair, and Miss Mimba had promised Junior last year that should Coney Island return to Montserrat, he would be allowed to attend.

Devora's mind flashed back to last year's Coney Island. Her daily vigil then had been to peek through the fence and watch the rides go up and down and round and round. Her fantasy was about riding one of the horses—the beautiful, sleek, black and white one with the kind and majestic look on its face. 'Buck, buck, buck, buck, and hold on tight lest you fall off,' she had thought last year as she watched her siblings ride. But surely that would be fun too, wouldn't it? Anyway, one couldn't fall off just like that, she thought, for she could see a belt or some kind of strap placed around the waist of the riders as a safety precaution. She yearned to ride a horse but was too scared to ride the ones in the paddock. Her brother Guy was so brave; she liked to watch him run from a distance and jump on the moving horse. The horse would then buck and buck, trying to shake him off while he hung on for dear life, slipping from side to side on the saddleless horse. That just made Guy more excited, and she could hear him shouting loudly, 'Hee-haw, hee-haw, hee-haw!' just like those cowboys in the Western movies. Their dad, who usually sat on a stone in the yard plaiting some rope, would look up calmly from what he was doing. As if just noticing what was going on for the first time, he would say, 'Stop your noise and ride the horse, boy. Go on, go on, giddy up, giddy up.' As the horse took off with front feet high in the air, Dad would smile widely. His smile was very brown from tobacco smoke, and a pipe would be hanging from the corner of his mouth.

The man she called Daddy was not really Devora's dad, but he was married to her mom. It didn't matter because they got on well. Her real dad was living in America now; he had moved there a few years ago with her half-sisters. He had left Montserrat for England before she was born, but she had met him and liked him. Her face lighted up as she thought of her upcoming trip. She was looking forward to the summer, when she would spend time with her half-sisters. Out of the corner of her eye, she saw her mom in her usual position, trying to make a point about Guy's riding skills. As was her custom, she looked up from her washing, hands akimbo on her hips, and declared, 'I tell you, Pete, that horse is dangerous, and the boy is just too impulsive. Mark my words, one of these days he will hurt himself. One day I will live to say I told you so.' Of course that never happened, for Guy was as good a rider as any of the men who worked in the paddock, or even better. He was totally fearless. Devora guessed boys were just made like that, never appearing to be afraid of anything; especially not horses.

On good days when his arthritis wasn't bothering him, Daddy would saddle up the horse, mount it, and then carefully bend over and pick up a squealing Geni. Sitting her in front of him on the horse for safety, he would say, 'Ride away, my girl.'

Once seated her excited little voice would start chanting, 'Moo-up, moo-up, come on, let' go, Daddy! Moo-up, moo-up!' Geni had these unique ways of expressing herself in toddler language that made people laugh. She was learning to talk and still trying to say things the proper way. They called it baby talk, so Devora guessed other babies might be able to understand what she was saying.

Devora often stood there dreamy eyed, watching the others riding the horses with no expression on her face to show what she was thinking. Secretly she wished she could get onto the horse and ride away into the wind. Dreaming of her dad, or her prince charming coming to get her on a white horse, was often the basis for her far-fetched fantasy. She would often look up to the skies when planes were passing over, hoping her dad was aboard and the plane would drop him off in Montserrat. Today she knew no one was going to offer to take her for a ride on the horse, and even if they did, she would decline. When she was younger, she would try to hide under Mom's skirt when the horses got close, like she always did when she was scared. Now she wanted to ride a horse with her prince charming someday, because she would trust him to keep her safe. She would wait, and when the time was right, she just knew he would come along.

Later that evening Mom and Dad announced during dinner that they were taking Guy and Geni to Coney Island. There was no mention of Devora. They wouldn't take her, because she was too afraid of going on the merry-go-round, and even the slides and see-saws. Ah, but what about the fun horses? She could ride the horses if someone came on with her. If only she were braver and not always such a coward when it came to riding. Even the toddler Geni enjoyed those things and showed no fear. She knew it was her fault that they weren't taking her, and she wasn't going to cry or beg or anything.

Coney Island came and went, and all her friends spoke of nothing else but the rides, marshmallow, and sweet popcorn for weeks. At home it was the same story over and over. Geni would chant, 'Round and round and round we go, round and round and round we go,' jumping up and down with excitement. Devora decided that she wasn't going to worry about it because she was leaving tomorrow to spend the end of the summer holidays in New York City with her four half-siblings. She knew that she would have loads of fun. She would make sure she enjoyed herself, and her real dad was there as well. She smiled to herself, her excitement well contained.

The anticipated trip came at last, and Devora excitedly took off in a thirty-eight-seat plane from Brambles Airport. As the plane glided smoothly over the sea, she marvelled at the blueness of the skies and sea. It was really beautiful from up here, and the weather was absolutely wonderful for flying, though a bit windy. There were always crosswinds between Montserrat and Antigua, but the journeys was very short and smooth, and no sooner were they in the sky than the plane started descending again. In fifteen minutes the plane was preparing to land at the VC Bird International Airport in Antigua, and she was heading towards the counter to check in. Aunty Ismay, who lived in Antigua, was meeting her at the counter to ensure everything went smoothly. She wished she didn't have to stop on her way to NYC, but Montserrat had only a small runway and no international airport. Antigua was the international gateway to a number of Caribbean islands.

The family would contact Aunty Ismay when passing through Antigua. She was the only relative living close to VC Bird International Airport, and Devora was always happy to see her smiling face. It was comforting to know she was close by, because there were no late flights into Montserrat, and one often had to overnight if delayed flights came in after 6.00 p.m. All checks completed Devora, waved good-bye to her aunt and boarded her flight to NYC, but this time it was a 747 jumbo jet on which she took her seat. She would be in NYC in about four hours and couldn't wait to see her siblings.

Most of all she was looking forward to the pizza, Chinese chicken, and ice cream she was going to eat. Everything tasted so good in America, and the portions were huge. She didn't have to worry about putting on weight because she would walk that off in no time. She was also an athlete who played netball and took part in the Amateur Athletics Associations inter-island meets, which were held in different Leeward Islands. She was a middle distance runner and had won a gold medal in Nevis for the 400 metre race. Her favourite was really the 1500, but she had only ever gotten silver medals for that race. The 200 metre race was another medal winner for her, but only bronze. She was not much of a sprinter at all. She fastened her seatbelt at the prompt from the air hostess, opened her novel, and settled down to read until the in-flight entertainment came on. She had also brought an outdated *Right-On*[8] magazine about Michael Jackson so that she could have a variety of things to keep her occupied. TV programmes didn't really interest her that much, although she liked to watch romance and comedies from time to time. Since they had turned thirteen, she and her mates had been borrowing *Right On* just to read about the Jackson Five. Some of her friends also had moms, dads, siblings, and other relatives in America who sent these magazines regularly. They were so lucky to have these overseas relatives who sent stuff and sometimes a bit of money, which made life a bit easier. Despite this, they would have preferred to grow up with their biological parents, as life wasn't the same with them living far away. Devora went through the usual in-flight process of eating her meals and hoarding her snacks for one of her sisters in the USA. She then fell asleep and slept for the rest of the flight. She hadn't been interested in the movie; it was *Grease*, and she had seen it many times before. Just before touch down at JFK International, she woke up and rushed to the washroom to wash her face. She danced around in the very narrow room singing softly, 'New York, here I come, yeah.'

She was very happy and couldn't wait to meet the family. The drive to the house was long, and there were loads of traffic like nothing she had ever seen in Montserrat. There were thousands of big cars along the way, and some drivers appeared very impatient. Everything was different here from her little Montserrat. She marvelled at the street lights and tried to understand how they were coordinated. They eventually arrived at the three-story house, which was situated at the back of the huge Hudson River, from where she could see the outline of New Jersey on the other side. One of these days she hope to go there just to see what it was like. Devora was so excited to be in NYC that she couldn't feel any jet lag after the long flight. She was ready to have fun and didn't want to miss a moment of it if possible.

And so it was that on one nice hot day, everyone at her siblings' home in New York left her at home with their cousin Connie. As they hugged and kissed her good-bye she stood at the back door looking at the huge ships passing up and down the Hudson River, taking in the sheer beauty of their movement on the rippling water. Huge trees lined the jersey horizon on

---

[8]   A US magazine that focused on Michael Jackson from his teen years.

the other side, and she could stand and watch this forever without getting bored. Connie tapped Devora on her shoulder. 'Let's go for a walk.'

'Where are we going to?' asked Devora.

'Let's go up to Teggy Square; it's boring here, and its beautiful outside.'

Devora hurriedly put on her sandals and grabbed her bag. Life was never dull around Connie; she really knew how to have fun. Connie was full of energy and excitement, and Devora watched her, curiously wondering what she had up her sleeves. They took the number 03 bus and came off at the last stop just before they got to the local shopping centre, Teggy Square. They then changed to the number 205 and headed to the Bronx. 'Where are we going?' asked Devora.

'To Coney Island on Long Island,' answered Connie.

'What if we get lost?' asked Devora.

'We won't; I've been there many times before,' she replied

Devora just watched her without asking any more questions. This was her opportunity to realise her dream of going to Coney Island.

Devora liked to observe people; people were unique in the way they did things, and she found this very interesting. Her elder sibling Emer often told her, 'You think too much.' How could she not think, she wondered. There was always something to plan and do, and she was a very creative and artistic girl. At that moment she was concentrating on the route and making contingency plans. She knew Connie had a wild streak in her, sometimes doing things that could get people into trouble. Well, she wasn't getting her into any trouble today, Devora thought. She was memorising the bus route now, taking note of landmarks and signs. She knew that at the first sign, she was finding her way back home with or without Connie. She had received her cautions at home before she left. She was told to be careful in NYC because persons of less than noble character could take advantage if she wasn't on the alert. 'Look out for yourself and cultivate no strange company or visit any strange places,' her mom had warned her.

As they got off the train they had boarded in the Bronx, she realised they had stopped right next to Coney Island, and she was overflowing with excitement. She was able to come to the fair and have fun like everyone else—for the first time she was feeling confident. Her face was flushed, and she wanted to try to do everything, including ride a horse. Connie grabbed her hand and asked, 'Which ride?'

'Oh, no, not yet. I'll just watch you for now. I'm going to have some marshmallow first, and then some ice cream,' said Devora. 'Woo hoo! Fun, fun, fun! I just love it.' She was surprised at herself; she was always too reserved to express her feelings openly. Today, though, she just let it all go. It must have been the extraordinary hot sun or being in NYC which had liberated her. It was about 105 degrees in the shade on this late July morning, and everyone was burning up with heat. Adults and children could be seen playing under garden sprinklers to keep cool. Ices, ice cream, and cold drinks were on sale everywhere.

The heat didn't bother Devora much because she was accustomed to the hot sun in Montserrat; which although not as extreme as NYC was prevalent all year round. The day was full of fun for Connie and Devora as they experimented with anything that took their fancy. There was so much to do and see and eat, but Devora didn't overdo it. She did everything in moderation, being ever cautious by nature. But Connie went wild giving new meaning to being over the top, loud, and wild in a very nice way. Devora loved her because she was considerate, easygoing, and genuine, and she made sure Devora had fun as well.

Devora didn't need to worry about going on the rides or the horses without her prince charming today. Connie's confidence had flowed over to her, and they did everything together. There were thousands of people milling about everywhere, and she noticed everyone appeared confident and concentrated on having fun. After today she knew she wouldn't be scared of anything again. She was going to ride! She had a wonderful day and was happy she had come to Coney Island. Devora hugged the huge teddy bear she had won shooting hoops at a stall. It was almost bigger than little Geni, but she was going to take it back for her. She knew her little sister would love that.

When Connie and Devora got back home, they received a good telling off for going away without letting anyone know where they were and not leaving a note. They were contrite and apologised humbly, promising to be more responsible next time. Meanwhile they were sneaking knowing looks at each other. For the rest of the summer, Devora had the time of her life, and it was an experience she would never forget. Never again would she feel left out, for now she had two families of equal importance to her. She would have fun in Montserrat with Guy and Geni, and even more fun in NYC with her other siblings in the summer. She realised if she waited patiently for the right time, she could have experiences like everyone else. A look of contentment was on her face that night as she lay down to sleep.

At the end of her long summer vacation, her newfound confidence was noticed and commented on by her family. Devora only smiled; she had learnt a lot in NYC, and next time she could travel on her own. She didn't miss her dad so much because she knew she would see him next year. Spending time with him had made her feel that she had a real dad of her own and wasn't sharing someone else's. For now Devora was content and vowed to make do with Daddy, her stepdad.

Two years later, Coney Island returned to Montserrat again. Devora raced home excitedly, begging to be taken. Her parents appeared surprised that she participated in rides and slides, but they put it down to being a bit older and more confident. Devora kept her little secret but knew she would remember her NYC trip that had brought her out of her shell. Had she not gone to that fun fair with Connie, she would still be a coward. Growing up in Montserrat, her parents had been so overprotective that they would not have allowed her to go off with Connie or any friend for that matter. They thought they were doing what was best for the children by ensuring no harm came to them, and they didn't pick up bad habits. In the meantime they allowed limited opportunities to socialise with friends. This reduced exposure to certain essentials of a child's development, including learning to argue and critique with others who see things from a different perspective. Their eyes on her also kept her away from boys of her own age, even reducing the ability to flirt and understand the opposite sex. Boys on the other hand were given unlimited freedom to socialise and interact with whomever they felt like. Fortunately schooling provided those opportunities, which helped kids like Devora to have a holistic upbringing.

The funfair experience had a positive impact on the way Devora treated her children later on in life. Despite advice to the contrary from her mom, she allowed her kids to be independent and to form ongoing social relationships with friends, not only at school but on weekends and evenings. She showed her children that she trusted them, which reinforced their trust in their parents and others. It also allowed them to form their own opinions based on personal experiences rather than those enforced on them. When they migrated to England, Devora encouraged friendships but hesitated at allowing sleepovers, because the risks were far greater than they were in Montserrat. She actively encouraged social networking with both sexes and encouraged her kids to value the opinion of others, ensuring that their views were expressed as well.

Children in England for the most part are allowed to make decisions, ask questions, and debate issues they need clarified. It is difficult to picture them accepting the 'children should be seen and not heard' motto that some Montserrat kids experienced. The rights of the child are taken very seriously, and breeches of this often result in serious recriminations. For Devora, she knew that an extremely important component of raising kids in modern England was the art of instilling confidence and self-esteem in her children, to enable them to balance their lives in a constructive way. Her trust paid off, and she hoped these values would be passed on through the generations, whether they remained in England or returned to Montserrat in the future.

Jumbie Taman Tree

Background

This story is set in the village of Trials and highlights how a young girl was sent to live with a lonely lady, referred to as a spinster. It focuses on how the young lady's parents made efforts to help her to become a lady who spoke only proper English, rather than the native dialect, and how she overcame this. It also highlights her escape from the mythical 'jumbie' at Jumbie Taman Tree, based on her cultural knowledge of how they responded to certain behaviours and actions.

A number of people from different countries have stories of their experiences with jumbies. Montserrat is no exception, and jumbies feature strongly in our island's culture. Jumbies are considered to be dark in appearance and are representatives of ancestors. I have not heard of jumbies speaking aloud except during the jumbie dance ritual. During the ceremony a ritualistic dance is usually performed when there is severe illness and where medicines appear not to help in its cure. Some folk then resort to seeking answers from the dead, who are thought to possess individuals during the ceremony.

The jumbie dance consists of four couples performing and dancing the quadrilles until someone is possessed by the spirit. The message is then relayed through the possessed person. Sometimes a sick baby might be given the name of a dead ancestor through this ceremony. Some folk actually believe that this ritual works, and the baby will miraculously recover and thrive following the new name. The new name is referred to as a 'jumbie name' and is not usually on the person's birth certificate. Many people claim to have seen jumbies, while others remain sceptical as to whether they exist. In fact the thought of jumbies can bring tears to the eyes and make the heart race fast with fear. Despite this people take great pleasure in telling and listening to jumbie stories.

The Story

As a teenager Gertie liked to dress up and would often use Kool-Aid added to milk to change her hair colour. Kool-Aid was used to make lemonade and was very popular in Montserrat. The sachets came in many different colours, but her favourites were red and orange. Children often took different flavours to school for lunch. Gertie's fake lipstick was usually a red carnation-type flower that grew wildly around the yard; she often rubbed this on her lips to make them pink.

She sometimes imagined she was a fashion model, although that was not what she really wanted to be when she grew up. She was often lectured by her parents about growing up to be to be a proper young lady, able to sew, cook, and act in a ladylike manner. They made a number of efforts to ensure she became a well-rounded lady by sending her off to other proper ladies to learn ladylike stuff. Additionally she attended typing classes at town hill and sewing classes in Kinsale. Cooking was enhanced through home economics classes, and socialisation and discipline at Brownies and Girl Guides. There was never an idle moment in her life.

All she wanted to do was dress up and have fun. At primary school she had been teased by older boys on the basis of being light skinned, but she never really took them on. She had wished and prayed to be dark-skinned then, but no matter how much sunshine she got, nothing changed. She also spoke a bit differently than the other children, which increased the teasing. Mom did not have a clue what was going on and made things worse by insisting that words like 'um' and 'yah' weren't to be a part of her vocabulary. Other forms of dialect were acceptable, although Mom preferred her children to speak proper English. Mom herself did not speak proper English, except when at work or when speaking to certain people. Still, she wanted to set high standards for her children. At times she struggled to keep her English perfect, but bits of dialect would often kick in. To add to her distress, Gertie was sometimes accused of coming from England, maybe because she had relatives living there who sent clothes and shoes from time to time, which she liked to wear. Her favourites were the platform and two-tone shoes, the clogs, and the bell-bottoms.

Gertie had the final straw when Mom, in her quest to turn her into a lady, sent her to live with a spinster. From time to time certain ladies would ask Mom if she would allow her bright little girl to keep them company. There was never any communication or efforts to gain consent from Gertie. She became more and more resentful of this as time went by but couldn't let Mom know. Now she thought of her first encounter with Miss Paula, who lived around the corner from her school. Her mom had packed her bag and taken her over to Miss Paula's, telling her only that the lady wanted her to stay with her. She wasn't happy and didn't want to go at all. She knew what Mom had in mind, but she couldn't question her because Mom would ask her to be quiet. After all, at home her parents had made it clear that children should be seen and not heard. As she walked alongside her mom quietly, she started planning her return home. She would show them that the only place she intended to live was at home with her siblings. Looking at her long fingers, she counted ten days—that was the longest she intended to stay with that woman. Maybe the woman pitied her and wanted to help her to be a lady, but she was going to show them she didn't want any pity. She was going to be all right and knew she was already a lady because she liked to dress up, colour her hair, and wear her own brand of lipstick.

As they got closer to Miss Paula's house, Gertie started to pout, which was something she often did when she was displeased and no one was watching. 'Why does it have to be me?' she wondered.

Her mom knocked on the door of the light blue house, which suddenly brought Gertie out of her reverie. A short, crooked-looking lady with a friendly smile opened the door and said, 'Good afternoon'. Gertie tried to hide behind her mom's back but returned the greeting all the same. The two adults chatted for a while, and her mom assured Miss Paula that Gertie would be no trouble. Then she said good-bye to Gertie and left.

'Mom doesn't even look remorseful that she is leaving her child behind,' thought Gertie. 'She will see me soon, though—just wait and see.' Had her mom looked back, she would have recognised that look of rebellion and daring that she had only seen a few times before.

Gertie was treated well by Miss Paula, and she couldn't complain as she got everything she needed. There was another little boy in the house, and all she had to do was play with him and keep him company when Miss Paula went shopping or ran an errand. Gertie would sometimes be sent to the shops to buy something Miss Paula had run out of, but she didn't mind this at all. She liked the smell of freshly baked bread coming from Richard's bread shop in Kinsale. However, she had enough of pretending she was okay here, and it was time to go home. She had been counting the days and had put a mark on her storybook each day. This was day ten, and she wasn't staying one day longer. Miss Paula went into her bedroom to rest as usual, and Gertie sat in the living room doing her homework. She wanted to get the homework out of the way because she enjoyed getting 100 per cent every time. The teachers loved her for this, and she always came first in class. English was her favourite subject, and she planned to be an English teacher when she grew up. She had taught herself to read at an early age, which had amazed everyone. It all started when she picked up her first newspaper, which was awfully smelly because it was used as wrapping for the salt fish her mom had bought at the local shop in Kinsale. She became fascinated by the words on the paper, which she couldn't yet understand. Gradually she started pronouncing the small words and got her older siblings to help with the longer words. She could still remember the surprised looks on their faces when she read bits and pieces here and there. She hadn't even started school then.

Now finishing up the last bit of her homework, she closed her books, placed them neatly into her rucksack, and walked quietly on tiptoes over to Miss Paula's bedroom. She could hear the woman snoring loudly like thunder. She concentrated on not making any sound. Gertie wondered what she would do if Miss Paula woke up and caught her. She imagined her troublesome brother, and how he would have teased with a *'Look e deh behine u'* ('Look, she is there behind you'). If she were to hear that tonight, Gertie vowed she would run off fast like lightning. She wasn't going to scare herself and lose her confidence, and she continued to focus on what she was doing. Everyone knew at home that when she set her mind to something, absolutely nothing could stop her from doing it because then she had no fear. Fear only came when she was uncertain and unfocussed. Tonight she knew exactly how she would carry out her planned return home.

Feeling safe to execute her plan, she grabbed her back pack, walked softly over to the door, opened it quietly, and slipped out into the dark. She left the door wide open because if she locked it, it would arouse the entire neighbourhood; the catch made such a loud sound when closing. Breathing a sigh of relief, she took off running at high speed across Aymers Ghaut. Not even a jumbie could catch her that night. When she got to Jumbie Tamarind Tree (Taman Tree), she was sure the jumbie that lived there was watching her, but she surely wasn't going to let it catch her. She had heard her parents talk about the jumbie many times, so she knew exactly what to do—run for her life. She had heard it over and over again: never walk past Jumbie Tamarind Tree late at night, because the jumbie was right there waiting for unsuspecting passers-by and would scare them.

As the thoughts passed through Gertie's mind, her feet were going faster and faster. She was running and thinking really hard, her eyes wide open with tears running down her red cheeks due to the strong wind blowing across her face. Eventually she started chanting aloud without realising it: 'Run for your life, run for your life, run.' As she soared past Jumbie Taman Tree, the sound turned into a shrill wail that would have frightened even the jumbie from which she was running. The only thing was she wouldn't have known that, because she hadn't looked back yet. *'Run, run for your life!'* she screeched as she ran.

Gertie whizzed past Jumbie Taman Tree and got to the crossroads in Trials in record time. She slowed down then and was just about to look back, when again she remembered the ominous warnings she had heard when eavesdropping on her parents conversations: don't look back! She swung her head back like a soldier at attention and increased her speed again. Gertie's eyes were popping wide with fright, determination, and defiance because she intended that when she got home, no one was taking her back to Miss Paula's home. No way was she going back there; she needed to be with her mother just like her other siblings. As she got closer to her parents' front door she squeezed her eyes tight and quickly spun around and started walking backwards. It was said that jumbies wouldn't follow if one walked backwards.

If she closed her eyes, no way jumbie would think she was looking back, unless it was a stupid jumbie who didn't know the difference between looking back with eyes open and looking back with eyes closed. Gertie sucked her teeth in annoyance at her lack of understanding of how the jumbie would be thinking. Still, her back was turned the wrong way, and she was walking backwards. She knew she had to do this to ensure that the jumbie didn't follow her inside the house. Careful not to fall, she walked as fast as she could backwards until she got to the front door. Wishing she had some sand to throw down, she knocked urgently, ready to do battle with whoever answered. She also knew that if she threw sand in front of the doorway, the jumbie had to count every grain before moving on, so the sand would distract it from following.

As her mother opened the door, Gertie couldn't see the surprised expression on her face because she was still walking backwards. She rushed past her, dropped her bag on the floor, and sat down chest heaving, out of breath. Her siblings Anique, Bim, and Emmanuel were already sound asleep. It was just her parents who were still awake, and they waited for her to catch her breath. Gertie's dad didn't say anything that night, but Mom said, 'You came home?' Gertie looked at her and nodded her head, saying nothing. Looking her over as if she was gauging her mood, her mom said without any fuss, 'Go get yourself ready for bed.' Gertie got up obediently and sorted herself out for bed.

When she got up the next morning, she noticed Mom looking at her with concern, and Mom asked her what had happened at Miss Paula's. 'Did she hit you?'

Gertie said, 'No, but I'm staying here, this is where I live.' Her mom looked at her long and hard, as if she could see straight through her. Appearing satisfied about something, she went in to prepare breakfast. On her way to school that day, Gertie was planning the speed at which she would run if she saw Miss Paula on her way there. She wasn't going to answer any questions if Miss Paula asked why she had left. The lady could ask her mom, because she hadn't asked her if she wanted to live with her in the first place, so now they were even.

Looking back, Gertie realised that her circumstances had been no worse than a number of other young ladies; it was just part of the culture that actually helped to shape who she was now. She had felt like a victim despite seeing other girls in similar situations sleeping over or living with lonely ladies. It turned out that spending time with these proper ladies was a good way of shaping girls into sophistication with proper etiquette and manners. Gertie admitted she had had a relatively easy life, for some girls had to tend animals and care for younger siblings or the children of other people. She didn't have to do any of those things, although she liked to sneak away to milk the cows with her brother and ride the big sheep and goats that had been imported from England. She fondly remembered her little sister pointing at the sheep and chanting, 'inglin shoop, inglin shoop,'[9] which generated many a teasing and laughter for her attempts.

From that day on Gertie has not had to run from jumbies again. She later learnt that they were all based on cultural beliefs and made very engaging stories for entertainment in families. As she thought things through rationally she realised she must have had her eyes opened at some point when walking backwards but had not seen anything called a jumbie. It was all in her imagination based on the stories she had heard of Jumbie Taman Tree. Later she was able to look back and have a good laugh at her folly. Rather it is just part of the Montserrat culture.

Lest I Forget

The next three chapters cover aspects of Montserrat culture and tradition that many of us hold dear and wish to keep in our memory, to pass on to our loved ones. The chapters focus on traditional celebrations such as Jouvert Jump Up and St Patrick's Day. My favourite Montserrat recipes have been detailed in one chapter, with reference to the Montserrat national dish, goat water, which has thrilled the palates of many over the years.

I could not complete the book without giving some insight into the Montserrat dialect or Creole sometimes, referred to as Montserrat English. Although there is no dictionary spelling for most of the dialect words, an attempt has been made to capture the words to mimic their sounds and tone. A number of phrases and words have been captured in the chapter, creating a travelling guide for the adventurous visitor to Montserrat who would like to have a go at talking like a Montserratian.

---

[9]   A toddler's attempt to say 'English sheep'.

CHAPTER 10

Traditional Celebrations

A number of annual traditional celebrations are held in Montserrat every year. This is where folk beliefs and customs surface in an entertaining and festive spirit. Overseas-based Montserratians from far and near enjoy coming home to enjoy the beat of the traditional steel pan, soca music, and the beat of the masquerade. The cuisine—including the goat water, the island's national dish, though to bear similarities to an Irish stew—delights the palate of all. The intent in the following stories is to recapture the essence of these celebrations in a vivid, candid narrative.

Jouvert Jump Up

The jump up is always something to look forward to and occurs in Montserrat routinely every first of January. Jouvert is especially important because it signals the end of the carnival, the island's annual festival held for three weeks beginning in December and ending in January, with a last lap jump up. When January 1 falls on a weekend, the following Monday is usually allocated as a public holiday and automatically becomes Jouvert. One of the things I miss about Montserrat is the calypso and soca music accompanying the Christmas festival, the jump up, and the costume bands. The reflection below is of the total enjoyment experienced in traditional Montserrat style by two young ladies and their friends.

'Gyel, get ready and come leh ah we go deh ah tung go jump up.'[10] The sound of excited young voices came from inside the four-bedroom house. Suddenly the door burst open, and Mary rushed outside, sat on the steps, and started doing up her laces. She was dressed in a red T-shirt marked 'Free up you bam bam', a pair of yellow colourful short pants from Arrow's Man Shop, and a pair of pink sneakers. She had a blue sun visor turned backwards on her head and a whistle hanging with a multicoloured string from her neck.

'Jill, come on, let's go,' shouted Mary impatiently. Suddenly Jill appeared at the door just as unceremoniously as Mary, one sneaker in her hand. She was dressed in bright, bold colours also obtained cheaply at Arrow's Man Shop, just like Mary, and a pink flute hung around her neck with a different set of colours. It was time to go into Plymouth, or Tung as the locals called the capital. They were going to play marse and jump up in the various brass bands. Chatting, laughing, and bantering along the way, Mary and Jill said good afternoon to everyone they met as they headed from the village into town. This type of courtesy was the custom of Montserratians; they said hello to everyone, even if they didn't like them very much. If they didn't there would be punishment to pay when their parents found out. The island was tropical all year round, and it was a perfectly hot day on Montserrat, but as January went it was not as hot as the summer days. The weather was perfect for jumping up behind the bands, and the music was going to be hot as usual. As they got to the crossroads in Trials, they stood close to the public bathrooms for a minute to debate which way to go. They had a choice of walking straight down the road past Marse Harry's shop, or walking the other way and going north. To decide they did the usual routine of 'Innie minnie minie mow, put the baby on the po'. On each word the index finger would change direction. Whichever direction the finger pointed last would be the right way to go. This method was always useful when a decision was difficult to make. Today the finger stopped in the direction of Marse Harry's.

In a rush Mary and Jill set off at a run down the hill and past teacher Mary's house, past Bell and Sarah' house. Teacher Mary's house was special because she was the first female politician of Montserrat, and every year around Christmas she held a huge children's party where all were invited

---

[10]   'Girl, get ready so we can go to the street jump up.'

and received many gifts. This was always something to which kids to looked forward. The girls didn't bother to shout out to their friends, Irene and Ivania, because their mom was on the island visiting from Canada, and they were out having loads of fun. Those two girls were always happy and knew how to enjoy themselves. Ivania and Sarah sometimes played lawn tennis together in town after school.

They hurried past Marse Harry's shop and said hi to the men pulling in their fish nets (a harl sian). Not many fish were in the baskets. The sea was rough and water was white, as they would say. The girls weren't bothered about any of that right now; they just wanted to get to Plymouth to join the action. Jacob's bus suddenly pulled up beside them, and they hopped in, saying good afternoon. They would get a free ride as usual, no questions asked. Jacob was really kind to everyone and gave rides to help out. As the small bus drove up the narrow street in Wapping, past John Bull' shop[11] and Kieth and Claude' Beauty Salon,[12] Fort Ghaut Bridge[13] came into view. Both girls had a phobia of Fort Ghaut Bridge, especially when it rained heavily. In fact Jill had had many a nightmare about the bridge. Today, just as her chest tightened, Miss Goosy loomed up on the other side of the bridge next to Cotton Ginnery. The girls huddled together with a mixture of excitement and anxiety. They were a little bit wary of Miss Goosy simply because they couldn't see the top of its head. Still, they loved to watch her dance on the very tall legs.

Miss Goosy was so tall that she rose up above the bus. They were sure she was wearing stilts, but they couldn't see under the trousers and so weren't entirely sure. Her face was painted like a beautiful brown doll with very red lips. They knew it was just an artificial face because its hair was made of brown wool. She was dancing up and down and shaking up her stick legs, which they could now see very clearly as the trousers rode up and then down in harmony with her movements. Mary always said one day she wanted to be a Miss Goosy anyway, so she was going to follow this one for a while. Putting their reserves aside, the girls shouted to the driver in unison. 'Driver, land me, land me, please,' they shouted. The bus stopped outside N & B Gas Station, and Mary and Jill shouted a thank you as they

---

[11]   A shop owned by an expatriate.

[12]   A hair salon owned by two extremely gifted French hairdressers.

[13]   Fort Ghuat Bridge divides Plymouth from the south of the island.

jumped out. As they raced around the bus to the opposite side of the road, they could see a number of cars lined up at the gas pumps. People were talking loudly like they were in a hurry or impatient to be served.

Suddenly there was a bit of shouting from one of the workers. He was yelling at a man in a car who had taken gas but didn't have any money to pay. Words were passing between them, and the girls could nearly grasp some of what was being said. Mary was not surprised at this set of events because she had witnessed it herself from time to time. The two men were cussing so loud that they drowned out the sound of the masquerades dancing to the sound of Bam-Chic-Alay.

Mary and Jill walked over to watch the masquerades in action. Some played the fife and drums, while others danced around in their colourful costumes with shiny mirrors hanging from them strategically. The girls were unable to resist the music and started singing and dancing in time. 'Bam-chica-lay-lay, chiga foot maya, mama sen me dung a riva fu warta; e tell mi no fu trouble no badie, damn neaga man go feel up mi lala; a who e be a chiga foot maya; damn neaga man go feel up me lala.' Fascinated, the girls watched and imitated the masquerades as they changed to the quadrilles. In couples the masquerades could be seen taking turns to dance and rest as they got tired. Each couple did a series of sets, consisting of five quadrilles with tempos that became swifter and swifter. Mary and Jill looked at each other and laughed as they imitated the heel and toe quadrille. Tired of this drill, though enjoyable to watch, they decided to move on to more action.

People were everywhere, filled with the festive spirit and determined to enjoy the last of the festivities eating, drinking, chatting laughing and having fun. There was hardly room to walk, but the two girls squeezed through the crowds as they moved bravely on. They were there to have fun, and nothing was going to stop them. The girls headed towards War Memorial and walked past the post office, looking at the time on the huge clock (sometimes called jetty clack) as they passed by. The taxi stand was empty today, so they guessed the drivers were all busy bringing people into town for the last lap jump up. As they got closer to post office, they made their way up John Street, passing Mercer's store on the way. They looked at the pointy-toed shoes[14] in the show case and had a good laugh. The girls

---

14   Those shoes are now called pumps in England.

exchanged stories of when their moms had bought them pointy shoes to wear to functions. Grimacing to emphasise the point, they shouted and said, 'They were tight, tight, really very tight!' They laughed and held on to each other, and then they walked up the one-way street towards Laps. Turning another corner, they headed past Walls and continued towards Osborne's offices and store. They marvelled at the long queue of people down at the ice cream parlour waiting for the delicious goodies to be served on a cone.

Looking at some shoes in the shoe case generated more stories and laughter. Every young girl dreaded the plastic shoes nicknamed Bata Bus. There was no joy wearing them in the hot sun. The transparent, plastic shoes got soft and hot and burned the instep. The other source of displeasure was that they often picked up horrible things like dog waste and mud in the sole grooves, which were awkward to clean. Mary joked about the first Bata Bus she owned. Her mom had bought the new pair of plastic shoes to wear to school. Knowing that people would have a laugh at her, she tossed them way up on the roof of their house, never to be seen again. For an entire week she walked barefoot to school. When her mom found out, she did get a sore bum, but also new shoes: pointed ones from Mercer. Luckily she didn't have to wear these for long because a package came from her relatives in England. Mary was expected to wear the shoes that came quickly before her feet grew too big for them, which saved her from the pointy shoes.

The girls headed up the road towards Evergreen Tree at the roundabout. They laughed loudly as some young boys hung out on the sidewalk and tried to chat them up. 'Psst, psst!' The sound was coming from Dema, the young guy who felt he was so good looking that no girl could resist him.

The girls looked his way and then at each other knowingly, and they burst into more laughter. As they got closer to the evergreen tree, they could hear the popular brass band Burning Flames playing 'Free up You Bam Bam'. They couldn't resist this tune, so as their steps sped up they were singing along with the musicians in the band. *'Never me again with no stiff waist woman . . . budum dudum dum . . . Diane cramping me style, dancing out a time . . . Whine you waist, free up you bam bam . . . Whine you waist, free up you bam bam.'*

Some friends the girls knew were sitting over at the Wade Inn Hotel waiting for the action, as they called it. They jumped up when they saw the two girls and joined them, dancing and singing along. As they crossed the roundabout, crowds sat under the evergreen tree. Some people danced, some ate fried chicken from Evergreen Restaurant, and others just socialised with people they knew. People from every village on the island were in town, and there were large numbers from overseas, young and old. One could tell the difference by the way people were dressed and the varying accents. Taking all this in, the girls headed down the crowded road towards Letts Appliance Store.

At last there it was; the big band with several colourful, costumed troupes following, and crowds and crowds of people coming up the road past Arrow's Manshop. In fact the crowds extended way down the road beyond Fisherman's Shed. As usual Burning Flames, the most popular band around that day, had come down from Antigua for Jouvert and pulled the crowds from the other bands. No one made a fuss about this because it was thought that Burning Flames had originated from Montserrat, and the good-looking young guys were very popular and much loved by the young ladies. It was mostly their style and the music they played that attracted people to them. They were thought to be the best band around these parts then. The calypso king and festival queen rode majestically behind the band on some big trucks and so did the road march king.

Unable to resist the music and crowds anymore, the girls jumped in behind the band and started moving their waists in the way only a Montserratian knew how. That evening they followed the patrol of bands up George Street and up to Glendon Hospital. People were on the verandas, some as patients some as visitors. The nurses were dressed in really neat, white uniforms with caps on their heads, looking like Florence Nightingale. They smiled and waved from the veranda along with the patients as the bands and troupes passed by. That night as the girls returned home, exhausted from following behind various bands, they chatted about who had won Road March King and who was the best band on the road. Boy, had they enjoyed themselves this year. They certainly couldn't wait for next year's festival, and this time they were going to join troupes for the fun of it. The festival activities were something Montserratians near and far looked forward to each year; they tended to bring together Montserratians from all over the world and helped boost the economy. Jouvert Jump Up in Montserrat culminated with all the activities as one big show for young and old to enjoy.

Whether one stands on the side streets observing, or moves one's waist behind the band, or just walks at a distance behind, it is still enjoyable. A large number of Montserratians from overseas look forward to this event and ensure that flights are booked very early in the year. Some people have said not even the increase in air fares can stop them from going home for Christmas and the festivities held around that time.

St Patrick's Day

I couldn't complete this book without adding a wee bit about St Patrick's Day.For Montserratians at home and abroad, this is a big celebration of culture. Needless to say I feel a sense of sadness every St Patrick's Day that I spend in England, because I have never had the opportunity to attend one of the ceremonies held by the Irish here in Britain. Montserratians in London somewhat lacks that cohesiveness held by Montserratians at home regarding the drive to celebrate St Patrick's Day. From time to time my associates have asked why Montserratians celebrate St Patrick's Day when they are not Irish. It turns out that a number of persons are still of the impression that Ireland is the only country to celebrate St Patrick's Day as a national holiday. As a result I have made it my business to explore a short history of its implications and meaningfulness for Montserratians.

Another related issue that may appear a bit petty to some, but is in fact important to others, is the name 'Emerald Isle of the Caribbean' which Montserrat is sometimes called. Some people have argued that Montserrat cannot be known as the Emerald Isle of the Caribbean since one of the Windward Islands is allegedly known by the same name. I am not sure of the history of that Windward Island in question, but according to documented history, the following occurred.

Montserrat was returned to the United Kingdom under the Treaty of Paris after being briefly captured by France during the American Revolution in 1782. A large number of Irish Catholics who were persecuted on other islands during the seventeenth century arrived at Montserrat seeking refuge. Around that time it is documented that the Montserrat population was comprised of 50 per cent Irish Catholics. The Irish ran the plantations on the island and owned the natives, who were slaves then. There was a subsequent failed slave uprising on 17 March 1869, which also coincides with St Patrick's Day. (I need to add here that slavery was abolished in

Montserrat in 1834.) Montserratians continue to enjoy a national holiday on St Patrick's Day, celebrated on the seventeenth of March every year. In Ireland, St Patrick's Day is a national holiday to celebrate the anniversary of of St Patrick, the patron saint of Ireland. During the fifth century St Patrick worked extensively with the Irish to reinforce Christianity in Ireland.

In Montserrat an entire week of activities is organised, including presentations and discourses on the history of St Patrick's Day. A creative writing competition is usually employed as a means of discovering new talent and creating opportunities for all writers. Montserratians of all ages are encouraged to write and submit pieces, which are then judged by a panel. Traditional food feasts, displays, and sampling are also aspects of the cultural celebration that draws interest from large numbers of visitors as well as nationals. It is very common to see huge pots of goat water on display at various stalls, especially in the village of St Patrick's in the south of Montserrat. Goat water is said to be a derivative of an original Irish stew much sought after by visitors and nationals alike. The delicious stew draws crowds to its stands because it fills the air with its unique, mouth-watering aromas. I just love the smell of cooking cloves in the atmosphere, not to mention the other favourites: salt fish, johnny cake, and dukna.

Other activities include hikes, races, and street dances to the islands traditional calypso and soca music. From various venues on the streets, one can see the very entertaining masquerades on the streets, dressed up in their colourful costumes and performing the quadrille. A favourite is the heel and toe, which people often try to mimic. Other performances are sometimes organised by the island folk singers, the Emerald Community Singers, and other artists.

The Montserrat national bird, the oriole, and the national flower, the Heliconia, can also be seen on display at various venues. The national dress is worn with pride by Montserratians and consists of a white peasant blouse, white cotton skirt with an overskirt of green yellow, and white kente. An optional green waistband and a head tie made of the kenke is optional. This can be accessorised with slingback black shoes or the wearer's choice. The national dress is symbolic of that worn by the ladies of the plantations.

Often referred to as a fusion of Afro-Irish culture, this yearly St Patrick's Day event is definitely something to look out for. I am aware that some Montserratians abroad do celebrate St Patrick's Day and have been fortunate to participate in the event in French St Marten. The day was celebrated with a cruise around the lagoon. A number of Montserratians living in St Marten met and enjoyed each other's company as they listened to music and reminisced about life in Montserrat. That experience was so unique in many ways that it is one I won't forget for a very long time.

CHAPTER 11

Favourite Montserrat Recipes

Food is an important aspect of the Montserrat culture, and our cuisine, like the rest of our culture, reflects the history of Montserrat because it embraces methods from a mixture of our Amerindian, African, Irish, and British heritage. It is difficult to tell in some instances which foods remain in their pure forms and which are derivatives or components of another. It is also difficult to determine which foods are purely native to Montserrat. There is no documented evidence of what foods the first natives, the Caribs and Arawaks, brought to Montserrat, although history suggests that some of their favourite foods included corn, prickly pears, paw paw, sweet potatoes, breadfruit, and yams. As with the rest of the Caribbean, the Spaniards were known to bring in pigs, cattle, and goats and introduced bananas, sugar cane, ginger, plantains, and coconuts. Some of these crops were introduced by the Indians to different Caribbean Islands and eventually made their way to Montserrat.

The meal patterns of the Montserrat folk are similar to that of the British. During the work week three meals are eaten over the course of the day. Breakfast usually consists of bread, a form of protein, and a cup of tea. (All hot drinks except coffee are referred to as tea in Montserrat and may consist of traditional milk and cocoa or real tea and coffee and herbal and local bush tea.) The more cultural practice of picking certain bushes fresh from their stalks and placing them in a cup or teapot of boiling water to extract the flavour of the bush (known as drawing) is a favourite morning and bedtime beverage option. Bushes such as soursop bush, pum coolie, tamarind bush, and hibiscus to name a few also have medicinal properties. When used to heal and soothe colds and coughs, the bushes are boiled to enhance their potency. Bushes can also be combined to address multiple illnesses. Like most Caribbean hot drinks, they are usually taken early in the morning to keep the gas out of the stomach and keep one invigorated for the day. Hot drinks are also taken as purgatives and gas relief for indigestion.

The lunch time meal may vary from individual to individual, but for the majority it usually consists of a light meal. The evening meal is the main meal of the day and usually consists of ground provision, rice and vegetables, and a protein in the form of a stew or gravy. Saturday normally consists of two meals, mainly breakfast and dinner. Dinner is usually eaten earlier on Saturdays, than during the week, and the island's popular 'Saturday soup' is the norm for most. Two meals are also taken on Sunday, and dinner is often a celebration of a variety of dishes done in various styles. Leftovers are usually thrown away or given to the pigs or dogs; a great difference to how many Montserratians now operate in England, where cooking for many is done once a week, and leftovers are eaten during the week. This is especially true for those who work full time. There are some who retain their tradition of cooking every day. Fruits and snacks are taken throughout the day, not as a desert. Mango and guava can be picked freely from anywhere because they are found all over the island.

On a different note, the ability to walk into a Caribbean shop in some areas of London is indeed a novelty and a privilege. Picking up an expensively priced quarter of a breadfruit, taking it home, cooking it, and consuming it is something longed for by many a Montserratian in Britain. Some of us know the little hideouts in London where one can buy a piece of breadfruit and other ground provisions now and then. It is with pleasure I share a few of my favourite Montserrat recipes below.

Goat Water

The Montserrat national dish.

Ingredients
1 quarter fresh goat meat
2 oz plain flour
2 onions, finely chopped
2 scallions
4 cloves of garlic, crushed
3 sprigs fresh thyme (or other herbs)
1 red pepper
1 green pepper
1 hot chilli pepper
1 Tbsp mace
1 oz marjoram
1 Tbsp crushed cloves
2 Tbsp tomato puree
Browning

Method
Cut off excess fat and cut up goat quarter into 2-inch squares (do not remove bones). Wash well with water and malt vinegar. Place in a saucepan with cold water and bring to a boil on medium heat. Add remaining ingredients and skim off fat accordingly.

Add boiling water to keep water levels up.

When meats is tender, lower fire and add cold water to flour and mix into a smooth paste. Stir paste into boiling goat stew to thicken. Add browning until brown in colour. Allow stew to simmer on low heat until done. Serve with fresh rolls.

Salt Fish (Sarlfish)

Montserratians enjoy having salt fish and johnny cakes as part of the Sunday morning breakfast. It can also be eaten at dinner or lunch time.

Ingredients
1 side salt fish or cod fish, soaked in fresh water overnight (to remove salt)
2 medium onions
1 green pepper
1 red pepper tomato ketchup vegetable oil
2 Tbsp water black pepper

Items Required
1 large frying pan/wok/shallow saucepan
1 saucepan for cooking fish
1 kitchen knife of choice cutting board plate or bowl

Method
Cook fish until tender and easy to flake off. While fish is cooking, remove outer skins of onion and cut the onions down the centre and into half-circle rings.

Cut peppers in two and remove the core; cut further into elongated pieces to the required size and set aside on a plate until ready to use.

Remove cooked fish from saucepan. Drain cooking water and run fish under cold water until cool.

Clean fish, removing any skin and bone (don't worry about flaking). Flake fish into desired size using finger tips and place in a plate or bowl. Heat frying pan on the stove on medium heat. Add small amount of vegetable oil and let it heat moderately. Add onions and peppers and stir, allowing to partially cook (do not allow to cook completely). Add fish flakes and mix with onions and peppers with a pot spoon. Add tomato ketchup and black pepper. Stir around and through the fish. Add small amount of water and cover the pan, allowing it to cook on medium heat for 10 minutes or as required. Remove from heat when complete. Serve with johnny cake or choice of staple.

Johnny Cake

Pronounced 'jannie kiak'; also known as bakes.

Ingredients
1 kg self-rising flour
1 Tbsp baking powder
1 Tbsp vegetable shortening
1/2 tsp salt warm water

Items needed
1 mixing bowl
1 sieve
1 scale for measuring flour
1 plate frying pan vegetable cooking oil

Method
Sift flour into mixing bowl using the sieve. Add baking powder and mix together thoroughly.

Add vegetable shortening to mixture. Using fingers, mix with flour until mixture looks rough. Add warm water in small amounts. Using fingers, mix the ingredients into a dough-like paste (do not knead like bread flour; should be handled lightly). Mixture is ready when it comes off the hands totally (if too wet and sticky, add flour). Roll mixture into golf ball sizes or required size and rest on a plate. Cover with a clean towel and leave to raise for 15 minutes to half an hour in a warm place (but not the oven or microwave). Place frying pan on fire and allow to heat until very hot. Add vegetable oil and allow to heat. Using pad of fingers, shape dough balls into a flat, round biscuit shape. Drop into hot oil and let fry. Brown both sides. Adjust heat to ensure johnny cakes are well cooked and do not burn. Remove when cooked and golden brown. Let cool before eating. Serve with salt fish or preferred accompaniment.

Saturday Soup

Some Montserratians cook this routinely on a Saturday.

Ingredients
2 chicken drumstick, chopped to required size
1 medium salted pigtail, chopped to required size (soaked overnight to remove salt)
1 salted pig snout, chopped to required size (soaked overnight to remove salt) root vegetables (ground provision), peeled and cut up to desired sizes:

- 1/2 medium dasheen
- 1 small sweet potato
- 1/2 lb pumpkin diced
- 1 christophene, any size
- 1/4 breadfruit
- 1 small onion
- 1 clove garlic
- 3 carrots thyme (or other herbs) salt white pepper

Method
Place a medium-large saucepan half filled with water on stove and bring to a boil. Add pigtail and pig snout and cover. Allow to cook until tender (should not be too soft). Test water for saltiness. (If too salty, drain off and pour boiling water over the pig tail and snout). Add chicken to boiling water and cook for 10 minutes. Add all other ingredients and allow to cook on medium heat. Soup is ready to eat when all vegetables are soft and soup is of a medium or desired consistency.

Small dumplings called droppers can be added and will thicken the soup. Other seasonings can be added for flavour. A variety of meats can be used in this soup.

Setting the Jumbie Table

A white linen tablecloth is placed on the table, where the food is set out attractively for the jumbies. Setting the jumbie table is a tradition practiced mostly among older Montserratians. This is a way of ensuring the dead ancestors are well fed so they continue protecting the household. The food on the jumbie table is expected to remain untouched until Christmas day, when it is cleared away from the table. The household can then have a feast of what's left of it.

Items
2 cassava breads
1 black cake
1 bottle rum punch (Perks)
1 plate of turn corn
1 bowl white rice
1 plate tart
2 black puddings (1 rice, 1 cassava)
1 bottle guava drink
1 bottle ginger beer
1 bottle sorrel
Caribbean cheddar cheese
1 bottle Mount Gay Rum

CHAPTER 12

Montserrat Dialect

I consider my language and dialect to be a strong part of my culture, which I maintain when I am with my friends and family. When I moved from Montserrat, I realised that we were different, that we spoke differently.

'Ayah mi barn, mi no bang no warta cumyah.'

'Hanum gi mi.'

'Dardi ohh.'

'Awah ya say.'

'Gi mi libit wa ya yet deh.'

I am sure many will agree with me that Montserratians have a very unique way of speaking. Further, when speaking to a fellow Montserratian, one can almost always tell from which area of Montserrat that person originates. The tone and broadness of speech is certainly a giveaway as to whether a person is from the west, east, north, or south of the island. The further away from, town the more pronuonced the accent. One can imagine the problems encountered in a place like England, where the accents, languages, and cultures are more diverse. Some people in England are very good at adapting to English accents, which are many and varied depending on where in the country one is living. Others tend to try to emulate the Queen's English, speaking at the rate and with the intonations of a BBC reader. My experiences with trying to be understood during the early days in England have been nothing short of hilarious at times. My emotions have ranged from embarassment to humour at the way my communication partners would say, 'What was that, my dear?' I suppose my accent sounded foreign then.

Of course I was speaking what I thought was the Queen's English, having had previous experiences on popular Montserrat radio station ZJB while presenting programmes. On a whole this experience did not help at all at that point in my life, as I struggled from time to time to make myself understood, especially during my first year in England. There were times when I couldn't quite figure out if people were just making fun of my Caribbean accent or were serious. It was difficult to differentiate between sarcasm and genuine misunderstanding due to my limited experience of the British culture. Eventually I took to apologising for my Caribbean accent prior to making public presentaions, which worked quite well until eventually I realised it just didn't matter, because within Britain itself there were so many different accents anyway.

Arguably the most frustrating moments in my journey to a British accent would be those times when individuals automatically jumped to the conclusion that I was of Jamaican origin. Some have been very nice about it, while others tried to soften what I would not necessarily call a faux pas with an opening statement such as, 'Jamaicans are very nice people.' So many times I've had to correct this assumption with, 'I hate to disappoint you, but I am 100 per cent Montserratian.' That would usually evoke an apology, but sad to say it is still surprising how many people I have come accross who associate the Caribbean accents only with Jamaicans. Despite the influx of Montserratians to England, it is even more surprising that many people claim never to have heard of the island. As time passed so has my original accent, which is now crossed between Caribbean and British. At times people have been curious about my new accent, over which I appeared to have little control no matter how I try. In humour I explain that the accent is in transition and is trying to be British. This became a running joke and caused me no embarassment, for it was exactly how I felt.

As time went by, I became adventurous and decided to try an audio programme that took me through the process of speaking with a clear British accent. I have finally put the programme to rest and am currently still in accent transition—I have given up trying to speak with a perfect English accent. My funniest experience has to be when I met fellow Montserratians and tried to speak my native dialect. I found that I just didn't sound right anymore, and therefore I felt I was losing a part of me that I held dear. Often sounding as if I was putting on the Montserrat accent rather than being Montserratian was something I couldn't allow to happen. I quit while

I was ahead. Sad to say the Montserrat dialect is not written anywhere, and despite living in England, there are many Montserratians who speak mostly dialect no matter what, while others; especially the young ; have shifted to speaking with a clear English accent only. Although this is not wrong, there is concern for the future sustainability of the dialect among the diaspora. The other significant issue relates to those who try to receive medical aid after certain illnesses. Some individuals such as stroke victims and those with certain neurological illnesses automatically revert to their mother tongue, making it difficult for care providers to understand what they are communicating. It is with this in mind that I make my first attempt to write the dialect as a guide only.

There have been many schools of thought as to the origins of the Montserrat dialect. It is supposed by some that it originated in Africa, while others are of the impression that it has been influenced by the Irish. In an attempt to clarify this, J. C. Wells carried out a phonetic study in Montserrat and published it in the *Journal of International Phonetic Associates*. Wells argues that the Montserrat dialect as a language 'has a great deal in common with other Caribbean English-based creoles. As in the other British or ex-British territories such as Jamaica, Guyana, Trinidad, Barbados and Antigua, there exists a continuum extending from the broadest Creole up to a local variety of Standard English' . . . as in the other British or ex-British territories such as Jamaica, Guyana, Trinidad, Barbados and Antigua, there exists a continuum extending from the broadest Creole up to a local variety of Standard English'. Wells' debatable conclusion was that the linguistic influence of the Irish and its contribution to Montserrat is not enough to have any significant impact. Unfortunately as with most things related to Montserrat, there is hardly any research to be found in this area.

Of some interest, though, is the similarity of sounds of some words used in the Jamaican dialect. When I studied in Jamaica, no individual except for my class mates knew I was not from Jamaica. I suspect that if I had spoken dialect, not adding or removing the 'h' sound from some words would have given the game away, and I would have been referred to as foreign. Of note also is the number of attempts made to use specific spellings when writing the Montserrat dialect. Many continue using spellings that are for the most part interchangeable with the spelling of the Jamaican dialect. However, when listening keenly, one can pick up clear phonetic distinctions between the Jamaican and Montserratian dialect, as pointed out by Wells. It is not surprising that some of the dialect sounds similar, as there are certain commonalities between some Caribbean islands.

The Irish influence is common to both islands and of course like most Caribbean islands more than 50% of their population is of black African descent. For that main reason among others I have decided to write the Montserrat dialect the way most people would rather than copying from another countries interpretation of the dialect. To capture this as accurately as possible I have been interested in a number of dialogues with fellow Montserratians on popular social networking sites. Unfortunately there's not much research available to validate the Montserrat dialect also known as Montserrat English, as a single language and no definite confirmation of its origins have been found to date. Yet the dialect is spoken with confidence by all Montserratians. When outside Montserrat it certainly brings a sense of comfort just to hear the dialect spoken. The purpose of this contribution is to preserve the dialect for the use of the young wherever they are and to remind those who might ultimately forget our culture, our heritage.

Dialect	English
shuldn	shouldn't
fule	fool
di	the
pikney	children
dem	them
jus so	like that
troot	truth
dat	that
cum/coom	come
dung	down
yah	here
nex	next
wid	will
um/oom	it
an	and
ooway/gooway	go away
mine you	be mindful
anyting	anything
dem pikney deh	those children

you hafoo bliarm you self-------you are responsible
wah----------------------------------what
evesdrapus/eavesdrapoos ---------eavesdroppers
u ---------------------------------- of (e.g., wan u dem)
demself ----------------------------themselves
a you ----------------------------you all; all of you
a you ----------------------------it's you
gout to in yah----------------------get out of here
no cum back yah -------------------don't come back here
an til me say so --------------------until I invite you back; until I say so
disubediunce/disoobeedioonce--disobedience (disoobeedioonce)
A u hear mi -----------------------do you hear me
A you look pan me wuk yah-----I can't believe what I am seeing/hearing;
I'm shocked
Marmi/Mooma------------------- Mother
Dardi/Poopa ---------------------- Father
peppa --------------------------- pepper
warta--------------------------- water
sarl ----------------------------- salt
out oo--------------------------- out of
cantrual/cantrooa ---------------- control
trear ----------------------------- discipline
mark mi wods --------------------- mark my words
ban you bellie an barl------------tie your belly and cry out in pain or
anguish
me ah go ------------------------- I can do; I will do
ah we---------------------------- we/us
tek------------------------------ take
wan------------------------------ one
nat now/nat eva/neva------------ never
hafu tek arl tree------------------- must take all three
arl ------------------------------- all
tree ------------------------------ three

Translations Used in Folk Stories

Dialect: You shouldn fool di pikney dem so.
English: You shouldn't fool the children like that.

Dialect: Tell dem di troot, dat when di jack e lantun come dung yah nex time, dem wid see um an hide ooway.

English: Tell them the truth so that when the jack o'lantern comes down here next time, they will see it and hide away.

Dialect: Mine u if anyting happen to dem pikney, deh you hafoo bliarm you self.

English: Be aware that should any harm come to those children, you are responsible.

Dialect: Wah ah you ah do in yah; eavesdrappus hear no good oo demself.

English: What are you doing in here; eavesdroppers hear no good of themselves.

Dialect: Ah u gout to in yah, and no coom back antil mi say so.

English: You all get out of here, and don't come back until I ask you to.

Dialect: Disubediunce, ah you hear me.

English: I hope you understand that I'm intolerant to disobedience.

Dialect: Ah u look pan mi wok yah.

English: I can't believe what I am seeing. (This is an expression of disbelief, usually said with hands on hips, head tipped to the side, and eyes partially raised to the sky.)

Dialect: Pickney no hear wah marmie say drink peppa warta, lime, an sarl.

English: Children who don't follow their mother's (parent's) advice will suffer and regret it later. (Basically pepper water, lime, and salt leave a bad taste in the mouth.)

Dialect: Dem pikney deh out ou cantrual.

English: These children have no discipline.

Dialect: If u no triarn, dem you ago ban you bellie an barl womun, mark mi wods.

English: If you don't discipline, then you will be crying in anguish later, mark my words.

Dialect: No jack e lantun ago kech awi, nat now, not eva, an if e tek wan, e ha fu tek arl tree u a-we togeda, and dat no passible.

English: No jack o'lantern can ever catch us, and if it does try, it has to take all three of us in one go, and that is impossible.

A Guide to Using Montserrat Dialect

Days of the Week

What day it is today	Ah wah deh tiday be?
Today is Monday	Tiday ah Monday
Tuesday	Choosday
Wednesday	Wenisday
Thursday	Tursday
Friday	Friday
Saturday	Sateeday
Sunday	Sunday

Months

What month is it now?	Wah mont e be?
January	January
February	Febuary
March	March
April	Earpril
May	May
June	Joon
July	Jooly
August	Argoos
September	Septemba
October	Actooaba
November	Noovemba
December	Decemba

What is today's date? ------------ A wah di diat be tiday?

Today is Wednesday, the second of November, nineteen ninety-three—Tiday a Wenisday, di secund u Noovemba, nineteen ninety-tree.

179

Time of Day

in the morning -------------------- nah di marnin
in the afternoon ----------------- nah di aftoonoon
in the evening -------------------- nah di evenin
in the night ----------------------- nah di nite
before dawn---------------------- before darn
When the clock strikes twelve--- When di clack strike twelve
last night ------------------------- larse nite
this week ------------------------- dis week
next ------------------------------- nex

The Weather

What type of weather will we have tomorrow? -- Wah kindu weda a we a get tumaro?
It is going to be cold------------------------------- Yah go be cooal
A storm is on its way ------------------------------ Wan starm pan di way
Is it going to be foggy? --------------------------- Yah go be faggy?
Is it going to rain?--------------------------------- Yah go rian?
What will the temperature be? -------------------- A wah di tempricha ah go be?
Do we expect thunder and lightning?------------- Ah we expec thunda an lightenin?

Personal Details

Surname--------------------------- curniarm
What is you surname? ------------ Ah wah you larse niarm be?
Christian name-------------------- chrischun niarm
What is your first name? --------- Ah wah u fus niam be?
Initials ---------------------------- inishuls
Where do you live? -------------- Weh u live?
Town------------------------------- tung
Sex/gender ----------------------- sex/genda
Are you a man or a woman?----- U ah wan man or wan oomun?
Nationality------------------------ nashinality
Where did you come from? ----- Ah weh you cum fan?

Date of birth----------------------diart ou birt
When were you born? -----------When u barn?
Place of birth ---------------------weh u barn

Greetings

How are you? ------------------------------------Ah how you do?
I'm fine, thank you, and you? -------------------Me ar-rite, tanks, an u?
Not very well ------------------------------------Me no too good tarl
I have a pain here in my stomach----------------Me belly ah hut me yah so so
I'm not too bad----------------------------------Me no too bad dardi
I am going ---------------------------------------Mi gan dardi
Someone is waiting for me; I have to go------Sumbady ah wiart fu mi, so mi hafu go.
Enjoy yourself ----------------------------------Enjaye youself
Have a good trip --------------------------------Hah wan good trip
Safe travel --------------------------------------siarf travel
Tell them hello for me--------------------------Say hallo fuh mi
Give them my regards ---------------------------Gi dem mi regards

Asking Questions

Who's that? ------------------------------------Ah who dat? Ah who e be?
What's there to see here? ----------------------Ah wah deh fuh see out yah?
What kind of hotel is that? --------------------Wah kine ou hotel dat?
Where? ---Weh?
Where is the toilet? ----------------------------Weh di tieloot deh?
Where are you going? ---------------------------Ah weh you ah go now?
Where are you from? ----------------------------Ah weh you cum fan?
How far is that? --------------------------------How far dat be?
How long does that take? -----------------------How lang dat ago tek?
How long is the trip ----------------------------How lang di trip be?
How much---------------------------------------Who mooch?
How much is that?-------------------------------Who mooch dat deh be?
What time is it? --------------------------------Wah time e be?
Which car is mine? -----------------------------Which wan ou di kiar dem ah mine?

When are we leaving here?------------------When ah we ah lef yah?
No, that's impossible --------------------Nah dat no passible nutten
tarl go so
I think so------------------------------Me tink so
I agree---------------------------------Me ugree
I hope so too---------------------------Me huap so too
No not at all --------------------------No nat u tarl
No, no one-----------------------------No nobady
No, nothing----------------------------Do nutten
That's right----------------------------Dats rite
I don't agree---------------------------Me disugree
All right -------------------------------Ar-rite
I don't know ---------------------------Me no no

Introduction

Let me introduce myself --------Leh mi intrujuce meself
My name's----------------------Mi nearm
I'm ----------------------------Mi ah
What is your name? -------------Wah you niarme?
May I introduce-----------------Leh mi tell u who e be
This is my husband--------------Dis ah mi husbun
wife----------------------------wife
daughter-----------------------darta
son ----------------------------son
little girl ----------------------li gyel
sister --------------------------sista
brother-------------------------bruddo
aunt ---------------------------antie
uncle --------------------------uncle
niece --------------------------mi
sista darta nephew -------------mi sista son
granddaughter-----------------grandarta
grandson ----------------------granson

Chatting Someone Up

I like you ------------------------------- Mi like you

I like spending time with you --------- Mi like fuh spen time wid you

I miss you so much -------------------- Mi miss you suh mooch

I think about you all the time --------- Mi ciarn stap tink bout you

I dreamt about you -------------------- Mi min ah dream bout you

You have such a sweet smile ----------- You smile sweet sah

You have such beautiful eyes ---------- You gat some nice eye

I'm in love with you -------------------- Mi luv you

I'm in love with you too --------------- Mi luv you too

I don't feel as strongly about you ----- Mi no feel di searm bout you

I already have a boyfriend------------- Mi gat wan bwoye fren u-ready

I'd like to go to bed with you---------- Mi want to sleep wid you

Only if we use a condom -------------- Only if ah we use wan candum

This is going too fast for me ---------- Dis ah go too fars fuh mi sah

Take your hands off me --------------- Tek you han dem arfu mi/No touch mi eh!

We have to be careful of AIDS------- Mi friad AIRDS/Ah we hafu careful bout di EARDS

That's what they all say---------------- Dat ah wah all you dem jus say

We shouldn't take any risks ----------- Ah we shuldn tek no riss

Do you have a condom? -------------- You gat wan candum?

No? In that case we won't do it ------- You no gat none? In ah dah kias deh ah we nar do nutten

Arrangements

When will I see you again? ----------- Wen mi a-go see you ugen/oogen?

Are you free over the weekend? ------- U free pan di weeken?

What shall we arrange?----------------- Wa ah we ah go do?

Where shall we meet? ----------------- Way ah we ah go mit up?

Will you pick me up?------------------- U ah go pik mi up?

Should I pick you up? ----------------- U want-mi fuh pik you up?

I have to be home by six o'clock ------ Mi hafu guh huam by six uclak

Saying Good-bye

I don't want to see you anymore --------- Mi no want fuh see you ugen you know

Can I take you home? --------------------- You want mi fuh tek you huarm?

Can I call you? ----------------------------- Mi cuh gi you wan carl?

Will you write me? ------------------------ You ah go write to mi?

Can I have your address? ------------------ Mi cuh have you address/Gi mi you address

Thanks for everything -------------------- Tanks fuh everyting

It was very nice --------------------------- Dat min very nice

Say hello to them ------------------------ Tell dem mi say hello

Good luck -------------------------------- Arl di bess

When will u be back? --------------------- Wen you ah cum back yah?

I'll be waiting for you -------------------- Mi ah go wiat fuh you

I'd like to see you again ----------------- Mi want to see you ugen/oogen

I hope we meet again soon -------------- Mi huap ah we ah go mit up ugen soon

Eating Out

I'd like to book a table--------------------- Mi want to book wan tearble

I'd like a table for two please ------------- Mi want wan tearble fuh two please

We haven't booked ------------------------- Ah we no book yet

Is the restaurant open yet? ---------------- Di resturant upn yet?

What time does the restaurant open? ---- Wah time di resturant ah upn?

Can we wait for a table? -------------------- Ah we coo wiat fu wan tiable?

Do we have to wait long? ------------------ Ah we haffu wiart lang?

Ordering

waiter --------------------------------- wearta

We'd like something to eat---------- Ah we want sudden fuh yet

Can we see the menu? --------------- Ah we cuh see di menu? Bring di menu

We haven't made a choice yet ------ Ah we no choose wah ah we want yet

I'd like ---------------------------------- Me want

I don't want a starter---------------- Mi no want no starta

Enjoy your meal--------------------- Enjarye you meal

The Bill

How much ford this dish cost?----- Ah huh much fuh dis yah?
Could I have the bill, please?------- Nring di bill deh?
Everyone pay separately ------------ Everybady ah pay fuh demself

Paying a Complement

That was wonderful ---------------- Dat min nice
The food was excellent -------------- Di food mi really good
The food was delicious-------------- Di food min dilishus

At the Doctor's

Could you call the doctor for me?------- Carl di dacta fuh mi?
When does the doctor's surgery open? -- Wen di dacta affice ah upn?
I'd like to make an appointment to see the doctor -------- Mi   want   wan
appintment fuh see di dacta
I've got an appointment to see the doctor-------- Mi gat wan appintment
fuh see di dacta

Ailments

I don't feel well --------------------Mi no feel good
I'm dizzy-------------------------Mi head ah spin
ill ----------------------------------sick
I've got a cold----------------------Mi gat wan cuarl
It hurts here-----------------------Yah so so ah hut mi
I've been throwing up -----------Mi min ah vamit
I've got------------------------------Mi gat
I'm running a temperature-------Mi feel hat, mi ah bun up wid fieya
I've been stung by a bee ----------Wan bee boong me
I've been bitten by a dog---------Wan darg bite me
I've been stung by a jelly fish ----Wan jellyfish sting mi
I've been bitten by a snake-------Wan sniark bite me
I've been bitten by an insect -----Wan insek bite me (sudden bite mi)

I've cut myself ---------------------- Mi cut meself
I've burned myself ---------------- Mi bun meself
I've had a fall---------------------- Mi farl dung
I've sprained my ankle------------ Mi sprearn mi ankle
I've come for the morning after pill   Mi cum fuh di marnin aftu pill

Medical History

I am a diabetic---------------------- Mi ah wan diubetic
I have a heart condition---------- Mi gat hart trouble
I have asthma ---------------------- Mi ah wan asmatic
I'm allergic to ---------------------- Mi alurgic to
I'm . . . months pregnant -------- Mi . . . monts pregnunt
I'm on a diet ----------------------- Mi pan wan diut
I'm on medication ---------------- Mi ah tek medison

At the Dentist

My tooth is hurting me ---------- Mi teet ah hut mi
A piece of my tooth broke off--- Wan piece ou mi teet bruk arf
My filling fell out ----------------- Mi fillin farl out
Can I come in today?------------- Mi cuh come een tiday?
I don't want a local anaesthetic-- Mi no want no injekshun
I don't want a root canal --------- Mi no want no root cannool

Asking for Help

help ------------------------------------- help,
sumbady help mi fire -------------------- fayah
police ---------------------------------- poolice
quick----------------------------------- fars
danger --------------------------------- dianjah
stop ------------------------------------ stap
don't------------------------------------ no dodat, no doom
let go ---------------------------------- leh go
Stop that, thief ------------------------ Stap dah tief deh
Could you help me, please? ----------- You cuh help me please?

Where's the police?	Weh di poolice deh?
Call the police	Karl di poolice
Call an ambulance	Karl wan amboolunce
Where is the nearest phone?	Way di nearis fooan be?
What's the emergency number?	Wah di emurjunsi numba
What's the number for the police?	Wah di numba fu di poolice?

Theft

I've been robbed	Somebady rab mi
My purse has been stolen	Sumbady tief mi pus
My car's been broken into	Sumbady bruk eenah mi kiar

Conversation between Two Montserratians

Below is the re-creation of a conversation in dialect between two Montserratians, one living in England and homesick, and the other still living in Montserrat. They are both trying to write the dialect the way they think words are spelt. Can you spot the differences?

Sue says: A ya mi barn a ya mi rare—good stuff.

Ba says: True that.

Sue says: Ye not for the title of the book.

Ba says: Oh, okay. Me understan' wah u mean.

Sue says: Gi mi libit wa ya yet deh.

Ba says: Han' um gi me.

Sue says: Put um dung a u look pan wok ya—dardi ohh.

Ba says: U gat me a larf so much. Dat wan pain nah me belly yah so so. Me like to write de dialec, but when me tark um, people start to larf artu me. Ah wah do dem?

Sue says: Ooh, mi gat wan problem too—a de accent—I jus mek di dialec soun wrang.

Ba says: Not u dardie. When u gat um inna you, you could um soun' um and listen um and understan' um.

Sue says: But di tarking soun betta when u wid monstration. But wen wid di English, it soun bad bweye.

Ba says: Dat ah true. Dem Englunt peeple tink ah-wee ah tark wan diffrent language.

Sue says: Do u know what they call a shub shub?

Ba says: Sure do! It's like the slugs up here.

Sue says: We used to say, 'Shub shub, shub shub, show mi u batoom. Shub shub, shub shub, show mi u batoom.'

Ba says: And it wriggle round and round.

Sue says: Yes, they tiny—I wish I had a photo of one for my story. They so small tho, they gone before u could catch them.

Ba says: Hmm, if u use a slug, I might be the only one who can tell it's a slug and not a shub shub.

Sue says: Boy, these slugs here are huge—almost big like rat.

Ba says: I know. I seen some when I was up there, almost ran for my life.

Sue says: Rfyl—man de scary fu true. Strange things they are, and not shy like our little shub shubs at all.

Ba says: Yes sah. Big man like me ah from wan teeny weeny slug. Me hav fu sah. Ah wah dat dey be.

Sue says: A dat me a say.

Ba says: Marmi, oh session!

Sue says: Dardie oh—mi head a hut mi how mi larf so, an warta in a mi yieye.

Ba says: Oh, ah u me hea a larf so. Me ah wander who de baddy be ah larf so hard.

Sue says: Wa di fart u a say—honestly, I have never spoken like this in my life.

Ba says: Me ah tell u, coz u hav me a larf so much me nearly drap siddung pan de floor. Me neither; I am always the well-spoken Queen's English guy, so much so Montserrat people used to call me English.

Sue says: Frowing up we had to speak kind of properly as well, My mother used to say not to talk bad language in the house. In primary school some people asked if we were from England. Being light skinned didn't help, either, so I was bullied by a few boys as a result. Thankfully I had friends to whom it didn't matter.

Ba says: Yes sah. Otherwise our teachers would bang ah-wee, and parents will bang ah-wee when we get home.

Sue says: Yep. Anyway, dear—sleep a kill me, so mi gan na mi bed.

Ba says: Ahh rite den. Ah we go tark again soon. Sleep gud u hear, and mark u enjay uself tomorrow. Wark good.

Common Myths Used in Montserrat

English: walk backwards
Dialect: wark backwoods
Meaning: If you walk backwards, you will cause confusion, and the jumbie will not follow you home.

English: Place two match sticks in the shape of a cross on the baby's head to stop hiccough.
Dialect: Put two match stik pan di bearbie head fu stap di hiccup.
Meaning: Two crossed match sticks will keep away evil spirits.

English: If you hear your name called once, don't answer.
Dialect: No ansoo pan di fus Karl.
Meaning: Hearing your name called once is an indication that an evil spirit is trying to lure you away, so don't answer. Wait for a second call (this is much like hearing voices or having hallucinations).

English: The baby needs an ancestral name.
Dialect: Di bearbie want niarm (jumbie name).
Meaning: When babies cry continuously for no apparent reason, it is an indication that they need a new ancestral name. It is usually the name of a dead relative.

English: You are being ridden by a ghost.
Dialect: Jumbie ah ride u.
Meaning: Having a nightmare is an indication that a jumbie is riding you.

Jumbie Dance: A means of communicating with the dead.
Meaning: A traditional dance ritual to aid the naming of a child. The dancer performs a ritual, dancing in a trancelike state to a specific drumbeat. During the dance a dead relative speaks to the family through the dancer and gives the name of the child. The child is known by that name from then on. The name is a house name or nickname.

English: Small donkey has big ears.
Dialect: Smarl donkey gat big ear.

Meaning: Children have better understandings than you think, so be careful what you say in their presence.

English: A kind heart makes goats carry what they have out the door.
Dialect: Kind hart mek gooat kiary wah e gat ah dooar.
Meaning: One can become a victim of one's own generosity.

English: Children who choose not to listen to their mother's advice drink pepper water, lime, and salt.
Dialect: Pikney no hear wah marmie say drink peppa warta lime an sarl.
Meaning: Children who do not obey parents will suffer and have bad experiences. It is good to follow parents' advice, as it is for your own good.

English: People who don't like you give you a basket to carry water.
Dialect: If nearga no like u dem gi u baskit fu kiary warta.
Meaning: People will try to work against you and make life difficult if they don't like you.

English: Stick broke in your ears.
Dialect: Stik bruk up nah u ear.
Meaning: You don't listen to correction; you're behaving as if you're deaf; you're impulsive.

English: Take a look at this!
Dialect: Ah u look pan mi wuk yah.
Meaning: Expression of amazement or shock at some occurrence that caused vexation.

English: Oh father.
Dialect: Dardi oh.
Meaning: An expression of shock at some calamity, calling upon the father as witness.

English: Oh mother.
Dialect: Marmi.
Meaning: As above, an expression of shock, calling upon mom as witness.

English: Something is up.
Dialect: Sudden out.
Meaning: Response to calamity.

English: What nonsense is this?
Dialect: Ah wah di fart is dis?
Meaning: Expression of displeasure.

English: Long grass carries news.
Dialect: Lang grarse kiary news.
Meaning: Speak cautiously because you do not know who could be listening.

English: The wall has ears.
Dialect : Di warl gat ear eh.
Meaning: Speak cautiously because you do not know who could be listening.

English: Spit in the air, and it will fall back in your face.
Dialect: Spit up nah di ear, an e ah go farl back nah u fias.
Meaning: What goes around comes around.

English: Bathe the baby in blue water.
Dialect: Beard di bearbie nah blue warta.
Meaning: Bathing the baby in blue water will keep away evil (used when the baby is crying nonstop). Blue is a cube of blue colorant used to enhance white clothing when placed in the sun after washing.

English: Wear your nightdress on the wrong side.
Dialect: Wear u nightie pan di rang side.
Meaning: Wearing you nightdress inside out will ward off evil and prevent nightmares.

English: The dead know who they beat when there is no light.
Dialect: Jumbie know who dem bang a dark night.
Meaning: Bullies will take advantage of the weak and vulnerable when there is no witness or help.

This is Montserrat culture, and we're proud of it forever!

AFTERWORD

Having read the preface and the various chapters of this book, you will notice that there is a similar, continuous theme: reflective narrations of the journey from the beginning of the volcanic eruptions, the adaptation process, and memories of aspects of the Montserrat culture. Montserratians continue to redefine their positions in England as British citizens with their own unique cultures and traditions. The exploration of different ways of addressing challenges has been and still is an essential component of the migration process in England. As such the various issues related to schooling, discipline, relationships, and employment have created many challenges for the island folk, who find themselves with little or no resources directly identified to tackle some of the ongoing issues.

As time passes so does the intensity of displacement issues felt by Montserratians, whose loss of land and kin resulted in their scattering across countries. Despite this, increased access to social networking sites has made it possible for direct and indirect contact, as well as the revival of otherwise dormant, though not forgotten, cultural and traditional representations. Living in England for some is not seen as an alternative to Montserrat, but rather a place where a people remain in transition, hoping to return to their homeland one day. It is hard to say whether the majority are still going through the grieving process for loss of land and relations; it could be that they are slowly coming to the realisation that something once tangible and valuable emotionally, as well as financially, has gone forever. For a large number there appears to be a state of resignation to the unchangeable.

A blending in rather than resistance to the modern British system has taken place over time. There was a plea for some thought to be given to the type of support required to save the Montserrat culture. This theme continues to be thrown about at every opportunity but remains hanging in the balance due to economic inequalities and support systems. It could very well be that the once-a-year visit to Montserrat at Christmas time has become the emotional response to a need to own and be a part of the rock, as Montserrat is so fondly referred. The festival runs for a period of about three weeks. Its blend of calypso shows, queen and teenage pageants, masquerade bands, and costumed troupes with brass and steel pan music serves as a vehicle to reunite Montserratians from all over the world.

The intent focus on the Montserrat cuisine, which includes goat water, the national dish of Montserrat; dumplings and salt fish; johnny cakes; and other favourites are much sought after by the visiting diaspora. For those living in rural areas of metropolitan countries, it is often virtually impossible to find the correct ingredients to cook these dishes, hence the novelty when accessed. Living in England with its easy gateway to Europe gives one the opportunity to explore numerous areas of nativity, beauty, and entertainment, most of which are not possible in Montserrat.

Yet the loss of places like Hot Water Pond, Great Alps Water Fall, Soufriere, and a number of beaches have left a deep, aching sadness felt by Montserratians. For those who left Montserrat, the adaptation process has brought many challenges, while the multicultural societies have resulted in mixed trends and uncertainties especially noticeable in the very young. Despite this, a large number of people have successfully embraced the opportunities offered by England, particularly in its much desired education system and an extensive variety of job opportunities.

The shift in the cultural paradigm of Montserrat is causing open debates among the diaspora in England and other countries. Those living in Montserrat are more reluctant to openly voice their concerns about this. I had a difficult conversation with a local living in Montserrat; he tried to convince me on the phone that it is people of our generation living in England who create issues related to cultural stagnancy, because we do not pass it on to our children. My response to this would be that perhaps he was speaking from a personal perspective. Given that we are from the same peer group, there must be some truth in what he is saying, but then again he appeared to be speaking on behalf of the diaspora, and to this end I cannot but discount his allegations as a bit of self-served guilt for whatever reason. It is hardly possible to speak on behalf of the entire Montserrat Diaspora, but needless to say there is obvious evidence on the social networking sites that people are anxious to save the Montserrat culture.

We must create awareness that culture is not necessarily taught in a formal way but is in fact passed down from generation to generation as a matter of course. Just as it is said that children live what they learn, hear, and see, so it is that the continuous practices of a people are passed on indirectly in some instances. So, is it too late to save the Montserrat culture? Is there even a way of saving it, and if so, who will take the lead? Who will pass on what makes us what we really are as a people? Will the *original* Montserratians be just a memory in the next hundred years, with the only true memory a few skeletons and pottery in a grave? If history were to repeat itself, then like the Caribs and Arawaks, the first known Montserratians to live on the island, *we* are now in danger of becoming extinct with the possibility of being replaced by a new generation of people who may or may not be inclined to learn more about the essence of our culture.

Documented evidence created in books, on the Internet, and in newspaper articles are readily available and show that this generation of Montserratians are very keen to leave a legacy behind, with everyone trying to make some type of contribution; be it the dialect, cuisine, or music. As a song admonishes, 'I'm warning you, my friend, hold on to your property and leave it for your children.' Could this be the time for the leaders to formalise a plan to save the culture, and if so, what angle will it take? We hear a lot of talk of sustainable development, so now what of sustainable culture? Now known as diaspora, we ask the question, 'Is there still a place to call home? Is it now just a tourist resource to visit?' Though some may get carried away into feelings of resentment and despondency about what Montserrat was and what could have been, there is still the hope that we can all embrace the new diversity of Montserrat and live together in unity for the good of the country.

Relationships have been affected both negatively and positively, but it is not possible to make a judgement of the benefits or lack thereof to the migrant Montserrat society. The Montserrat society has always been influenced by subcultures due to its close proximity to the United States of America, as well as the highly developed island of Antigua. Despite this the area of discipline for children came as quite a shock to the Montserrat community. There is some need for in-depth research into the needs of the youth of Montserrat, who are part of the diaspora. Issues such as teenage pregnancy, crime, employment, and elderly care are areas of some concern for the Montserrat community in England. Other areas that could benefit from research are the cancer rates among Montserratians, which for all intents and purposes is thought to be on the increase. The health care system in England, with its access to quick diagnostics and specialist services, has been noted and well appreciated. One of the drawbacks of living in Montserrat has been the lack of resources, resulting in long waiting times for results and delayed diagnosis. Access to specialist services on the island should be a priority in order to enhance the efficiency of health care provision. The main limitation to conducting research within the Montserrat community, both on the island and abroad, has always been the cost. Lack of other resources such as office space, transport, and access adds to the challenges associated with this.

The Montserrat government's UK office alluded to making several attempts to highlight the need for these resources. Despite their efforts, these attempts have yet to reach fruition. It is therefore imperative that resources be made available to allow for more in-depth research to be conducted about the experiences of Montserrat migrants and the unresolved issues that affect their integration into British society.

APPENDIX 1

Main Volcanic Events and Activities, 1995—

18 July 1995	First public awareness of volcanic activity (teaming and venting commences)
21 August 1995	Volcanic eruption; the south of Montserrat and Plymouth are given orders to evacuate (first evacuation)
7 September 1995	End of evacuation
30 November 1995	Dome growth found at English crater
2 December 1995	South of Montserrat evacuated (second evacuation)
2 January 1995	End of evacuation
29 March 1996	First pyroclastic flow down Tar River
3 April 1996	South of Montserrat evacuated (third and final evacuation)
17 May 1996	First pyroclastic flow reaches the sea
17 September 1996	First volcanic explosion
30 March 1997	Great Alps Waterfall destroyed by a pyroclastic flow
29 May 1997	Pyroclasic flow heads north into the ghauts
25 June 1997	Day of Death: villages in the east and central corridor are destroyed by pyroclastic flows; nineteen people die
25 June 1997	The only airport and the main access to Montserrat is shut down following pyroclastic flows and deaths. Montserrat practically shut off from the world
3 August 1997	Pyroclastic flows reaches the capital, Plymouth
7 August 1997	I left for England

26 December 1997   Plymouth and west coast are destroyed by pyroclastic flows

11 February 2010   Large pyroclastic flow throws ash more than twenty thousand feet in the air, affecting nearby islands Antigua and Guadeloupe. Flight paths are disrupted

Assistance & Withdrawal

19 August 1997   Assisted Passage Scheme becomes available to Montserrat

21 August 1997   Assisted Regional Voluntary Redundancy Relocation Scheme becomes available for Montserratians

23 August 1997   Montserrat Building Society can't take the heat and pulls out

28 August 1997   Insurance companies withdraw; all claims will be invalid from henceforth and no refunds announced

1998   Montserrat folk granted full residency rights in the United Kingdom

2002   British citizenship granted to Montserrat folk

End of Life in Montserrat as We Knew It

5 September 1997   1,580 people are living in schools and churches (the era of living in shelters begins)

26 December 1997   Plymouth and west coast are destroyed by pyroclastic flows

1995-1998   Approximately 8,000 people are said to have left Montserrat following the start of the volcanic crisis

17 March 1999   United Kingdom publishes its white paper on overseas territories

February 2005   A new, smaller airport (named John A. Osborne Airport in 2008) was opened in Gerald's by Princess Anne, allowing Montserrat access to air travel once again

APPENDIX 2

Background Research

This appendix has been added with the kind permission of the researcher and captures results of a study carried out by Udwal T Aymer in Birmingham England (2003) as part of a MA dissertation in social work to evaluate the social, economical, and cultural experiences of Montserrat migrants to the United Kingdom.

Montserratians who migrated to Birmingham after the 1995 volcanic eruptions in Montserrat were asked to volunteer as participants. The aim of the research was to evaluate the effects of the volcanic crisis and the experiences of Montserratian migrants who relocated to Birmingham as a result of the crisis.

Names and work places have been omitted for purposes of confidentiality. Only aspects of the interview response relevant to this book have been added.

This is an analysis of the results obtained from the interviews in order to provide insight into the effects of the volcanic crisis on Montserratians and the experiences of Montserrat migrants who relocated to Birmingham as a result of the volcanic crisis. It will be highlighting the impact of this transition on individuals. The findings will be presented under the different subheadings used in the interviews. The main subsections are as follows:

- Social Effects
- Economical Effects
- Cultural Effects
- Personal Effects

Section 1

Social Effects

This section focused on revealing when and why the participants relocated to Birmingham and their experiences of accommodation (housing) and support upon arrival in the UK and Birmingham. Upon undertaking the main interview questions it was important to clarify why the participants migrated to the UK. This revealed that all the participants migrated to the UK as a result of push factors generated by the volcanic crisis.

For some participants migration was due to the cut-off access to public services such as education and training services. Participants migrated to continue education and training.

'I came to the UK because life back home was nearly forces to a halt. There were no schools or education services as most schools were destroyed by the volcano.'

For some there was a very strong sense of the emotional and psychological impact of the volcanic crisis. It was revealed that migration was due to psychological issues triggered by the conditions created by the volcanic crisis in Montserrat.

'I came to the UK in 1997 because I was tired of living under the volcanic conditions. It was coming to the point where it was becoming too stressful for me.'

The participants highlighted that there was a level of continuous uprooting where many were practically homeless.

'We lost our home as a result and couldn't cope with moving around all the time. The situation on the island was really bad.'

Discussions around the participants' experience of housing before they migrated to Birmingham revealed that all of them owned their own homes on Montserrat before the crisis started, but had to abandon their properties to live in temporary relocation accommodations and rented properties with friends and families. There were indications that some participants lived in overcrowded circumstances but felt less a sense of comfort due to the atmosphere generated by the people who they were sharing these accommodations with.

'I lived in a village in my own house before the volcanic eruptions started, but had to move to a rented property in another village when the volcano started erupting. The accommodation was good because there was a family atmosphere there.'

'We were living in our own house before and during the volcanic eruption but we had to move to live in a school in the safe area when our village was declared unsafe. There were too many people living there though, but we felt comfortable. Everyone looked after each other.'

'We lived in our own 5 bedroom home but we moved from our area due to the volcanic eruption, to live with our family in the safe area in their two bedroom house. There were about 9 of us living there at the time which was very uncomfortable; it wasn't that bad for us.'

Further discussions on the issue of housing focused upon the participants' experiences of support and housing when they arrived in Birmingham. The discussions revealed differences in the way the participants were distributed upon arrival in Britain and supported towards finding accommodation when they arrived in Birmingham. Many revealed that they had little information about where they were going or where they were going to be accommodated.

'When we arrived in the UK we had a hard time. We were not given any information about where we were going and no one really asked us anything. One person did at the airport; he asked us if we had money and my mom told him £90. He said that was enough for us. They then put us onto a bus and we ended up in Birmingham. We had no clue that we were going to Birmingham.'

'When we came to Birmingham we went straight to a church that other Montserratians attended. We were taken to a live in a hostel and we were left there and didn't see any official for a couple of weeks.'

'When were temporarily put in a two bedroom flat with two other families.'

'We stayed with my uncle and his partner in their two bedroom flat—my mom, my two sisters, my brother and I. When I got to my uncle's flat I realised I had to sleep on the floor. For God knows how long before my mom was given her own place. I did nothing but cry for I was not used to this way of living and the sudden adjustment made me feel really depressed
.

The discussion also revealed that finding accommodation was a slow process. Many indicated they were offered accommodation in poor conditions, some of which they had to refuse and accept later.

'We moved accommodation about three times before settling in a house because the accommodation we received was in very bad condition. It was two months before something suitable was found.'

Section 2

Economical Effects

This subsection focused on analysing the participants' welfare status in Birmingham in terms of financial security and the extent to which they were able to meet perceived needs.

The discussion revealed that the majority of participants are employed in low earning jobs. They highlighted their dissatisfaction with their income as they were unable to meet their entire needs.

'I work as a Custom Advisor for . . . and I get £250 per week before tax. I struggle a lot with bills and I am left with nothing after I pay them.'

'I work as a fulltime—and earn £200 per week before tax. I find it difficult to pay bills. I am not coping well because things are quite expensive here and If you have a low wage coming in it is difficult to meet your needs.'

Comparisons were made between the participants' level of welfare in Birmingham and level of welfare in Montserrat. The participants felt that they were much more financially secure when they lived in Montserrat given that they were able to meet their needs through the income generated via their employment. They thought that life was more difficult in Birmingham.

'I was a full-time—in Montserrat and my salary was—. This was good times because I had more than enough money to meet my entire needs and plus save. I find work in Birmingham more stressful and less rewarding.'

'I am not coping very well here because it is difficult to save money as things are quite expensive.'

Section 3

Cultural Effects

The focus in this area was on revealing the impact life as a migrant in Birmingham had on participants' cultural practices. The main emphasis of the questions was to reveal the participants level of access to cultural amenities and to reveal whether or not they were able to continue their cultural traditions.

Discussions around access to cultural amenities such as foods revealed mixed feelings. Some participants thought that traditional foods were not readily available, while others thought that they were not entirely available.

'Caribbean foods are available in Birmingham, but some foods we are used to eating a lot of are not here. As time goes by you do find them here and there.'

'You can get Caribbean foods in Birmingham, but these foods are not as good as back home. We used to go to the forest and get fresh foods. We used to cultivate fields with fruits and vegetable.'

'You can get certain Caribbean foods in Birmingham, but I don't like the taste of them. They taste very different to what we are used to in Montserrat. They are quite expensive as well, so you cannot always buy all the foods we used to eat back home.'

Within the discussions there was a strong sense of a loss of community contact among participants. The participants spoke of the notion of direct interaction and togetherness that was operated within the Montserratian communities and indicated that they recognised that this was not the case in Birmingham among their predecessors.

'Moving from Montserrat has had a big effect on my way of life because I can no longer do the things I used to do when I was in Montserrat. We are friendly people and we are used to saying hello to people in the streets, living with our neighbours as if they were family and socialising with other people. It is hard to do this because people don't socialise with you if they don't know you.'

'When I think of Montserrat I think of a community. People were always looking out for each other and everyone treated you like family . . . everyone trusted everyone and everyone knew everyone. It is different here; people look out for themselves . . . you don't even know who your neighbours are and you cannot trust anyone.'

Participants expressed a loss in areas such as cultural practices where it was revealed that none of the participants engaged in traditional cultural practices. It was indicated that they did not have access to practices such as traditional celebrations and various forms of socialising. However, participants highlighted that they still engage in certain practices such as religion and preparing certain foods on certain days.

'Moving from Montserrat to Birmingham has affected my way of life in that there is less freedom. There are no beaches near where you live and I have a less social life because we don't have cultural celebrations anymore and we don't get to socialise with fellow Montserratians like we used to. Everyone's busy trying to make it.'

'When I was living in Montserrat I used to attend church a lot, speak a lot of dialect and celebrate certain things during Christmas time (such as carnival, Easter Monday road relays, and fishing competitions). In Birmingham I only attend church regularly and speak a lot of dialect.'

'I consider my language (dialect) to be a strong part of my culture which I do maintain when I am with my friends and family. The way we eat too is maintained; like we have soup on Saturday and salt fish and vegetables on Sunday morning and a big dinner in the afternoon. I also listen to a lot of Caribbean music such as reggae, calypso, and dancehall music. We play these in my house on a regular basis.'

There was also a strong awareness of the issues affecting ethnic minorities in Birmingham such as exclusion and inequality. One of the participants indicated that she was aware of this and the importance of maintaining a strong sense of self within Birmingham.

'When I moved from Montserrat and came to Birmingham I realised that we were different; we speak differently, think differently and act differently. Montserratians are hard working people and we have integrity. I hope I haven't lost that. The culture in Britain is so different . . . you've got to contend with so many different things in this society such as issues affecting multiculturalism such as exclusion and inequality."

Section 4

Personal Effects

The focus in this area was on revealing the personal views, feelings and opinions of participants migrating to Birmingham. The aim of this was to highlight how cultural displacement through migrating affects individuals on a personal level and how it has affected their attitudes towards life.

Upon discussions the participants expressed a sense of loss/ bereavement, and at some points regret, as a result of leaving what I would term their entire life behind to settle into a different country and different norms and values to their custom.

'Like anyone leaving their home where they grew up to live in a different place, I had mixed feelings such as anger, loneliness and so on. This move has affected my way of life totally.'

'I feel a sense of loss because when I was in Montserrat I didn't have anything to worry about. I miss the freedom and the security.'

'Initially, within the first six months of being in Birmingham I hated it. I regretted coming here. It took me about six months before I settled in. The move from Montserrat is not affecting me now. I look at it as my home away from home.'

In some areas the discussion revealed that the feel of loss/bereavement was influenced by disappointments experienced by the participants as their high expectation of what Britain was, was different to what they were experiencing. This came as a shock to many of the participants.

'Before I came here to live I was excited because of what people used to say about England. People used to say that England was a nice place to live but when I came here it was totally different. When I arrived here I wanted to go back home.'

'Personally I think access to my cultural needs in Birmingham is very poor considering they claim to be a multicultural society.'

There was also the awareness that none of the participants received professional help/input to overcome their feelings of loss and bereavement or even psychological distress their experiences of the volcanic crisis and migrating had on them.

'I had no professional help to overcome my feelings of moving from Montserrat to Birmingham. If I was going through anything (distress, hardship, etc.) I

would phone my friends because they identified with me. This made me feel better. Mixing with other Montserratians at church also helped me a lot.'

'I had no support to overcome my feelings; I just had to accept what happened. This helped me to move on slightly.'

'I had no support to overcome my experiences of the volcanic eruptions in Montserrat and the stress I got when I moved to Birmingham. I just tried to cope with it and accepted what I was going through . . . I had to have faith and believe that things were going to get better.'

Discussions also revealed that many of the participants have future plans which are aimed at improving their standard of life in Birmingham. There was a sense of need to fully integrate as British citizens and the need to live as traditionally as possible (as Montserratians).

'I would like to make life better for myself and live as a British citizen.'

'I don't want to settle for less than I deserve. I want to get married, have children, and travel the world . . . I used to travel a lot when I was back home.'

'My future plan is to complete my studies, find a good job, and hopefully one day buy a home in the UK that I can finally set up as a home away from home.'

'My future plan is to complete my studies, find a good job, and set up a home away from home. I also want to have kids and educate them about my experience of life in Montserrat and migrating here.'

Appendix 3

Advice for Support

There are a number of support systems available in the United Kingdom for individuals who have experienced trauma of any kind. Counselling services are also available via general practitioners and some work places. GPs can also recommend useful contacts for support.

Some useful contacts to consider:

Assistance Support and Self Help in Surviving Trauma (ASSIST), Helpline: 01788560800

British Association for Counselling and Psychotherapy (BACP), Tel: 01455883316

Citizens Advice Bureau—kindly check you yellow pages or directory for numbers in your area

MIND, Tel: 0300123 3393

APPENDIX 4

A Brief History of Montserrat

Nickname   Emerald Isle of the Caribbean, as a result of its
                resemblance to Ireland

                Said to have been named *Santa Maria de Montserrate*
                by Christopher Columbus, after the blessed virgin
                of the Monastery of Montserrat

                Also thought to have been named for the mountain
                in Catatonia, Spain. There is some resemblance to
                its rugged terrain

Location   Located in the Caribbean Sea, it is a part of the
                Caribbean chain of islands called the Lesser
                Antilles

Discovery   Montserrat was said to have been discovered by
                Christopher Columbus in 1493, on his second
                voyage to the West Indies

Ownership
1632   Controlled by Irish Catholics, who were allegedly
                forcibly removed from Ireland and sent to the
                Caribbean as indentured servants

1782	Montserrat is under French rule during the French Revolution but returned to the United Kingdom under the Treaty of Paris
1798	St Patrick's Day celebrations become part of the Montserrat cultural celebrations following failed slavery uprising in the Caribbean.
1834	Slavery abolished in the Caribbean and Montserrat
1871-1958	Montserrat forms part of the Federal Colonies of the Leeward Islands
1958	Montserrat becomes part of the West Indies Federation, which collapsed in 1962
Population	Prior to the volcanic eruptions, the population was said to be about 12,000. Post migration figures in 2008 were estimated at around 5,879. The population originally consisted of an Irish-African mix. Migration pre—and post-volcanic eruptions have resulted in a large mix of Africans, Dominicans from the Dominican Republic, Americans, East Indians, British, Jamaicans, Guyanese, and Haitians.
Budget	Subsidised by the British and administered by the Department for International Development (DIFID)

Culture

Celebrations and festivals include the street parade held on the first of January with street jump up and costume bands on the streets throughout the day. It is part of the Christmas festivities, which are celebrated for three weeks in Montserrat from early/mid December to early January. There are various competitions including the popular festival Queen Show and Calypso, or Monarch Show. Costume band competitions are also a part of the festival.

Boxing Day and St John's Day are both public holidays with similar cultural celebrations involving music, costumed bands on parade, and masquerade performances.

St Patrick's Day is the annual celebration of Montserrat's Irish heritage, with emphasis on wearing the national colours, especially the green and white combination; focus on cultural cuisine includes the national dish, goat water, and traditional music.

Calypso or soca is the main music choice for competitions, dances, and entertainment. Made popular by Montserrat's internationally renowned artist, the late Alphoso 'Arrow' Cassell with the song 'Hot, Hot, Hot', many of the Caribbean island share a similar love for this type of music.

Steel band music is another popular form of music which has been added to the schools' curriculum. Steel pan music is very popular in Trinidad.

Masquerade music is quite unique and relates to the island's African heritage, with its use of goatskin drums (called kettles) and booms and fife. Masquerade performances include five **quadrilles** dances and the heel and toe polka. Their costumes consist of brightly coloured apparel with voluminous adornments. A whip is carried which is cracked in a fierce and scary fashion during the performance.

The string band is less widespread but still a popular form of music, with its use of ukulele, shak, bass boom pipe, fife, guitar, triangle, and gradge.

Folk dances include the popular **jumbie dance,** which combines folklore, music, and dance ritual. It has been described as a pure manifestation of Montserrat folk religion. The jumbie dance is no longer practiced but remains a source of discussion and reference as a result of its uniqueness. A combination of African and Irish heritage, the dancers are described as performing Irish steps and move their upper bodies like Africans. Performed by four couples, the dance occurs as an aspect of crisis intervention for individuals who have life-changing issues or serious illnesses for which there is no obvious medical cure. The dances, mainly the quadrilles, are accompanied by fife, tringle, woo woo drum (jumbie drum), skin drum, tambourine, and French reel.

BIBLIOGRAPHY

Aymer, U. (2003). The Effects of the Volcanic Crisis on the People of Montserrat Viewed through the Experiences of Montserrat Migrants in Birmingham. (Masters of Arts degree) Unpublished. London.

Chessum, L. (2000). *From Immigrants to Ethnic Minority.* London.

Chin, P. L., & Kramer, M. K. (2004). *Integrating Knowledge Development in Nursing, 6th ed.* St. Louis: Mosby.

Clifford, J. (1988). *The Predicament of Culture-Twentieth Century Ethnography, Literature and Art.* London: Harvard university Press.

Fergus, H. (1994). *Montserrat: History of a Caribbean Colony.* London: Macmillan.

Fergus, H. A. & Markham A. (1989). *Hugo versus Montserrat.* London.

Geertz, C. (1993). *The Interpretation of Cultures.* London: Fontana Press.

Knight, W. K., Emmer, P. C. & Higman, B. W. (1997). *General Histories of the Caribbean: The Slave Societies of the Caribbean.* Hong Kong: UNESCO.

Kwsesi, O. (2000). *Black Irish Culture & Society.* London.

Leininger, M. & MacFarlane, M. (2006). *Culture Care Diversity & Universality: A Worldwide Nursing Theory, Second Edition.* USA.

Markus, H. R., & Kitayama, S. (1991). Culture and the Self: Implications for Cognition, Emotion, and Motivation. *Psychological Review, 98,* 224-253.

McEwen, M. (2002). *Theoretical Basis for Nursing.* Philadelphia: Lippincott Williams & Wilkins.

Palmer, W. (1990). *In Search of a Better Life: Perspectives from the Caribbean.* London.

Olsen, F, (1973). *On the Trail of the Arawaks.* University of Oklahoma Press.

Patullo, P. (2000). *Fire from the Mountain.* Constable. England.

Philpott, S. B. (1973). *West Indian Migration: The Montserrat Case.* London.

Roy, C. (1970). Adaptation: A Conceptual Framework for Nursing. *Nursing Outlook,* 18:3, 42-45.

Shaver, P. R., Wu, S. & Schwartz, J. C. (1991). Cross-cultural Similarities and Differences in Emotion and Its Representation: A Prototype Approach. In M. S. Clark (Ed.), *Review of Personality and Social Psychology, 13,* 175-212. Newbury Park, CA: Sage.

Skinner, J. (2003). Montserrat Place and Mons'rat Neaga: An Example of Impressionistic Autoethnography. *The Qualitative Report,* 8(3) 513-529. Retrieved (30/05/2011) from http://www.nova.edu/ssss/QR/QR8-31Skinner.Pdf

Taylor, D. (2009). The Island Caribs of Dominica, BWI. *American Anthropologist,* 37:2. Wiley.

Thompson, K. (2010). *A Look at the Caribbean and Its People and Culture.* New Africa Press.

Thompson, S. (2009). *Reflections to Stir the Mind, Body, and Soul: An Exploration of History, Culture, Passion, and the Untamed Imagination.* Indiana: AuthorHouse.

Warnes, A. M. (1997). The Health and Care of Older People in London: A Report to the Kings Fund London Commission. London: Kings Fund.

Wells, J.C. *(1980).* The Brogue That Isn't. *University College London. [Originally published in the Journal of the International_Phonetic Association, vol. 10, 74-79.]*

Wolcott, H. *(1999). Ethnography: A Way of Seeing. London: Altamira Press.*

Media

www.thedailymail.co.uk
www.themirror.co.uk
www.theMontserratreporter.com
www.telegraph.co.uk
www.thevoicenewspaper.com
www.zjbradioonline.com

Plymouth destroyed by Pyroclastic flow

pyroclastic flow

pyroclastic flow

Roseanne celebrates her 80th birthday in England

Evergreen Tree round about in Plymouth

Brambles airport totally destroyed by pyroclastic flows

MAP OF MONTSERRAT

FLAG OF MONTSERRAT

The **Montserrat Flag** came into being on 25th January, 1999 which is also the date for Coat of Arms adoption. Montserrat is a territory of the United Kingdom. The overall setting of the flag is blue in color which symbolizes awareness, trustworthiness, determination and righteousness. The British Union Jack is present on the upper left section of the flag, known as Canton. The Montserratian emblem is located on the right half of the **Montserrat Flag**, which represents Erin, the sign of independence for Ireland. The symbol on the **Montserrat Flag** shows a woman standing very close to a yellow harp embracing a black cross. To show respect to the earlier European settlers the Montserrat flag bears the shamrock as its insignia.

http://www.mapsofworld.com/flags/montserrat-flag.html

Journal contributions

The author has made contributions in journals under the name Thompson. Although in no way related to the contents of this book she has decided to share the links as she thinks professionals and others could find this a useful resource.

Patient inclusion in goal setting during early inpatient rehabilitation after acquired brain injury

Catherine Dalton, Rachel Farrell, Annette De Souza, Evelyn Wujanto, Ann McKenna-Slade, Sharmen Thompson, Clarence Liu, and Richard Greenwood Clin Rehabil published 21 September 2011, 10.1177/0269215511405230 http://cre.sagepub.com/cgi/content/abstract/0269215511405230v1

Developing Leaders through Work-based Learning, Back-casting and Partnership
Ian Scott, Chipo Takavarasha and Sharmen Thompson. *Learning and Teaching in Higher Education, Issue 4-2, 2010.* resources.glos.ac.uk/ . . . /502ECF4BBCD42A039A3D0F4D9D184DBD

Incontinence after brain injury: prevalence, outcome and multidisciplinary management on a neurological rehabilitation unit.
Leary SM, Liu C, Cheesman AL, Ritter A, Thompson S, Greenwood R. Clin Rehabil 2006; 20: 1094-9.

Poetry published by the same author using the name Sharmen D Thompson

Reflections to stir the mind body and soul: An Explosion of History, Culture, Passion and the Untamed Imagination